Contributing Author
Rabbi David J.B. Krishef

Editor
Dona Herweck Rice

Editor-in-Chief
Sharon Coan, M.S. Ed.

Illustrator
Agnes S. Palinay

Cover Artist
Keith Vasconcelles

Art Director
Elayne Roberts

Product Manager
Phil Garcia

Imaging
Alfred Lau
James Edward Grace

Publisher
Mary D. Smith, M.S. Ed.

Interdisciplinary Thematic Unit

World Religions

Grades 6-8

Author

Gabriel Arquilevich

Teacher Created Resources, Inc.
6421 Industry Way
Westminster, CA 92683
www.teachercreated.com
©1995 Teacher Created Resources, Inc.
Reprinted, 2006
Made in U.S.A.
ISBN-1-55734-624-0

Table of Contents

Table of Contents *(cont.)*

Introduction

Why Teach Religion?

If, for example, your students were asked what they know about Hinduism—an ancient faith claiming about 700 million followers—they would likely respond with an overwhelmingly small amount of information. Though they see religious images every day, they often know little about the religions themselves or the lives of the great spiritual leaders.

But why such ignorance? Why has the study of religion been neglected? In the early 1960's, the Supreme Court declared state-sponsored religious activities within the schools to be unconstitutional. However, the Court emphasized that learning about religion is essential. Despite the importance of religion in history and culture, most schools have kept a distance.

Fortunately, this distance is being bridged.

In a world which continuously grows more intimate and interdependent, there is a need for everyone to awaken to one another's spiritual heritage. To a great degree, the world has been shaped by religion. To teach history without religion is equivalent to teaching biology without reference to the human body. School boards across the nation are beginning to recognize this fact, advocating religious studies within the framework of history.

Besides the obvious profit of knowledge, religious studies foster tolerance. This is, perhaps, the most valuable lesson. After all, racism and stereotypes are born largely out of ignorance. How wonderful, then, to give students the opportunity to listen to a Buddhist speak or to visit a synagogue and ask questions of a rabbi. These kinds of direct contacts are invaluable.

Many people may wonder if students in the middle grades are too young to begin studying religion. Absolutely not! In fact, such a unit may provide spiritual nourishment missing in many students' lives, or it may strengthen the students' ties to their own faiths. Some may finally have the chance to wonder out loud about the meaning of life. They might return home and ask questions of their parents. Students are usually genuinely inspired by such a topic. Parents are likely to be appreciative, because in many cases, they will learn along with their children.

About the Curriculum

The ultimate goal of this curriculum is threefold: an appreciation of the history and culture of major world religions, an appreciation of the spiritual foundations of major world religions, and a personal exploration into matters of spirituality. Of course, these three translate into *tolerance*.

This book contains two main sections, beginning with the Semitic religions of Judaism, Christianity, and Islam, and followed by the Indian religions of Hinduism, Buddhism, and Sikhism. These are supplemented by a chapter on Taoism. The final chapter is activity based, dedicated to comparison and reflection. At the end of the book, there is a bibliography.

Each chapter focuses on one religion and features each of the following areas:

- origin
- maps
- branches
- worship and prayer
- myths, stories
- symbols
- calendar
- quiz and review
- leader or prophet
- basic teachings, belief system
- sacred text (excerpt and background)
- rites of passage
- place of worship
- places of pilgrimage
- holidays, festivals

Introduction *(cont.)*

About the Curriculum *(cont.)*

In addition to these topics, each chapter presents an opportunity for self-reflection and artistic response. Among other things, these include an essay on forgiveness, a personal pilgrimage, and inventing one's own spiritual symbol. There are many possibilities for these kinds of activities.

Obviously, the scope of this curriculum is limited. Although it introduces the world's "great" religions, it does not include some significant faiths, just as it cannot address each religion in great detail. Rather, this curriculum should be thought of as the starting point. While it is written for middle grades, it can easily be used in high school or adjusted for younger students.

How To Use the Curriculum

The time frame of this unit depends on the instructor. Attending to every religion is crucial, but using every lesson would probably be tedious. It may be beneficial to have the students choose partners and report on a religion. Besides an essay, they might give an oral presentation complete with visual aids and some kind of cultural features. For example, the pair presenting Judaism might demonstrate for the others how to play with a Chanukah dreidel, while the Hindu pair might teach the others how to draw popular Indian designs. Not only will this bring the religion to life, but it will reduce the teacher-based lecture style so common to the study of history.

For young students, film and historical literature are invaluable supplements to the study of religion. Your students may greatly enjoy watching *The Ten Commandments*, listening to *The Ramayana* read aloud, and reading *The Cat Who Went to Heaven*. More than anything, focus on the living, breathing world of religion. Beware the temptation to lecture and explain.

Finally, teaching religion presents the educator with a tremendous responsibility. The teacher must always be sensitive to his or her own religious and social conditioning, as well as that of the students and parents. If this sensitivity exists, today's students will begin to harbor a deeper understanding of and respect for one another's faith.

About the Author

Gabriel Arquilevich is a middle-school teacher in Southern California. He developed this curriculum initially for use in his own classroom due to the sparsity of prepared information available. As he writes, "I decided to create a religions unit for my sixth graders. They had expressed interest in this subject, an interest I shared. But when I set out to structure the unit, I was surprised by the limited amount of age-appropriate resources in the field of religion. Although I was able to find helpful books, my search for a comprehensive middle-grades curriculum was futile. It became clear that I would be doing the bulk of the work, assembling information from a variety of sources. From this research and in-class experience, this book was born."

Mr. Arquilevich would like to thank his 1993-1994 sixth grade class for their feedback on this curriculum and for their wholehearted participation.

Introduction

Time Line

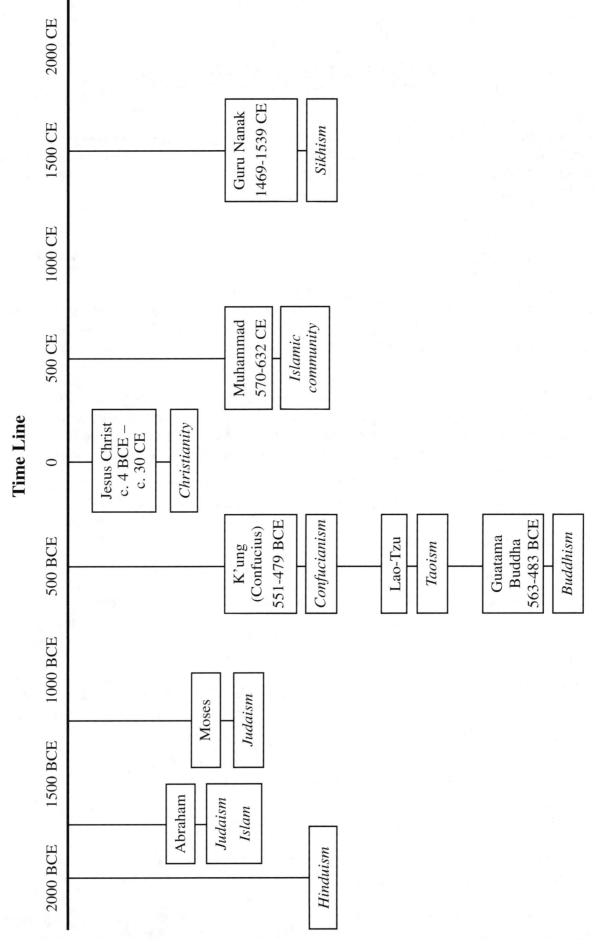

Name _____

Reading a Time Line

If you have ever read about something that happened long ago, then you are probably familiar with the abbreviations BC or BCE and AD or CE. Look at the time line on the previous page. Notice that Buddha was born in 563 BCE. Muhammad died in 632 CE. Both BC and BCE represent the years before the birth of Jesus. CE and AD mean the years after the birth of Jesus. The abbreviations stand for the following:

BC = Before Christ

AD = Anno Domini (in the year of our Lord)

BCE = Before the Common Era

CE = Common Era

In this book, only BCE and BC will be used. This is because BC and AD relate all dates to the birth of Jesus. Referring to Jesus as Christ or using dates that are based on the birth of Jesus are part of the Christian religion, while this book focuses on many different religions and belief systems.

You have probably also read of events happening, for example, in the 5th century or even in the 5th century BCE. A century is 100 years. If people lived in the 1st century, they lived in the first 100 years CE, or in the first 100 years after the birth of Jesus. So, if we say something happened in the 19th century, we mean it happened during the years 1801-1900 CE. The same rule applies to the centuries BCE, only we count backwards from the birth of Jesus. For example, Buddha was born in 563 BCE, which would mean he was born in the 6th century BCE.

Here are some practice questions. You will need to refer to the timeline and use your math skills.

Answer:

1. Who is older, someone born in 1760 BCE or someone born in 1450 BCE?

   _____

2. In what century was Guru Nanak born?

   _____

3. How many years difference is there between 250 CE and 250 BCE?

   _____

4. How many years difference is there between 1524 CE and 1436 BCE?

   _____

5. You visit a cemetery. One of the tombstones reads: "Born in the 15th century, died in the 16th." Make up possible dates that this person may have been born and died.

   _____

6. What century are you living in now?

   _____

Distribution of World Religions

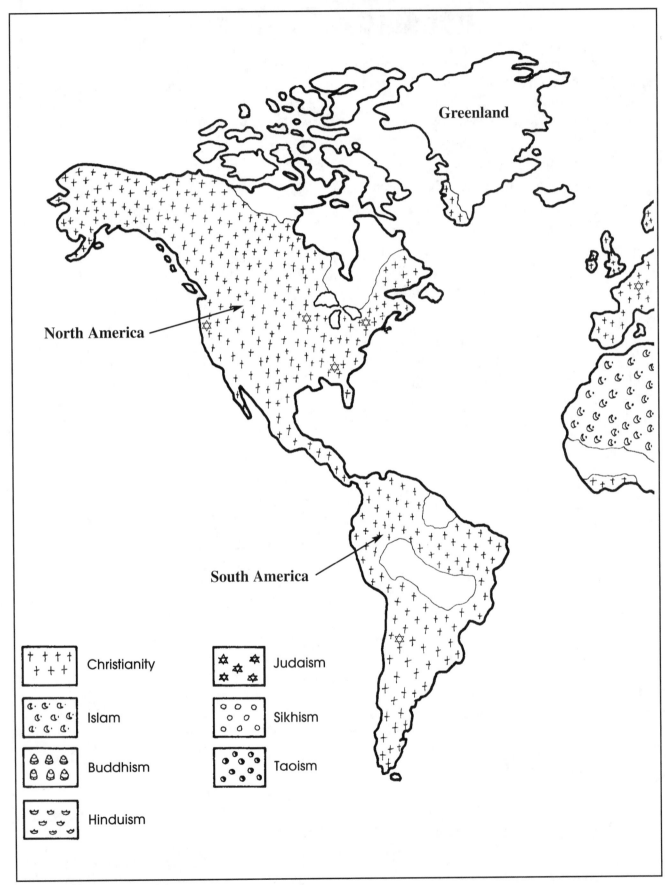

Distribution of World Religions *(cont.)*

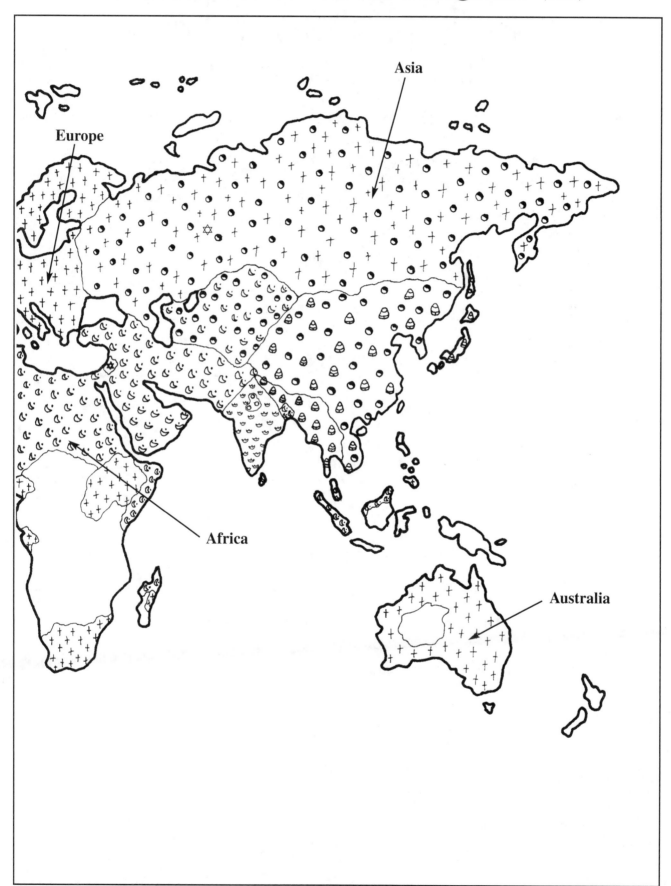

Name_____

World Distribution and Size of Major World Religions

Using the diagram below and the map on pages 8 and 9, answer the questions below. You might need an atlas to help you.

It is important to remember that this map shows only where each religion is most popular. You can find followers of almost every religion in different parts of the world. For example, more Jews live in the United States than in Israel, but they represent the majority in Israel while Christians represent the majority in the United States.

Answer:

1. Name one country where Hinduism is popular. _____

2. In which countries would you be most likely to meet a Muslim? _____

_____

3. List the continents where Christianity is widespread._____

_____

4. In what area of the world is Judaism predominantly found? _____

5. If you wanted to visit a Buddhist country, where might you go?_____

6. Name one country dominant with Taoists. _____

7. Which major religion is most widespread throughout the world? _____

8. Which major religion has the most followers? Which major religions have the fewest followers?

_____

Relative Sizes of the Major World Religions

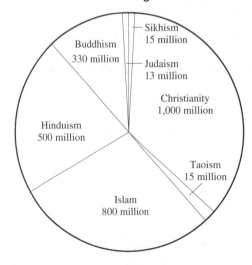

Belief, Fact, and Opinion

When learning about any subject, especially history or religion, it is important to know the difference between a fact, a belief, and an opinion.

A **fact** can be proved true. For example, it is a fact that Mars is the fourth planet from the sun. A fact can be proved either by actually observing something or by consulting a reliable source such as an encyclopedia.

An **opinion** is a statement or idea that tells how a person feels about something. If your friend says, "Pizza is the best food in the world," he or she is stating an opinion. However, opinions supported by facts are more convincing. If your friend took a survey and discovered that more people ate pizza than any other food, he would have some support for his opinion.

A **belief** is an idea or conviction that someone accepts as true or real. Some people, for example, believe that walking under a ladder is bad luck. Can this be proven? Probably not. But the person may still believe it true. Another person may believe in certain gods, while others do not. For them, these beliefs are like facts.

A **belief system** is a collection of ideas or teachings which influence a person's understanding of life. It usually gives instructions on how to live. As you will see, religions are a blend of both facts and belief systems. It can be proven that at least some of the religious leaders actually existed. The ideas they taught and some of the things they did, however, cannot be proven.

Recognizing Beliefs, Facts, and Opinions

Read each sentence and decide whether it is a belief, a fact, or an opinion. Write B for belief, F for fact, or O for opinion before each sentence.

_____ 1. Finding a penny means good luck.

_____ 2. *The Declaration of Independence* was signed in 1776.

_____ 3. There are seven continents on Earth.

_____ 4. The mountains are more beautiful than the desert.

_____ 5. If you are born in April, you will become rich.

_____ 6. Seals are the cutest animals.

_____ 7. Oranges have lots of vitamin C.

_____ 8. The rain forests in Brazil are being destroyed.

_____ 9. Rabbits make great pets.

_____10. You should stay home on Friday the 13th.

Name _____

The Semitic Religions

When we speak about the Semitic religions, we are referring to Judaism, Islam, and Christianity. The word *Semitic* describes the people who came from the Middle East and their languages. Arabs and Jews are both Semitic. Christianity is a Semitic religion because it originated in the Middle East.

Another feature Semitic religions share is monotheism. The prefix mono means *one* while theism means *belief in God or gods*. So although these religions differ greatly, they each believe in only one God. Later, you will be reading about polytheism, or the belief in more than one god.

Look at the map on the next page of the Middle East. The writings of the Hebrew Bible originated in the land between the Jordan River and the Mediterranean Sea. As you will see, both Judaism and Christianity are rooted in these writings.

This area is now the modern state of Israel. Its capital, historic Jerusalem, is sacred to all three Semitic religions.

Now find the cities of Mecca and Medina in the Arabian Peninsula. The prophet Muhammad was born in Mecca, now the world center of Islam. Every year, millions of Muslims, members of Islam, make pilgrimages to this sacred city. Medina is where Muhammad set up the first Muslim state. These cities are now part of Saudi Arabia.

Questions:

1. What does the word *Semitic* describe?

   _____

   _____

   _____

2. Which religions are considered Semitic?

   _____

   _____

   _____

3. Are the Semitic religions monotheistic or polytheistic?

   _____

Name _____

The Semitic Religions *(cont.)*

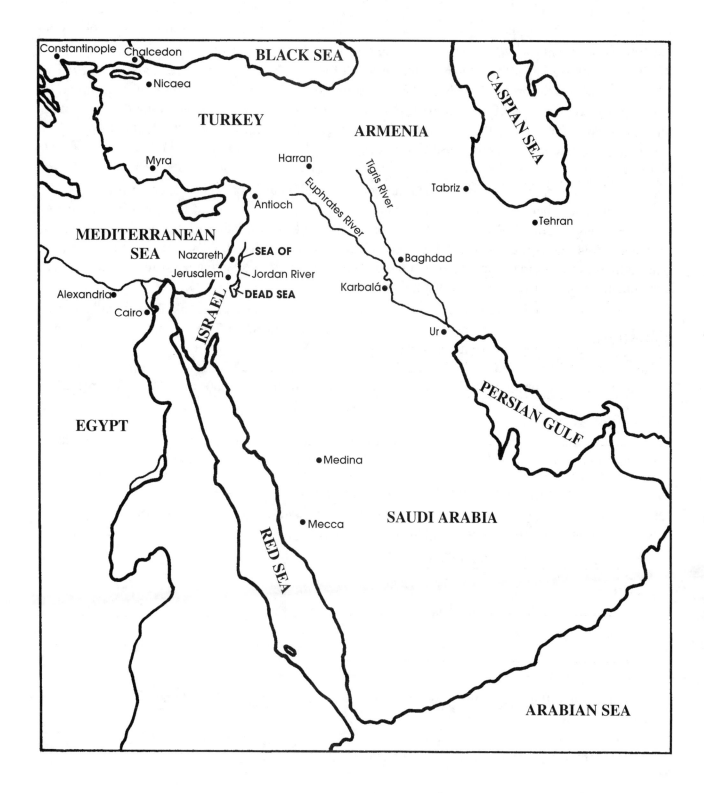

Name _____

The Bible

The Bible is the most famous book in all of history. It has sold more copies than any other book ever written. It has been translated into every major language and can be found in almost every hotel room.

The Jewish Bible was originally written in Hebrew, which is a very old language from the Middle East. Hebrew is written and read from right to left instead of from left to right as we read and write English. Another Jewish name for the Bible is *Tanakh* (kh is pronounced by rattling the back of your throat, like the German pronunciation of the composer Bach). Tanakh is a word created by taking the first letters of the Hebrew names for the three sections of the Hebrew Bible—*Torah* (the first five books); *Nevee'eem* (Prophets—books like Joshua, Samuel, Isaiah, Jeremiah, Ezekiel, and others); and *Ketuvim* (Writings, including books like Proverbs, Psalms, Esther, Ruth, Lamentations, and others).

The kind of Bible that you find most often in bookstores and hotel rooms is a Christian Bible. There are two differences between a Jewish Bible and a Christian Bible. First, the Christian Bible arranges the books from the Jewish Bible in a different order. Second, the Christian Bible contains 27 extra books that tell the story of Jesus and the spread of Christianity, such as the Gospels and the book of Acts. These books were originally written in Greek, another very old language. You will learn more about the Christian Bible in the section on Christianity.

Sometimes, you hear Christians refer to the Jewish part of their Bible as the "Old Testament" and the Christian part as the "New Testament." Christians usually call the second part of the Bible the "New Testament" because they believe it has replaced the "Old Testament." Jews do not use these terms because they do not believe that the Tanakh has been replaced. Therefore, Jews and some Christians refer to the two parts of the Christian Bible as the "Hebrew Testament" and the "Greek Testament."

Citing The Bible

Before continuing, you should understand how to refer to chapters and lines of the Bible. If you have ever read a quote from the Bible, you will notice it is followed by something like this:

Genesis 7: 1-4

What this means is that the quote comes from the book Genesis, chapter 7, verses 1 through 4. Try looking up this quote. What famous Bible story is in this chapter?

Now, use the Bible to answer the following questions.

Questions:

1. What is the Torah? List the books it contains. _____

   _____

   _____

2. What is the difference between the Hebrew Testament and the Greek Testament? _____

   _____

3. What famous speech is found in Matthew 5: 3-12? _____

   _____

Reading from the Bible: Adam and Eve and the Garden of Eden

There are many theories, stories, and myths that explain how the world began. One of the most famous creation stories is told in Genesis, the first book of the Tanakh. The word *Genesis* actually means *coming into existence*.

Following is the story of Adam and Eve and the garden of Eden as taken from Genesis. If you have never read directly from the Bible, you may find it a little difficult. You will probably need to read it more than once and keep a list of vocabulary words.

According to the Bible, God created the universe, including the heavens and earth, in six days. On the seventh day God rested. During this time, God created man from dust, breathing life into him. The garden of Eden, or paradise, was also created. Our story begins at Genesis 2:15.

[15] The Lord God took the man and put him in the garden of Eden to till and keep it. [16] And the Lord God commanded the man, saying, "You may eat of every tree in the garden; [17] but of the tree of the knowledge of good and evil you shall not eat, for in the day you eat of it you shall die."

[18] Then the Lord God, said, "It is not good that man should be alone; I will make him a helper fit for him." [19] So out of the ground the Lord God formed every beast of the field and every bird of the air, and brought them to the man to see what he would call them; and whatever the man called every living creature, that was its name. [20] The man gave names to all the cattle, and to the birds of the air, and to every beast of the fields; but for the man there was not found a helper fit for him. [21] So the Lord God caused a deep sleep to fall upon the man, and while he slept took one of his ribs and closed up its place with flesh; [22] and the rib which the Lord God had taken from the man he made into a woman and brought her to the man. [23] Then the man said,

> "This at last is bone of my bones
> and flesh of my flesh;
> she shall be called Woman,
> because she was taken out of Man."

[24] Therefore a man leaves his father and mother and cleaves to his wife, and they become one flesh.
[25] And the man and his wife were both naked, and were not ashamed.

3

Now the serpent was more subtle than any other wild creature that the Lord God had made. He said to the woman, "Did God say, 'You shall not eat of any tree of the garden'?" [2] And the woman said to the serpent, "We may eat of the fruit of the trees of the garden; [3] but God said, 'You shall not eat the fruit of the tree which is in the midst of the garden, neither shall you touch it, lest you die.'" [4] But the serpent said to the woman, "You will not die. [5] For God knows that when you eat of it your eyes will be opened, and you will be like God, knowing good and evil." [6] So when the woman saw that the tree was good for food, and that it was a delight to the eyes, and that the tree was to be desired to make one wise, she took of its fruit and ate; and she also gave some to her husband, and he ate. [7] Then the eyes of both were opened and they knew that they were naked; and they sewed fig leaves together and made themselves aprons.

Reading from the Bible:
Adam and Eve and the Garden of Eden *(cont.)*

[8] And they heard the sound of the Lord God walking in the garden in the cool of the day, and the man and his wife hid themselves from the presence of the Lord God among the trees of the garden. [9] But the Lord God called to the man, and said to him, "Where are you?"   [10] And he said, "I heard the sound of thee in the garden and I was afraid because I was naked; and I hid myself." [11] He said, "Who told you that you were naked? Have you eaten of the tree which I commanded you not to eat?" [12] The man said, "The woman whom thou gavest to be with me, she gave me fruit of the tree, and I ate." [13] Then the Lord God said to the woman, "What is this that you have done?" The woman said, "The serpent beguiled me, and I ate." [14] The Lord God said to the serpent,

> "Because you have done this,
> cursed are you above all cattle,
> and above all wild animals;
> upon your belly you shall go,
> and dust you shall eat all
> the days of you life.
> [15] I will put enmity
> between you and the woman,
> and between your seed and her seed;
> he shall bruise your head,
> and you shall bruise his heel."

[16] To the woman he said,

> "I will greatly multiply your pain in childbearing;
> in pain you shall bring forth children,
> yet your desire shall be for your husband,
> and he shall rule over you."

[17] And to Adam he said,

> "Because you have listened to the voice of your wife,
> and have eaten of the tree of which I commanded you,
> 'you shall not eat of it,'
> cursed is the ground because of you;
> [18] in toil you shall eat of it
> all the days of your life;
> thorns and thistles it shall bring forth to you;
> and you shall eat the plants of the field.
> [19] In the sweat of your face
> you shall eat bread
> until you return to the ground,
> for out of it you were taken;
> you are dust,
> and to dust you shall return."

Name _____

Reading from the Bible: Adam and Eve and the Garden of Eden *(cont.)*

[20] The man called his wife's name Eve, because she was the mother of all living. [21] And the Lord God made for Adam and for his wife garments of skins, and clothed them.

[23] Then the Lord God said, "Behold, the man has become like one of us, knowing good and evil; he must not be allowed to reach out his hand and take also from the tree of life and eat, and live forever." So the Lord God sent him forth from the garden of Eden, to till the ground from which he was taken. [24] He drove out the man; and at the east of the garden of Eden he placed the cherubim, and a flaming sword which turned every way, to guard the way to the tree of life.

Questions:

1. What is the one commandment God gives Adam in the garden of Eden? _____

2. What is Adam's first "job" in the garden? _____

3. How is Eve created? _____

4. How are Adam and Eve like children? What does their nakedness symbolize? _____

   _____

5. The serpent is called "subtle." What does this word mean? _____

6. Why do you think some people refer to the serpent as the "tempter"? _____

7. What finally convinces Eve to eat from the tree? _____

8. Describe what happens to Adam and Eve immediately after they eat. How do they feel? _____

   _____

9. In this story, God punishes. What are the punishments for the snakes, for Eve, and for Adam?

   _____

10. What happens to the language of the story when God delivers these punishments? Why?

    _____

11. What reason does God give for casting Adam and Eve out of the garden? _____

12. Describe what it was probably like for Adam and Eve before they are punished. Draw a picture of the garden of Eden. _____

    _____

13. Many people believe this story is an allegory. An allegory is a story that is not true but has a moral or religious meaning. What might this story mean if it is allegorical? What could a person learn from it? _____

    _____

Abraham the Patriarch

In order to understand the origins of Judaism, we must travel back almost 4000 years to the land of Ur. It was here that a boy named Abram was born. According to the Torah, God chose Abram to be the father of a great nation. Before the time of Abram, all people believed that there were many gods, such as a god of rain, a god of wind, a god of sun, and a god of the land. God made a covenant, or a sacred agreement, with Abram that he would worship only one God. As a sign of that covenant, Abram's name was changed to *Abraham*, meaning exalted father of a great nation.

When Abraham was young, his family moved north from Ur to the land of Haran. (Use a modern atlas and the map below to discover where Haran would be today.) It was in Haran in about 2000 B.C.E. that God made a covenant with Abraham. Abraham was about 75 years old when God said to him:

> "Go from your country and your kindred and your father's house to the land that I will show you. And I will make of you a great nation, and I will bless you, and make your name great, so that you will be a blessing." (Genesis 12: 1-3)

So Abraham and his wife, Sarah, along with a small caravan, journeyed hundreds of miles to the land of Canaan. This is the home where God promised Abraham a great nation. And though the land of Canaan has changed hands many times since Abraham's arrival, today it is the land of Israel, the Jewish homeland.

Sarah and Abraham grew old, but God granted them the miracle of a son, Isaac. In Genesis 22, God tests Abraham's faith by commanding him to sacrifice Isaac. Though Abraham's heart is breaking, he takes his son to the hills, binds him, and lays him on an altar of wood. As the old man reaches for the knife to slay his only son, an angel calls out to him, telling him to release Isaac.

> "Do not do anything to him. Now I know that you fear God, because you have not withheld me from your son, your only son."

The angel comes to Abraham a second time, assuring him that because of his faith he will have many descendants, and they will be blessed and prosperous.

Through these stories, it is easy to understand the importance of Abraham. You can read about all of the Jewish patriarchs and matriarchs in the book of Genesis. Interestingly, the Muslim religion also descends from Abraham's family. Before Isaac was born, Abraham had fathered a son with his maidservant Hagar. His name was Ishmael, and according to Jewish and Muslim tradition, he is the ancestor of the Arab people.

The Journey of Abraham

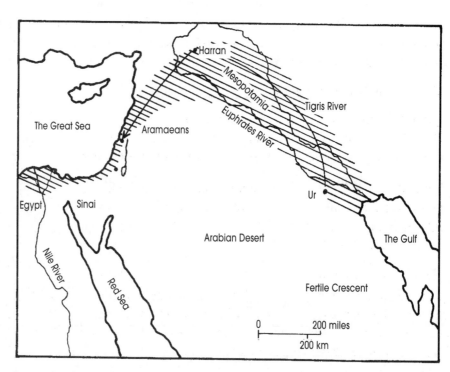

Exodus: The Story of Moses and the Ten Commandments

One of the most important chapters of Jewish history is told in Exodus, the second book of the Torah. It is the story of how God freed the Hebrews from slavery in Egypt and led them back to the land of Canaan. The word *exodus* actually means a *mass departure*.

As you will see, God chooses Moses to go before Pharoah, the king of the Egyptians, and demand freedom for the Hebrew slaves. After Moses leads the Hebrews out of Egypt, he takes them to Mount Sinai where they receive the 10 commandments and the rest of the Torah. The Torah forms the bedrock of Judaism, containing detailed instructions on day-to-day living, rules by which Jews still live today. Thus, Moses is revered as the most significant Hebrew prophet, and the Exodus as the most significant event in Jewish history.

Many scholars think the Exodus took place around 1250 BCE. According to the traditional Biblical story, the Hebrews were enslaved in Egypt four hundred years before the "going out."

The Birth of Moses

Before the time of Moses' birth, Hebrew tribes had lived and prospered in Egypt. But the new Pharoah of Egypt felt threatened by the strength and influence of the Israelites.

Pharaoh ordered his soldiers to enslave the Hebrew people. He set cruel taskmasters over them. Without a moment's rest, the Hebrews were forced to build the stone-cities of Pithom and Raamses.

Now, though they were oppressed, the Israelites continued to multiply. They remained a proud and spirited people. The king of Egypt, sensing their resilience, grew determined and finally commanded his people to cast every newborn Hebrew son into the Nile. He allowed the daughters to live.

During this time, in the tribe of Levi, a son was born to a couple named Amram and Jochebed.

Just then, Pharaoh's daughter, with her maidens beside her, came down to bathe at the river. She saw the basket in the reeds and sent her maid to fetch it. When she saw the crying child, the Princess felt great pity and compassion.

"This is one of the Hebrews' children," she said.

Seeing this, the baby's sister, Miriam, came forward and asked if the Princess would need a nurse to care for the child. She agreed, and so Miriam went to fetch her mother.

"Take this child," Pharoah's daughter said to Jochebed, "and nurse him for me. I will give you wages." Unknowingly, the princess had asked the baby's own mother to raise him!

So the mother took her child and nursed him. The child grew and was brought to Pharoah's daughter and became her son. She named him Moses, which means *drawn out*, because she drew him out of the Nile. Moses grew up as an Egyptian prince in the luxury of Pharaoh's court.

Exodus: The Story of Moses and the Ten Commandments *(cont.)*

Moses in Midian

Moses was now grown. Fortunately, his mother, Jochebed, was at his side, teaching him compassion and justice. One morning, he came upon an Egyptian taskmaster mercilessly whipping a Hebrew, one of his own people. Making certain none of Pharaoh's men were watching, Moses killed the Egyptian and hid him in the sand.

The next day, Moses attempted to settle a dispute between two Hebrews who were arguing. When he asked one of them why he hit the other, the first responded, "Will you kill me as you killed the Egyptian?" Soon after, Pharoah learned of the murder and ordered the death of Moses. Fearing for his life, Moses escaped to the land of Midian.

Traveling one day, Moses came upon a well where seven women were filling troughs. These were the daughters of the priest of Midian. When some shepherds tried to drive the women away, Moses protected them. The priest heard of the Egyptian's kindness and invited him to share his home. Soon, Moses married Zipporah, one of the seven daughters. Together they had a son, Gershom, which means *a stranger there*. Moses chose that name because he, too, felt like "a stranger in a strange land."

In time, the king of Egypt died, but the oppression of the Israelites continued.

The Burning Bush

One day when Moses was tending his father-in-law's flock, he came to Mount Sinai deep in the desert. Suddenly, he saw a bush on fire. Strangely, though the bush burned, it was not being destroyed. When Moses came forward, God spoke to him from inside the bush.

"I have seen the misery of my people who are in Egypt. I have come to deliver them out of that land, into a land flowing with milk and honey. Come now, I will send you to Pharaoh. Lead my people, the children of Israel, out of Egypt."

Moses wondered why he should be the one to free the Hebrews, but God reassured him. Then, God told him to gather the Hebrew elders and to beg Pharaoh to allow them three day's journey in the desert to worship the Lord God. Then God added,

"I am sure the king of Egypt will not let you go, but I will stretch out my hand and strike Egypt with all my wonders. After that he will let you go."

"But they will not believe me," answered Moses.

Then, God asked Moses to cast his shepherd's rod to the ground. And when he did, the rod became a snake. But when Moses retrieved the rod, it returned to its original form. Next, God had Moses place his hand to his breast. When he removed it, his hand was white and decayed like a leper's. Again he put his hand against his breast, and it became normal.

"If they believe neither of these signs," instructed the Lord, "pour water from the river on the land. The water will become blood."

Because Moses had difficulty speaking, God told him that his brother, Aaron, would speak on his behalf.

Moses Returns to Egypt

And so Moses returned to Egypt with his family and his brother, Aaron. Moses and Aaron went before

Exodus: The Story of Moses and the Ten Commandments *(cont.)*

Pharaoh and said to him, "These are the words of the God of Israel: 'Let my people go, so that they may hold a feast to me in the wilderness.'"

But Pharaoh did not believe them and sent them away. His heart hardened, and that same day he gave these orders to the taskmakers: "No longer give the people straw to make bricks. Let them gather straw for themselves. But demand the same number of bricks they made before, for they have grown lazy."

After Pharaoh's command, the misery of the slaves was multiplied. Though they worked relentlessly, they could not make enough bricks. For this they were beaten and even killed. The Hebrews felt great resentment toward Moses and Aaron, for the brothers had made their plight even worse.

Moses returned to the Lord and asked him why his people had been treated so badly. Why had they not been saved? God assured Moses that the people of Israel would be freed and instructed him to return to Pharoah.

"Tell Pharaoh to send the children of Israel out of his land. Pharaoh will not listen, so I will perform many miracles and bring my people out of Egypt. And the Egyptians will know that I am the Lord."

The Ten Plagues

Moses was eighty years old and Aaron was eighty-three years old when they went before Pharaoh. Upon instruction from God, Moses handed his shepherd's rod to Aaron. Aaron cast it on the ground, and the rod became a snake.

But Pharaoh was not impressed. He sent for his wise men and magicians who turned their rods into snakes. But Aaron's rod swallowed up all the others.

Because Pharaoh would not listen, God told Moses to go out in the morning to the river Nile. There, in the presence of Pharaoh, Moses handed his rod to Aaron, who struck the water. The water turned to blood. The fish died, the river smelled foul, and the Egyptians could not drink.

But again Pharaoh called upon his wise men and magicians. They, too, could turn the water to blood, and his heart remained unmoved.

Seven days later, God sent another plague. This time, when Aaron struck the river, thousands of frogs came from its banks. They swarmed Egypt, entering every corner of every house and covering the land.

Seeing this, Pharaoh called upon Moses:

"Pray to the Lord to take the frogs from my people, and I will let your people go worship in the wilderness."

Moses prayed to God accordingly, and God answered his prayer. The frogs died. But when Pharoah saw the plague had ended, he changed his mind. He would not let the people go. So God sent a plague of lice to infest the animals and people. Yet Pharaoh remained unmoved.

The plague of flies came next. Swarms descended upon the land and the houses. Only this time, the land of Goshen, where the Hebrews lived, was untouched. Seeing this, Pharoah agreed to let the Hebrews go into the wilderness. Again Moses prayed that the plague be lifted and the flies disappeared. And once more, Pharaoh did not let the Hebrews go.

Even after witnessing the next plague—the death of all Egyptian cattle—Pharaoh would not budge.

Exodus: The Story of Moses and the Ten Commandments *(cont.)*

The sixth punishment was the plague of sores. Sores appeared upon the bodies of all people and beasts of Egypt. Still, Pharoah did not set the captives free.

The next plague caused terrible hail, the worst ever in Egypt. Many witnessed the death of their live-stock. Pharoah agreed he had sinned and that he would let the people go. But again, he broke his promise.

When swarms of locusts invaded households and fields, the same process took place. The ninth plague caused three days' darkness to fall upon Egypt; yet still Pharoah did not listen.

Although warned of the tenth plague, Pharaoh responded only with anger. All the first-born in Egypt will die, Moses told him, including the first-born cattle. But none of the children of Israel would die.

The Night of Passover

That night, Moses instructed his people to wipe lamb's blood upon the doorways of their houses. He told them to eat the lamb and be ready to depart thereafter. The Lord, Moses said, would not bring death to their houses. Seeing the lamb's blood, God would pass over their homes.

Pharoah woke that evening to the sounds of great cries. There was not a home in Egypt where some-one was not dead. Even his own son died. Finally, after ten plagues, Pharoah set the Hebrews free.

That very night, after over four hundred years captivity, the Hebrew people journeyed on foot from Raameses to Succoth.

Crossing the Sea of Reeds

God guided the Israelites as they traveled. By day, the Lord went before them in a pillar of cloud. By night, a pillar of fire protected them. But it was not long before Pharoah's anger rose against his former captives. He took his army and his best armored chariots to retrieve the Hebrews. Camping beside the Sea of Reeds, the Israelites saw the Egyptians marching upon them. Frightened and bitter, they asked their leader if they had escaped to the wilderness only to die. But Moses reassured them.

Moses turned in prayer to God, and God answered:

"Why do you cry to me? Tell your people to go forward. Lift up your rod and stretch out your hand over the sea, and divide it. And the children of Israel will go through the middle of the sea."

So Moses stretched out his hand and a strong wind blew all night. The sea divided, and the Israelites walked into the middle of it, a wall of water on either side.

The Egyptians followed, but God made the wheels of the chariots get stuck in the muddy sea bottom, slowing them down.

And when the Hebrews had crossed the Sea, God told Moses to stretch his hand over the waters again. As he did, the Sea collapsed on the pursuing Egyptians, drowning them all.

The Ten Commandments

For three months they traveled the desert. They passed through the wilderness of Shur, through Marah and Elim, the wilderness of Zin, and Rephidim. Though they were weary and the land was parched, God always provided. Finally, they came to Sinai and camped before the mountain.

Exodus: The Story of Moses and the Ten Commandments *(cont.)*

Moses went up Mt. Sinai to talk with the Lord. God told him to prepare his people for a special treasure. Moses told his followers to prepare themselves with prayer, that in three days the Lord would appear on the mountain.

When the third day came, a thick cloud with thunder and lightning lay on the mountain. A trumpet called so loudly that the people trembled. Moses led them to the foot of the mountain. Then, God called the prophet to the top and delivered to him the Ten Commandments:

> *"I am the Lord your God.*
> *You shall have no other gods before me, you shall not make for yourself a graven*
> *image . . . you shall not bow down to them and worship them.*
> *You shall not take the name of the Lord your God in vain.*
> *Remember the Sabbath day, to keep it holy.*
> *Honor your father and mother.*
> *You shall not murder.*
> *You shall not commit adultery.*
> *You shall not steal.*
> *You shall not bear false witness against your neighbor.*
> *You shall not covet your neighbor's house . . . or anything else that belongs to your*
> *neighbor.*

For forty days and forty nights, Moses stayed upon Mount Sinai listening to God's instructions. God told Moses laws regarding criminal behavior, destruction or theft of property, proper treatment of other people, and celebrating the Sabbath and other holidays. In addition, God instructed Moses to build a special Ark to carry the tablets of the Ten Commandments, and a holy Sanctuary, called the Tabernacle, to house the Ark and in which to make offerings of grain, fruit, and animal sacrifices to God.

The Making of the Golden Calf

Now, while Moses was upon the mountain, his people grew uneasy. Though they had been led out of Egypt, though they had witnessed miracles, they felt insecure without their leader. They turned to Aaron and begged him to make them a god so that they might not be alone.

Aaron told them to gather all their gold jewelry. Then, he melted it down and sculptured a golden calf and built an altar before it. The Israelites made offerings to the idol and celebrated.

Seeing this, God grew very angry.

"I will destroy them," God said to Moses, "and make a great nation of you alone."

But Moses pleaded with God not to destroy the Israelites, and God listened. Moses descended the mountain. He looked angrily upon his people who were dancing and singing before the golden calf. In fury, he hurled the stone tablets from his hands, and they broke at the foot of the mountain. Then he took the calf and burned it. He ground it into a powder, sprinkled it in water, and made the people drink. The children of Israel mourned in shame.

Again, Moses climbed Mt. Sinai to ask forgiveness for his people. God granted them permission to continue their journey through the wilderness. God told him to make two more tablets of stone and return in the morning, and the words would again be written upon them. Moses did so and remained again forty days and nights. Though punishment came upon the guilty, God promised to have mercy and lead the Israelites into Canaan, driving out all the inhabitants of the land.

Name _____

Exodus: The Story of Moses and the Ten Commandments *(cont.)*

After forty years of traveling the desert wilderness, Moses finally delivered the children of Israel to the River Jordan, bordering the land of Canaan. Their entire journey can be seen on the map on page 25.

It was at the River Jordan, at one hundred and twenty years of age, that Moses completed his work. God told Moses he would not go into Canaan. After freeing the Hebrew slaves and leading them through the desert, it was time for him to die. He climbed Mt. Nebo, near Jericho, and God showed him the land the Israelites would inherit. The children of Israel wept for their great leader.

Questions:

1. Why is this story called Exodus? Approximately when did it occur? _____
   _____

2. Why did Pharaoh's daughter choose to call her adopted son Moses? _____
   _____

3. Why do you think God chose Moses to be a prophet? _____
   _____

4. List the ten plagues in order. Why was Pharaoh so stubborn about setting the captives free?

   a. _____   d. _____   h. _____

   b. _____   e. _____   i. _____

   c. _____   f. _____   j. _____

   g. _____

   _____
   _____

5. Why did the Hebrews make a golden calf? Which commandment does this worship break?
   _____
   _____
   _____

6. What two structures were used to house the Ten Commandments? _____
   _____

Traditional Route of the Exodus

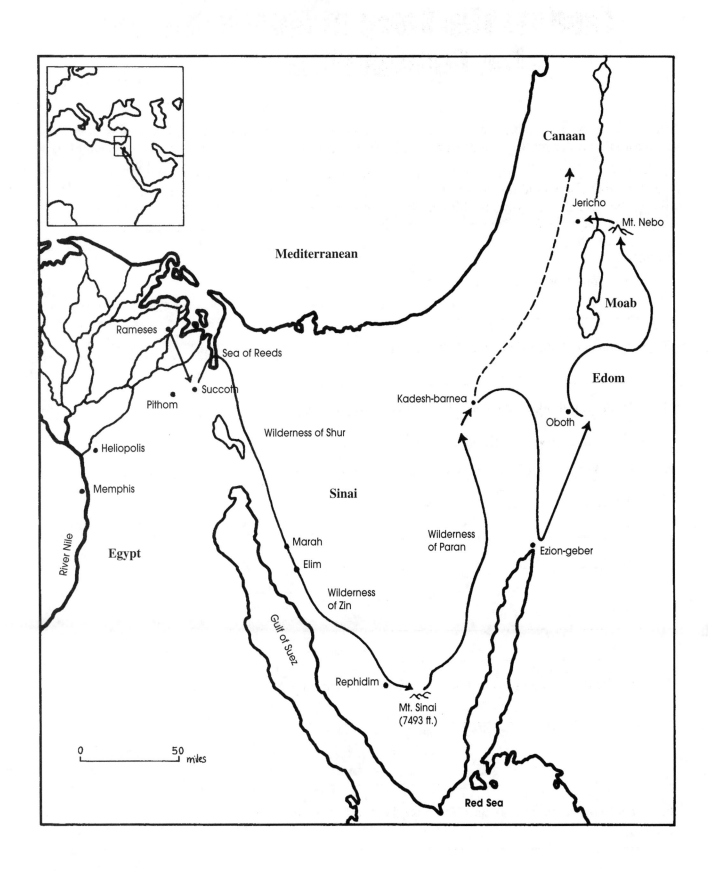

Name _____

The Ten Commandments

Jews believe that God delivered the Torah to Moses along with 613 commandments! Some of them, such as commandments concerning animal sacrifices, no longer apply today. The most famous of those commandments are the Ten Commandments, which form an important part of Judaism and Christianity.

After reading each commandment, write down what you think it means. (For a more complete version, read from Exodus 20: 1-17.) Next, get together with a classmate and discuss the Ten Commandments. Are they reasonable? Why do you think each is a commandment? Which ones could you live by? Do you think these rules should apply only to Jews or to all people?

Once the two of you have discussed your ideas, share them with the class.

1. I am the Lord your God.

   _____

2. You shall have no other gods before me, you shall not make for yourself a graven image . . . you shall not bow down to them and worship them.

   _____

3. You shall not take the name of the Lord your God in vain.

   _____

4. Remember the Sabbath day, to keep it holy.

   _____

5. Honor your father and mother.

   _____

6. You shall not murder.

   _____

7. You shall not commit adultery.

   _____

8. You shall not steal.

   _____

9. You shall not bear false witness against your neighbor.

   _____

10. You shall not covet your neighbor's house . . . or anything else that belongs to your neighbor.

    _____

Name _____

My Own Commandments

Now that you understand the Ten Commandments, here is a chance to decide on some of your own. Remember to ask yourself if your commandments are really something you can live by.

Name _____

The Proverbs

Proverbs is the twentieth book of the Tanakh. Written by King Solomon around 960 BCE, this is a collection of sayings which contain pearls of wisdom to follow. The purpose of the book of Proverbs, according to Solomon, is the following:

For learning wisdom and instruction, for understanding words of insight;

For acquiring the discipline for success, righteousness, justice, and fairness. (Proverbs 1:2-3)

Here are five proverbs from the Tanakh. Choose two of them and write what each one means to you. Then, write your own proverb and discuss it with a classmate.

1. "Happy is one who finds wisdom, and one who gets understanding, for the gain from it is better than the gain from silver and its profit better than gold." (Proverbs 3:13-14)

2. "One who seeks love overlooks faults, but one who harps on a matter alienates a friend." (Proverbs 19:7)

3. "A fool does not want to understand, but only to express an opinion." (Proverbs 18:2)

4. "A person's spirit can endure sickness, but low spirits—who can bear them?" (Proverbs 18:14)

5. "One who digs a pit will fall into it, and a stone will roll back upon the one who rolled it." (Proverbs 26:27)

A. _____

   _____

   _____

   _____

B. _____

   _____

   _____

   _____

C. _____

   _____

   _____

   _____

Respond:

Can you apply these three proverbs to your daily life? Respond on the back of this paper.

Jerusalem and the Western Wall

About 200 years after the Israelites entered the land of Canaan, in about 996 BCE, King David moved the Tabernacle and the Ark of the Covenant to Jerusalem and made it the Capitol of his kingdom. David's son Solomon, the next King of Israel, built a magnificent Temple to replace the portable Tabernacle used while traveling through the wilderness. He chose to build it on Mount Zion, which some believe is the same mountain where Abraham was asked to sacrifice his son Isaac. Some of the largest stones that made up the wall around the Temple weigh as much as 40 tons and are still visible today! This Temple was destroyed in 586 BCE, when the Babylonians, led by King Nebuchadnezzer, captured Jerusalem and exiled the Jewish population to Babylonia.

In 516 BCE the Temple was rebuilt when the Jews returned from exile, and it remained in use until 70 CE, when the Romans captured Jerusalem and destroyed the Temple. The only part which remained was a portion of the external wall around the Temple mountain. This last remnant of the Second Temple became the holiest of Jewish places. Before Israel gained control of Jerusalem in 1967, some referred to this wall as the "Wailing Wall" because Jews would go there to mourn the loss of the Temple. Since then, it has simply been called the Western Wall and has become a common place to visit. Many people write notes and leave them in the cracks of the wall, and some young people travel to Israel to celebrate a bar or bat mitzvah at the Wall.

Jerusalem has become one of the most famous cities in the world. Within the walls of the old city of Jerusalem are three of the world's most sacred religious sites. In addition to the Western Wall, there are Islam's Dome of the Rock, where the holy prophet Muhammad is believed to have ascended to heaven and Christianity's Church of the Holy Sepulcher, where Jesus was crucified.

Extensions:

1. Chapter VI and most of chapter VII in the First Book of Kings contain detailed descriptions of King Solomon's Temple. Read these chapters and write a report on your findings.

2. Read Psalm 13:7. What does this tell you about the Jews' exile into Babylon? Describe the feeling and language of the Psalm.

Anti-Semitism and the Holocaust

Throughout history, Jews have suffered anti-Semitism, acts of violence and hatred against the Jewish people. Some of the worst incidents occurred during the Middle Ages, when Jews were accused of using the blood of Christian children to make Passover matzah. During the crusades, Jews were massacred by Christians on their way to liberate the Holy Land from the Muslims, and in late 19th century Russia Jews were victims of pogroms, organized attacks. But the most tragic and horrifying of all may be what happened in Germany prior to and during World War II, known as the *Shoah,* or the Holocaust.

Adolf Hitler, leader of the Nazis, blamed Germany's problems on the Jews and other minority groups. As his army swept through Europe, they attempted to erase the Jewish population, imprisoning and murdering millions. Jews were placed in concentration camps where they were systematically killed. In total, about 6 million Jews, out of a world population of 18 million, were murdered during the Holocaust. The map below shows the estimated deaths in the countries besieged by the Holocaust.

Each year about a week after Pesach, Jews observe a special day called *Yom Hashoah,* Holocaust Remembrance Day, as a reminder of the horrifying consequences of hatred.

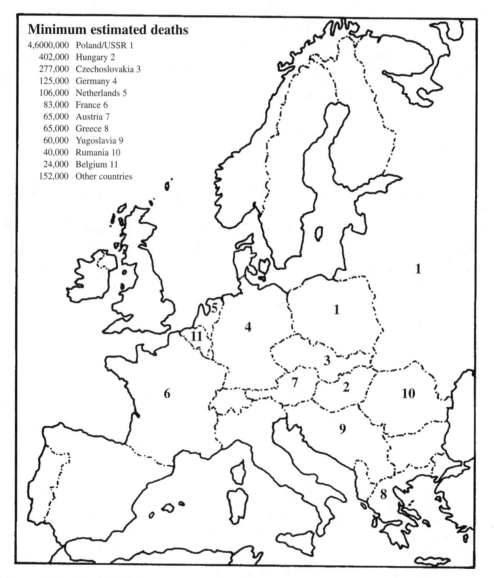

Minimum estimated deaths

4,6000,000	Poland/USSR 1
402,000	Hungary 2
277,000	Czechoslovakia 3
125,000	Germany 4
106,000	Netherlands 5
83,000	France 6
65,000	Austria 7
65,000	Greece 8
60,000	Yugoslavia 9
40,000	Rumania 10
24,000	Belgium 11
152,000	Other countries

Basic Beliefs and Observances

Monotheism

The most basic belief of Judaism is monotheism. A *midrash*, a Jewish legend, teaches that Abraham's father was an idol-maker; and one day when Abraham was young, his father left him in charge of the store. Abraham took a wooden club and smashed every idol in the store except for the largest one, and placed the club in its hand. When his father returned and asked Abraham what had happened, Abraham told him that the idols got in a fight, and the largest one smashed all of the smaller ones! His father said, "Do you expect me to believe that an idol can do that? They are just wood and stone. Tell me what really happened!" Abraham responded, "If you really believe that idols are only stone and wood, why do you worship them?"

Chosen People

Another belief of Judaism is that the Jews are the "chosen people." This does not mean that Jews believe they are better than other people or that people need to convert to Judaism in order to be loved by God. Rather, it means that God chose the Jewish people for the special responsibility of receiving the Torah and observing all of its mitzvot and passing the special ethical messages of the Torah to the rest of the world.

Messiah

Both Judaism and Christianity believe in a *Messiah*. The word Messiah is a Hebrew word which means "anointed." In Biblical times the coronation of a new king involved pouring a small amount of oil on his head, called *anointing*. Christians believe that Jesus was the Messiah (the name *Christ* comes from a Greek word meaning messiah) and that he will return. Christians also believe that the Messiah is the son of God. Jews believe that the Messiah will be a human being, a descendant of King David, who will bring the world to a time of complete peace in which every person will recognize and worship one God. Some Jews also believe that the Messiah will gather all Jews to the land of Israel, the Temple will be rebuilt, and there will be a resurrection of the dead.

Basic Beliefs and Observances *(cont.)*

Mitzvot

Jewish observance is structured around doing *mitzvot* (commandments; singular, *mitzvah*). Mitzvot cover all areas of the life of a Jew, including religious obligations and other kinds of ethical behavior. Some examples of mitzvot follow.

Prayer: Jews are obligated to pray certain prayers three times a day—morning, afternoon, and evening. These prayers include the *Shema,* the most important statement of Jewish belief (see the section of Tallit and Tefillin for two excerpts from the Shema) and the *Amidah*, a silent prayer in which they might ask God for certain things like health, wisdom, protection from enemies, and the coming of the Messiah. Some kinds of prayers are included only when praying with a *minyan* (10 people over the age of Bar or Bat Mitzvah; 10 men in Orthodox Judaism), so Jews are encouraged to pray with a community.

Tzedakah (charity): Jews are obligated to give a certain percentage, generally at least 10–15% of their income, to tzedakah.

Kashrut (dietary laws): According to the laws of kashrut, only split-hooved animals that chew their cud, certain types of fowl (like chicken, turkey, and duck), and fish with fins and scales are kosher—that is, proper to eat. Jews are also forbidden to mix dairy and meat products together at the same meal. In addition, animals (not fish) must be killed in a special way called *shechitah,* kosher slaughter, so they die with as little pain as possible. One of the purposes of the Kashrut laws is to sensitize Jews to proper treatment of animals.

Shabbat (The Sabbath): On Shabbat, from sundown on Friday night until dark on Saturday night, Jews set aside time to rest. It is symbolic of God's seventh day of rest, after taking six days to create the world. On Friday nights and Saturday afternoons, Jews have special Shabbat meals, including blessings over wine and special braided egg breads called *challah.* In a traditional observance of Shabbat, Jews refrain from creative acts which change the state of the world, including cooking, shopping, lighting fires (including using electricity), sewing or knitting, writing or coloring.

Branches of Judaism

Pre-Enlightenment Judaism

In the early 18th century, there were no formal movements within Judaism. Belief and practice varied (e.g., hasidic and non-hasidic, Ashkeai and Sephardi), but since Jews, no matter what their personal practice, had no chance of being accepted into the Christian world, it was unthinkable and nearly impossible for a Jew to leave the Jewish community. Therefore, there was no need to create a strict definition of what it meant to be a proper Jew.

Reform Judaism

In the post-enlightenment 19th century, the Reform movement changed significant parts of Judaism to make it more compatible with a changing world. For example, in the United States the language of prayer became English instead of Hebrew. In addition, Reform Jews believe that the mitzvot in the Torah are only meaningful if they add to one's relationship with God. Most of the traditional restrictions of Shabbat and Kashrut are not observed by Reform Jews.

Orthodox Judaism

In response to the changes that Reform Judaism was introducing, the traditional Jews, led by one particular Rabbi named Samson Raphael Hirsh, asserted that the only acceptable Jewish belief was that every letter of the Torah was given to Moses by God on Mount Sinai, along with a detailed commentary. Therefore, all traditional practices of Judaism reflect the will of God and cannot be changed in any way. Note that it was not until the birth of Reform that the traditionalists saw the need to create strict boundaries around the definition of a proper Jew. Thus Orthodoxy, which literally means "correct thought," was not born until after the advent of the Reform movement.

Conservative Judaism

Conservative Judaism responded to Orthodoxy by saying that there has always been a way to change Jewish law and tradition, but the basic system of mitzvot cannot be changed. Most of the observances of Shabbat and Kashrut, for example, remain unchanged, although most Conservative Jews tend to treat them more liberally than do Orthodox Jews. Examples of changes include giving women an equal role in synagogue ritual (in most, but not all, Conservative synagogues) and more flexibility to change the traditional prayers to reflect modern concerns.

Reconstructionist Judaism

Founded in the mid-20th century, Reconstructionism is the most recent of the major movements of Judaism. It operates under the principle of "The tradition has a vote, not a veto." In other words, unlike Reform, the entire basic system of mitzvot is still an important part of Judaism; but unlike Conservative, an individual mitzvah can be modified or rejected if the community no longer finds it meaningful.

Rites of Passage

Circumcision

During circumcision, a piece of skin (called the foreskin) which covers the front of the penis is surgically removed. In the United States, it is very common for babies from many religions to be circumcised for medical or personal reasons several days after birth. For Jews, however, circumcision is called *Brit Milah*, "the covenant of circumcision," and is done when the baby is eight days old, fulfilling the commandment God gave to Abraham in Genesis 17:10-12:

Such shall be the covenant between Me and you and your offspring to follow which you shall keep: every male among you shall be circumcised. You shall be circumcised in the flesh of your foreskin, and that shall be the sign of the covenant between Me and you. And throughout the generations, every male among you shall be circumcised at the age of eight days.

There are also special ceremonies to welcome baby girls into the religion. Although there is no surgical procedure for girls, they are welcomed into the covenant with most of the same basic language as the Brit Milah ritual of the boys.

Bar Mitzvah and Bat Mitzvah

When a boy reaches the age of 13 years plus one day or when a girl reaches the age of 12 years plus one day, according to their birthdays on the Jewish calendar, they become Bar Mitzvah (for a boy) or Bat Mitzvah (for a girl). Literally, this means "son (or daughter) of the commandments." From that day on, they become responsible for observing all of the mitzvot (commandments) of Judaism. Prior to becoming bar or bat mitzvah, their parents were responsible for their religious behavior.

Preparing to celebrate a Bar and Bat Mitzvah in the synagogue requires years of study. The content of the synagogue celebration varies, but it commonly includes one or more of the following: reading from the Torah scroll, reading a selection from the prophets, leading a portion of the service, and delivering a speech, called a *d'var Torah* ("word of Torah") about the scriptural readings. In Orthodox synagogues, only boys celebrate Bar Mitzvah by taking part in the synagogue service. Following the conclusion of the service, family, friends, and the congregation join together for a festive meal.

Marriage

Marriage in the Jewish tradition is called *kiddushin*, which means sanctification. A wedding is a public ceremony in which the bride and groom commit themselves exclusively to each other. It is done publicly because the community is expected to help the couple live a life of loyalty and devotion to God and Jewish traditions.

Before the wedding ceremony, the bride and groom formally accept the provisions of the *ketubah*, the Jewish marriage contract which stipulates, among other things, that they agree to cherish, honor, and maintain each other (physically, emotionally, and spiritually) according to the customs of Jewish marriage. The ketubah is then signed by two witnesses.

Rites of Passage *(cont.)*

Marriage *(cont.)*

Following the signing of the ketubah, the groom places a veil over his bride's face. The origins of the veil go back to the matriarch Rebekah, who, when she saw Isaac for the first time, "took her veil and covered her face." (Genesis 24:65). The veil is symbolic of Jewish traditions of modesty.

The marriage takes place under a *chupah*, a wedding canopy representing the home that the bride and groom will create together. The rabbi recites blessings, the couple drinks wine and exchanges rings (in an Orthodox ceremony, the groom does not receive a ring), and the rabbi recites seven special blessings comparing the couple to Adam and Eve, the two original human beings of creation. At the end of the ceremony, the groom breaks a glass, recalling the destruction of the Temple and reminding the couple that it is their responsibility to help fix the imperfect world in which they live.

Death

The Torah, at the beginning of Genesis, teaches us that human beings were created when God took a clod of earth, formed it into a human figure, and breathed life into it. When the breath of life leaves a body for the last time, Jewish tradition teaches that the body should be returned to the earth as quickly and naturally as possible.

For this reason, Jewish funerals do not permit cremation or embalming (except in the Reform movement), and they use coffins that are made entirely of wood. Most funerals take place within a day or two of death. The body is carefully washed and dressed in plain linen garments by a special group called the *Hevra Kadisha*, meaning "the holy society" because of the special nature of their responsibility.

Following the funeral, the family returns home for *shiva*. The word shiva means "seven" and refers to the first seven days following the funeral. During this time, mourners are prohibited from excessive grooming and pampering of the body, such as taking long baths, shaving, or trimming nails. In addition, it is customary to cover the mirrors in a shiva home. The reason for these customs is to allow the mourners to focus on their grief, instead of having to spend time worrying about their physical appearance. Mourners also do not go out of their homes during shiva; rather, the community comes in to comfort them by bringing them meals and leading services so the mourners can recite the *Kaddish*.

The mourner's kaddish is one of the most famous Jewish prayers. It is recited by mourners at the funeral, during shiva, and then for up to a year following the death. It is also recited on a *Yahrtzeit*, the anniversary of a death according to the Hebrew calendar. Interestingly, it does not mention death. Rather, it is a prayer affirming one's belief in God even after experiencing the tragedy of the death of a loved one.

Name _____

The Synagogue

The Jewish house of worship is called a *Synagogue.* Many Reform synagogues (and some others) are also called temples. In addition to being a place where Jews gather to worship, the synagogue also serves as a community and education center. The main services each week are Friday night (especially at Reform Temples) and Saturday morning, although many synagogues have services every morning and evening.

The rabbi is the religious leader and teacher of a congregation and usually speaks about the weekly Torah portion during Sabbath services. Services are usually led by a cantor who leads the singing or chanting of prayers and reads from the Torah scroll. However, anyone who is familiar with the prayers and the melodies may lead a service or read from the Torah.

In the center of the *bimah* (raised platform) at the front of the sanctuary is the *aron kodesh* (holy ark), holding the Torah scrolls. Each Torah is handwritten in Hebrew on parchment (animal skin). Above the aron is the *ner tamid* (eternal light) representing the constant presence of God and reminding us of the *menorah*, the seven-branched candle holder that illuminated the Temple in Jerusalem. There is also a podium, from which the rabbi speaks, and a table, at which the cantor sings and the Torah is read.

Below you will find a diagram of a common synagogue and a list of features. Locate them on the diagram.

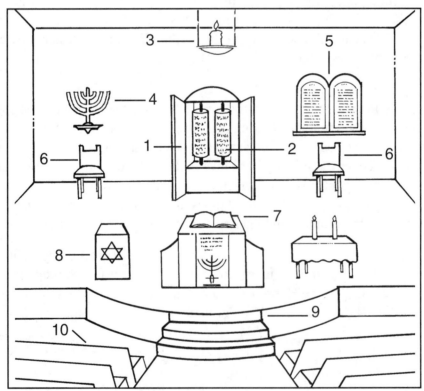

A. Congregation seating
B. Torah Scrolls
C. Ten Commandments

D. Menorah
E. Rabbi's and Cantor's seats
F. Bimah

G. Ner Tamid
H. Ark
I. Rabbi's podium
J. Cantor's and Torah reading table

Important Jewish Objects and Symbols

Tallit

A *Tallit* is a four cornered garment that is worn during the morning prayers. The important part of a tallit is the *tzitzit*, or fringes, tied onto each of the corners. The commandment to attach tzitzit to the corners of clothing comes from the Shema. The three paragraphs of the Shema contain the most important statement of belief in Judaism. Here is a portion of the third paragraph of the Shema, Numbers 15:37-41:

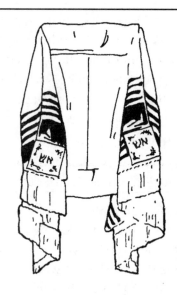

The Lord said to Moses: Instruct the people Israel that in every generation they shall put fringes on the corners of their garments . . . . Looking upon the fringes, you will be reminded of all the commandments of the Lord and fulfill them and not be seduced by your heart or led astray by your eyes. Then you will remember and observe all My commandments and be holy before your God . . . .

Some Jews wear a small four cornered undershirt, called a tallit katan (small tallit), so they can fulfill the commandment of wearing tzitzit all day.

Tefillin

Tefillin (called *phylacteries* in English) are small leather boxes with straps that can be tied on the arm and around the head. They contain verses on parchment from four sections of the Torah, including the first two paragraphs of the Shema. Tefillin are worn during morning prayers, except on Shabbat and Festivals. Wearing tefillin is a reminder of God's commandments. The tefillin on the arm (see illustration for two wrap methods) represents the opportunity to serve God with the body through doing commandments, and the tefillin on the head represents the opportunity to serve God with the mind through study and belief. The first paragraph of the Shema (Deuteronomy 6:4-9) is as follows (the commandment to wear tefillin is underlined):

Ashkenazim Wrap

Sephardim Wrap

Hear O Israel, the Lord our God, the Lord is One. You shall love the Lord your God with all your heart, with all your soul, and with all your might. These words which I command you this day shall be in your heart. You shall teach them diligently to your children. You shall recite them at home and away, morning and night. <u>*You shall bind them as a sign upon your hand, they shall be a reminder above your eyes,*</u> *and you shall inscribe them upon the doorposts of your home and upon your gates.*

Important Jewish Objects and Symbols *(cont.)*

Mezuzah

A *Mezuzah* is attached to the right side of the doorpost as you enter a room. Many Jews only put a mezuzah on the front doorway, but some Jews put one on every room of the house (except closets and bathrooms), in accordance with Deuteronomy 6:9 (see the first paragraph of the Shema on page 37). Inscribed on a small piece of parchment inside the mezuzah case are the first two paragraphs of the Shema.

Kippah

A *Kippah*, sometimes called a Yarmelka (Yiddish) or a skullcap, is a small round cap worn on the head. The Kippah is worn by men and women, although in Orthodox synagogues it is only worn by men. Some Jews wear the kippah all day; some wear it only while eating, praying, or studying; some wear it only during prayer; and some Jews (in Reform synagogues) do not wear one at all. It signifies that human beings are beneath, or dependent on, God.

Shofar

The *Shofar* is a ram's horn blown during the month prior to Rosh Hashanah (the New Year) as well as during Rosh Hashanah services and at the end of Yom Kippur (the Day of Atonement) services. Rosh Hashanah and Yom Kippur, also known as the High Holidays or the Days of Awe because of their importance, is a time during which each person is judged by God. The purpose of the loud sounds of the shofar is to wake people up and remind them of their responsibility to ask forgiveness for their sins. If a person hurts another person, the first person must ask the second person for forgiveness before God will forgive him or her. If a person has committed a sin against God, then he or she may ask God directly for forgiveness.

Star of David

The six-pointed star, called a *Magen David* ("shield of David") is a relatively new symbol of Judaism, becoming popular only in the last 200 years. It is named after King David, whom legend tells us had a shield with this star on it. A Magen David appears on the flag of the State of Israel.

The Jewish Calendar

The Jewish calendar is different from our calendar in some important ways. First, our calendar is a solar calendar, based on the length of time it takes the earth to circle the sun. The Jewish calendar is a lunar calendar, so every month begins with the appearance of a new moon, called *Rosh Hodesh* ("the beginning of a month"). A month is either 29 or 30 days long. The 12-month lunar year is about 12 days shorter than the solar year. Therefore, every two or three years the Jewish calendar adds a "leap month," an extra month to adjust the calendar so the holidays continue to fall in the proper season.

Second, the Jewish counting of years is based on the number of years since creation according to the Tanakh. For example, *Rosh Hashanah*, the Jewish new year, fell on September 21, 1998, which corresponded to the first day in the Jewish year of 5759.

Finally, each day on the Jewish calendar begins at sundown. That is why Rosh Hashanah of 5759 actually began at sundown on September 20, 1998.

Jewish Months

Tishri (Sept./Oct.)	Heshvan (Oct./Nov.)	Kislev (Nov./Dec.)	Tevet (Dec./Jan.)
Shebat (Jan./Feb.)	Adar (Feb./March)	Nisan (March/April)	Iyar (April/May)
Sivan (May/June)	Tammuz (June/July)	Ab (July/August)	Elul (August/Sept.)

Some Significant Holidays and the Months in Which They Fall

Tishre: *Rosh Hashanah* (New Year), *Yom Kippur* (Day of Atonement), and *Sukkot* (the harvest Festival of Booths, a reminder of the huts in which the Israelites lived during the travels in the desert)

Kislev: *Chanukah* (The festival of the rededication of the Temple)

Adar: *Purim* (celebrating the story of Esther and the rescue of the Jews from Persia)

Nisan: *Pesach* (Passover, the Exodus from Egypt), *Yom Hashoah* (Holocaust Memorial Day), *Yom Ha'atzma'ut* (Israel Independence Day)

Sivan: *Shavuot* (festival celebrating the giving of the Torah)

Passover (Pesach)

In the story of Exodus, you will recall how the Israelites smeared lamb's blood on their doorposts on the night of Passover. They did this to avoid the tenth plague God sent to Pharaoh, the death of all first-born Egyptian children. Seeing the sign, God literally "passed over" their houses.

The Festival of Passover, or *Pesach,* as it is called in Hebrew, falls in the Hebrew month of Nisan (see page 39 for a list of Jewish months and holidays) in late March or April. It commemorates freedom from slavery and the Exodus from Egypt. Families and friends gather to share a special meal called a *Seder* and to tell the story of Passover from a special book called a *Haggadah.* Special foods are also eaten that remind them of the hardship of slavery and the miracle of being taken out of Egypt.

At the center of a Seder table is a special plate known as a Seder plate, containing five (or sometimes six) items of food.

Maror: a bitter herb, usually horseradish, representing the bitterness of slavery

Charoset: a mixture of apples, walnuts, cinnamon, and wine, resembling the mortar which the Israelites used to build the Egyptian cities

Z'roah: a roasted bone, often a shankbone of a lamb, representing the Passover offering

Beitzah: a roasted egg representing the new life of springtime

Karpas: a green vegetable, usually parsley, representing spring and eaten dipped in salt water, representing the tears of slavery

Hazeret: Some Seder plates have a sixth place for another bitter vegetable, usually romaine lettuce, also representing the bitterness of slavery.

You also find the following items on a Seder table:

Matzah: unleavened bread representing the bread which did not have time to rise when the Israelites left Egypt in a great hurry (Matzah also represents bread of poverty, reminding Jews of the hardship of slavery.)

Wine or grape juice: Each person drinks four cups, representing God's promise to the Jews to take them out of slavery.

Passover (Pesach) *(cont.)*

Make a Seder plate to learn about the Passover symbols. Color the plate pictured below and cut it out. Next, cut a circle the same size as the plate out of a separate sheet of paper. Then, cut along the bold lines to divide the Seder plate into sections. Attach the centers of the two circles with glue or a brass fastener. (The Seder plate should be on top.) Finally, lift up each section of the plate and on the paper under it write a brief description of the food that is pictured and what it symbolizes.

Seder Plate

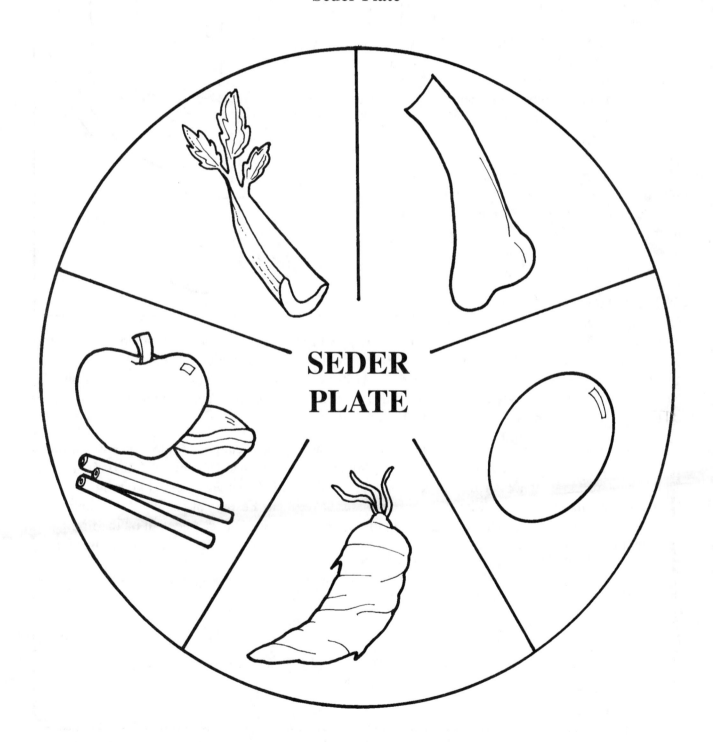

Chanukah

The festival of Chanukah (also spelled Hanukah) celebrates the defeat of the Syrian Greeks and the rededication of King Solomon's Temple by the Maccabees in 165 BCE.

The Syrians, ruled by King Antiochus, tried to force the Jews to worship the Greek Gods. He forbad them, under penalty of death, to keep the Sabbath or celebrate any Jewish holidays, circumcise their sons, or keep any other traditions of Judaism. He desecrated the Temple by placing statues of Greek gods in it, and he ordered the people to bring sacrifices of non-kosher pigs. King Antiochus sent inspectors to every town to make sure that the people carried out his instructions. The inspectors burned Torah scrolls and put to death anyone who violated the King's orders.

In the small town of Modi'in, a priest named Mattityahu (Mattathias) and

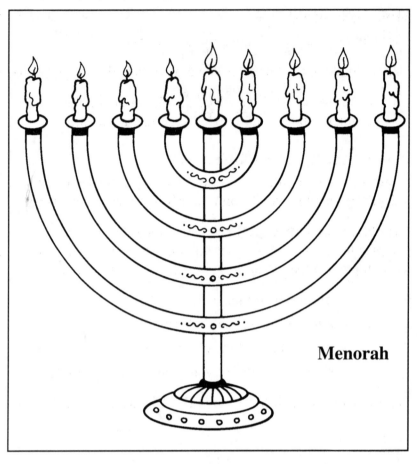

Menorah

his four sons refused to obey the King's orders. They fled to the hills and called for others to join them in fighting the Syrians. When Mattityahu died, the rebellion continued under the leadership of his son Judah, who had been given the name *Maccabee*, a Hebrew word meaning "hammer," because of his strength. Although Judah Maccabee and his followers were poorly equipped and outnumbered, they defeated the Syrian armies and recaptured all of Jerusalem.

The Temple was cleansed of idols and rededicated with feasting and great joy. A tiny container of oil was found in the Temple, enough to last one day. Miraculously, it burned for eight days and nights. That is why a special eight branched menorah (candle holder) called a *chanukiyah* is lit during Chanukah, and that is also why Chanukah is sometimes called "The Festival of Lights." The ninth candle, called the *shamash*, is used to light each of the other candles. One candle is lit on the first evening, two on the second, three on the third, and so on until all eight candles are lit on the last night.

In addition to the lighting of the chanukiyah, children receive gifts and play a top-spinning game called the *dreidel* game. See the next page to make your own dreidel.

Chanukah *(cont.)*

Making a Dreidel:

1. Cut out the dreidel along the bold lines.

2. Fold along the fine lines and glue or tape them together so you have a box shape.

3. Make two small holes where the circles are on the top and bottom and push a short pencil through. Spin the dreidel by twirling the pencil.

Playing the Dreidel Game:

A dreidel is a four-sided top. Each side has a Hebrew letter on it: *nun*, *gimmel*, *hay*, and *shin*. These four letters stand for the Hebrew words that mean "a great miracle happened there [in Israel]."

The players sit in a circle. Each player receives an equal number of tokens (nuts, candles, or coins) and puts five tokens from his or her pile into the center. Everyone takes turns spinning the dreidel. The letter on top when the dreidel stops spinning tells what to do.

> **nun:** Do nothing.
>
> **gimmel:** Take the center pile.
>
> **hay:** Take half the center pile.
>
> **shin:** Give half of your pile to the center pile.

Players who lose their tokens are out. The last player with tokens is the winner.

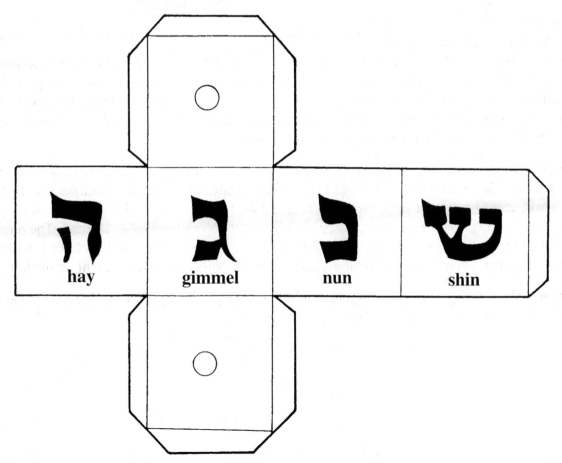

hay   gimmel   nun   shin

Chanukah *(cont.)*

One traditional Jewish food is called *latkes*. Latkes are crispy brown potato pancakes enjoyed on Chanukah and all year. Some people also celebrate Chanukah by eating jelly doughnuts. Both of these holiday treats are fried in oil. Remembering the story of Chanukah, why would it be important for the food to be fried in oil?

Here is a recipe for latkes. Be sure to cook with safety!

Ingredients:

- 4 large potatoes
- 1 teaspoon (5 mL) salt
- 2 eggs
- 3 tablespoons (45 mL) flour
- 1/2 teaspoon (3 mL) baking powder
- vegetable oil for frying
- applesauce or sour cream

Utensils:

- potato peeler
- grater
- paper towels
- hand beater
- skillet
- bowl
- spoon
- spatula
- plates and forks

Preparation:

1. Wash, peel, and grate the potatoes.
2. Drain off the liquid.
3. Beat the eggs.
4. Mix everything together, except the oil.
5. Heat the oil in a skillet.
6. Drop the mixture by tablespoons into the hot oil.
7. Fry the latkes on both sides until brown.
8. Drain the latkes on paper towels.
9. Serve the latkes with applesauce or sour cream on the side.

The Jewish Population

Despite the great impact that Judaism has had on the world, there were only about 13 million Jews in the world in 1995. That amounts to about .2% of the world's population. The map below shows the distribution of Jews around the globe in 1995.

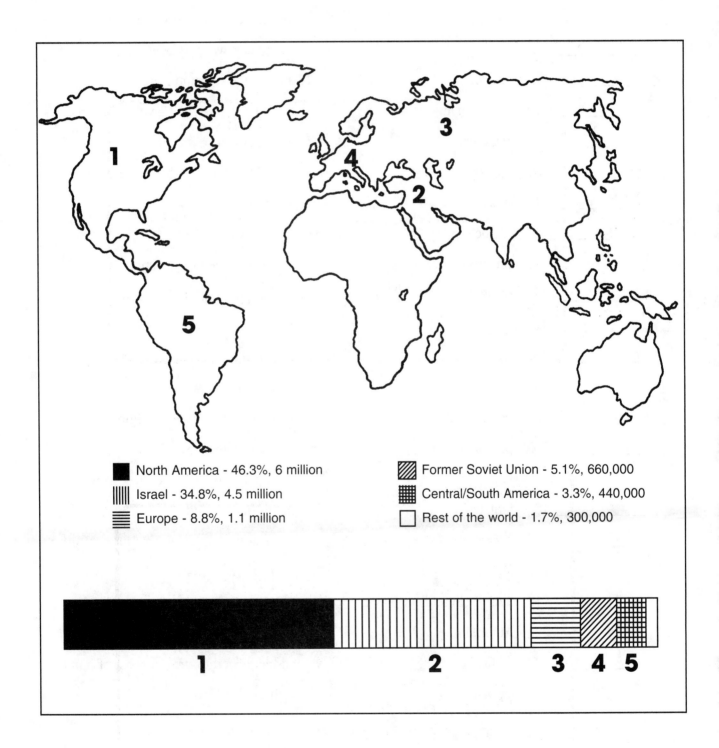

North America - 46.3%, 6 million

Israel - 34.8%, 4.5 million

Europe - 8.8%, 1.1 million

Former Soviet Union - 5.1%, 660,000

Central/South America - 3.3%, 440,000

Rest of the world - 1.7%, 300,000

Name _____

Vocabulary

Place the appropriate letters in the blanks to match the vocabulary words.

_____	1. synagogue	a.	saying that contains wisdom
_____	2. menorah	b.	the founding father of Judaism
_____	3. BCE	c.	small cap worn by Jews
_____	4. Tanakh	d.	before the Common Era
_____	5. polytheism	e.	rite of passage for 12-year-old girls
_____	6. Passover	f.	four-sided top
_____	7. shofar	g.	first five books of the Hebrew Bible
_____	8. mezuzah	h.	king of Egypt
_____	9. Holocaust	i.	potato pancake
_____	10. pharaoh	j.	eight-branched candlestick
_____	11. proverb	k.	worshipping an image or idol
_____	12. monotheism	l.	Common Era
_____	13. CE	m.	belief in more than one god
_____	14. Moses	n.	place where Jews worship
_____	15. bat mitzvah	o.	symbol of the Jewish religion
_____	16. patriarch	p.	murder of Jews by Nazis
_____	17. latkes	q.	spiritual leader of a congregation
_____	18. idolatry	r.	belief in one God
_____	19. Torah	s.	prophet who lead the Exodus
_____	20. dreidel	t.	ram's horn
_____	21. Star (or Shield) of David	u.	holiday commemorating the Exodus
_____	22. Abraham	v.	father of a tribe or nation
_____	23. rabbi	w.	case attached to the doorpost of homes
_____	24. kippah	x.	Hebrew Bible

Name _____

Quiz and Review

Part One: In questions 1-10, fill in the spaces with the correct answer.

1. Jews believe that God made a _____ , or sacred agreement, with Abraham.

2. The Jewish Sabbath takes place from _____ night just before sundown to _____ night after dark.

3. The Exodus took place around _____ BCE.

4. God first spoke to Moses on Mount _____ .

5. It took ten _____ before Pharoah let the Hebrews go.

6. _____ wrote the Proverbs.

7. Two foods eaten on Passover are _____ and _____ .

8. Chanukah celebrates the Maccabee victory over the _____ .

9. Jews were imprisoned in _____ during the Holocaust.

10. "Bar Mitzvah" means _____ .

11. There are about _____ million Jews in the world.

12. Two countries bordering Israel are _____ and _____ .

13. The _____ first destroyed King Solomon's Temple.

14. About 46% of the world's Jews live in _____ .

15. _____ is a rite of passage during which the foreskin of the male organ is removed.

Part Two: Respond to the following questions in full sentences. Be sure to use details to support your answers.

1. Summarize in your own words what is at the heart of the Ten Commandments. If you could take one guiding principal from them, what would it be?

_____

_____

_____

_____

_____

Name _____

Quiz and Review *(cont.)*

Part Two *(cont.)*

2. Why is the Western Wall sacred to Jews? How does it capture the essence of their history and religious heritage?

_____

_____

_____

_____

_____

_____

_____

_____

3. Briefly explain the origin of Judaism and its basic beliefs. In what ways were the beliefs unique or new to the world?

_____

_____

_____

_____

_____

_____

_____

_____

The Roman Empire

By the 1st century CE, the Roman Empire ruled a large part of the known world. In 63 BCE, General Pompey conquered Jerusalem, capital of Judea. The Romans renamed this area Palestine and ruled over it for nearly 700 years. The Empire's sophisticated system of roads helped aid the fast spread of Christianity. The map below shows the Roman Empire in the 1st century CE.

From 39-4 BCE, Herod the Great was made King of the Jews by the Romans. When he died, he divided the territory among his three sons: Archelaus, Antipas, and Philip, who also used the title "Herod." Archelaus ruled over Judaea, but in 6 CE he was deposed and a Roman governor took control. At the time of Jesus' death, Pontius Pilate was governor of Judaea.

The map on page 50 shows Palestine in the time of Jesus. Many places may already be familiar to you. You will want to refer to the map as you read about the life of Jesus.

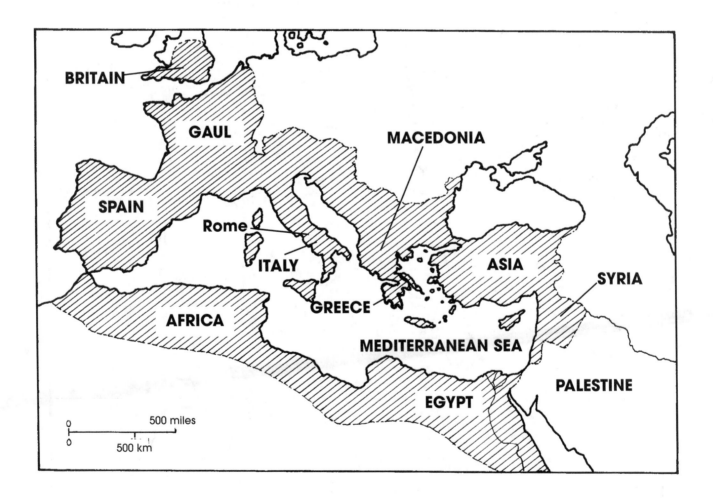

Palestine in the Time of Jesus

The Life of Jesus

The central figure in Christianity is Jesus Christ, whose life inspired what was to become the world's most popular religion. In order to understand Christianity, one must be familiar with the life of Jesus. Here is a retelling of his life, focusing only on the main events.

The Virgin Mary and the Birth of Jesus

The birth and childhood of Jesus is told in Luke, the third book in the New Testament. The story begins when God sends the angel Gabriel to Mary, a young woman who lives in the city of Nazareth in Galilee. She is betrothed, or engaged, to Joseph the Carpenter.

Gabriel tells Mary that she is blessed and that she will give birth to a son named Jesus. When Mary becomes fearful, Gabriel assures her that Jesus will be great. Since she is not married, Mary wonders how she will conceive a child. Gabriel tells her that Jesus will be the Son of God, and so the Holy Spirit will make the birth possible. Christians call this the immaculate conception. Mary sees the truth of her calling and says, "I am the handmaiden of the Lord."

At the time of Jesus' birth, Mary and Joseph travel to Bethlehem. The emperor of Rome, Caesar Augustus, had ordered everyone to register for taxes in the town of their birth, thus Mary and Joseph go to Bethlehem where Joseph was born. The town is so full that when Jesus is born, Mary places him in a manger (a food trough for animals) in a stable.

That evening, in the hills of Bethlehem, some shepherds see a new star in the sky. An angel tells them it is a sign that the savior, Christ the Lord, has come. The shepherds follow the Star of Bethlehem until they find Mary, Joseph, and the baby Jesus. The shepherds then speak throughout the land of what they have witnessed.

The Wise Men Visit

Knowing of the holy birth, three wise men come to Jerusalem to find Jesus, the newborn King of the Jews. Herod, the king, is threatened and wants to dispose of the child. He asks the wise men to find Jesus so that he may worship him. Rejoicing, the men follow the Star of Bethlehem until they find Mary and Jesus. But they were warned by God not to return to Herod.

Afterwards, an angel appears to Joseph in a dream, warning him that Herod will try to destroy Jesus. The angel tells him to take his family and flee to Egypt.

When the wise men do not return, Herod is furious. He orders the death of all male children in Bethlehem under two years of age.

After Herod dies, an angel again appears to Joseph in a dream, telling him to take his family into the land of Israel. Since Archelaus, Herod's son, still reigns in Judea, Joseph goes to the city of Nazareth in the region of Galilee. Therefore, Jesus grew up in Nazareth.

Jesus and John the Baptist

Luke 1 describes the birth of John the Baptist, son of a priest named Zacharias and his wife, Elizabeth. Like the birth of Jesus, John's birth is blessed. The angel Gabriel tells Zacharias that John will be full of holiness, turning many others towards God.

Now in his twenties, John begins fulfilling the prophecy. He lives simply, dresses in camel skins and eats locusts and wild honey. He wanders through Jordan, preaching to the people about the coming of the Messiah and urging them to repent their sins and live a just life. Before he preaches, he baptizes people by immersing them in the water of the River Jordan.

When Jesus arrives to receive baptism, John knows that here is the Messiah. After Jesus is baptized, the Holy Spirit comes to him in the form of a dove, and a voice comes from heaven:

> "This is my beloved Son, in whom I am well pleased."

Herod, hearing of John's influence, shuts him up in prison. Some time later, John the Baptist is beheaded.

From this time, baptism has grown into an important religious rite for Christians. It is said to cleanse followers of their sins.

Many people went to John for baptism and wisdom. He spoke of generosity, honesty, and non-violence. To the people he said, "He who has two coats, let him share with him who has none; and he who has food, let him do likewise." To the tax collectors he said, "Collect no more than is appointed you." To the soldiers he said, "Rob no one by violence or false accusation, and be content with your wages." (Luke 3: 10-14)

Extension:

Read Mark 6 and explain why John the Baptist is beheaded.

Name _____

Reading from the New Testament: The Temptation in the Wilderness

After receiving baptism from John, Jesus left for the desert where he fasted forty days and nights. This story, from Matthew 4: 1-11, tells of the temptations Jesus faced during his retreat into the wilderness.

[1] Then Jesus was led up by the Spirit into the wilderness to be tempted by the devil. [2] And he fasted forty days and forty nights, and afterward he was hungry. [3] And the tempter came and said to him, "If you are the Son of God, command these stones to become loaves of bread." [4] But he answered, "It is written,

'Man shall not live by bread alone,
but by every word that proceeds from the mouth of God.'"

[5] Then the devil took him to the holy city, and set him on the pinnacle of the temple, [6] and said to him, "If you are the Son of God, throw yourself down; for it is written,

'He will give angels charge of you,' and
'On their hands they will bear you up, lest you strike your foot against a stone.'"

[7] Jesus said to him, "Again it is written, 'You shall not tempt the Lord your God.'" [8] Again, the devil took him to a very high mountain, and showed him all the kingdoms of the world and the glory of them; [9] and he said to him, "All these I will give you, if you will fall down and worship me." [10] Then Jesus said to him, "Be gone, Satan! for it is written,

'You shall worship the Lord your God
and only him shall you serve.'"

[11] Then the devil left him, and behold, angels came and ministered to him.

Questions:

1. In this story, Jesus spends forty days and nights in the desert. List other famous religious stories in which the number forty is significant._____

_____

_____

2. List the three temptations Satan offers Jesus. _____

_____

_____

3. In this story, why do you think Jesus fasts? _____

_____

_____

The Apostles and the Sermon on the Mount

Soon Jesus had chosen twelve apostles (chosen followers). He wanted to give these twelve the power and wisdom to caste out evil and to heal sickness. His apostles were the following:

- Simon Peter
- James
- Philip
- Thomas
- Thaddaeus
- Simon the Zealot
- Andrew
- John (James's brother)
- Bartholomew
- Matthew
- James (son of Alphaeus)
- Judas Iscariot

Along with the disciples, thousands from all over Judea came to hear Jesus preach and to be healed. Once, upon seeing the multitudes, Jesus ascended a mountain and delivered what is now called "The Sermon on the Mount" (Matthew 5: 3-10), one of his most beloved teachings. It includes the *Beatitudes,* statements on being blessed. They are as follows:

> Blessed are the poor in spirit, for theirs is the kingdom of heaven.
>
> Blessed are those who mourn, for they shall be comforted.
>
> Blessed are the meek, for they shall inherit the earth.
>
> Blessed are those who hunger and thirst for righteousness, for they shall be satisfied.
>
> Blessed are the merciful, for they shall obtain mercy.
>
> Blessed are the pure of heart, for they shall see God.
>
> Blessed are the peacemakers, for they shall be called the children of God.
>
> Blessed are those who are persecuted for righteousness' sake, for theirs is the kingdom of heaven.

Extensions:

1. Memorize and recite the Beatitudes.

2. Write a short essay on the meaning of the Beatitudes.

Miracles

Jesus is known for performing many miracles. Usually these miracles involved healing the sick or even raising the dead. These unusual deeds, along with the power of his words, brought Jesus many followers. But he also threatened the religious and political establishment.

Here are a few of the miraculous episodes related in the New Testament.

Jesus in Galilee

At about the age of thirty, Jesus began to preach in Galilee. One day, walking by the sea of Galilee, he saw two brothers, Simon and Andrew, casting fishing nets. Jesus took a boat out to them and began to teach. Though they had caught nothing all day, Jesus told the brothers to cast their nets again. This time hundreds of fish rose in the nets. Simon and Andrew were astonished and immediately became disciples of Jesus. Soon they were joined by another pair of brothers, James and John.

The Marriage in Cana

Jesus and his disciples were invited to a wedding ceremony in the city of Cana of Galilee. Mary, Jesus's mother, also attended. She told her son that there was no more wine. So Jesus instructed the servants to fill six stone water pots with water and to give them to the master of the feast. The water was turned to wine.

Jesus Heals the Leper

Jesus spent much time preaching in the synagogues and healing the sick. One day a leper came to him and, kneeling down, asked to be healed. Jesus, moved with compassion, touched the leper's face, and the leper was healed. Then, Jesus instructed the man to tell no one of this miracle but to go straight to the priest to show proof of the power of God.

But the man could not keep quiet. Soon thousands of people sought Jesus until he was forced to depart into the wilderness.

The Pharisees and Healing on the Sabbath Day

The Pharisees, Jewish religious leaders, were traditional in their interpretation of the laws of Moses. Feeling threatened, they began to challenge Jesus and to try to entrap him with their questions. For example, Jesus forgave the sins of a paralyzed man and the man walked. The Pharisees challenged Jesus, saying that only God has the power to forgive. But Jesus answered that the power of forgiveness is also man's.

One day, Jesus entered a synagogue on the Sabbath and saw a man with a withered hand. He healed the man, though it was unlawful to heal on the Sabbath day. He explained that it was lawful to do good on any day. This angered the Pharisees, and soon they began plotting to destroy Jesus.

Miracles *(cont.)*

The Feeding of the Multitude

As Jesus' fame spread, throngs of people sought his presence. One day, he and his disciples were followed by multitudes of seekers. Jesus was moved with compassion, seeing them as sheep without a shepherd. He began to teach them.

Later in the day, the disciples advised Jesus to send the people away so they might feed themselves. But Jesus told them to bring what food was available. They did this but collected only five loaves of bread and two fish.

Jesus took the loaves and the fish and gave thanks. He distributed them to his disciples who, in turn, distributed them to the people. This continued until everyone, about five thousand people, were fed.

Jesus Walks on Water

Jesus sent his disciples into a boat to cross the sea of Galilee. He went alone up a mountain to pray until the evening. But soon the sea became rough and the boat was tossed about. Seeing this, Jesus walked on the water toward the vessel.

Sighting Jesus, the disciples were afraid, thinking he was a spirit. But Jesus spoke to them and calmed their fears. Peter then answered, "Lord, if it is you, let me come to you on the water."

"Come," answered Jesus. Peter walked on the water towards his Master. But when a strong wind came, Peter began to sink. Jesus took him by the hand, and said to him, "O you of little faith, why do you doubt?"

Raising Lazarus from the Dead

In a village called Bethany lived two sisters, Martha and Mary, and their brother, Lazarus. Jesus was close to this family. One day, Mary sent word to Jesus that Lazarus was sick. Two days later, Jesus went to Bethany, knowing already that Lazarus was dead.

"Lord," cried Martha, "if you had been here my brother would not have died. But I know that even now God will give to you whatever you ask."

Then Mary came to Jesus, weeping. She took him to the grave of Lazarus, which was a cave with a stone in front of it. Jesus wept for his friend, who had already been dead for four days.

"Lord," Martha cried, "by this time he is decaying."

"Did I not say to you," answered Jesus, "that if you would believe, you would see the glory of God?"

So Jesus had them roll away the stone. He thanked God and said, "Lazarus, come forth."

And Lazarus rose from the dead.

The Last Supper and the Crucifixion

In the spring of his third year of ministry, Jesus traveled to Jerusalem to celebrate Passover. According to Matthew's Gospel, crowds of people welcomed him into the city, proclaiming him to be the Messiah. Immediately upon seeing this, the Pharisees began plotting against Jesus. These religious leaders demanded that people conform only to the laws of Moses. Because Jesus disregarded their traditions in order to meet human needs, and because his following was growing, he threatened the Pharisees.

Once inside the walls of Jerusalem, Jesus made even more enemies. He went to the Temple built by Herod the Great. Instead of finding a quiet place of worship, Jesus found the Temple was crowded with the noise of merchants and money-changers. Outraged, Jesus overturned their tables and drove merchants from the Temple, shouting, "Make not God's house a marketplace." The Sadducees, who controlled the Temple worship, then joined the Pharisees in their opposition of Jesus.

That evening, Jesus and his disciples gathered to have supper together. In an act of humility, Jesus washed his disciples' feet. Then he took some bread, broke a piece, and said, "This is my body which is for you. Do this in remembrance of me." And when he blessed the wine, he said, "This cup is the new covenant in my blood. Do this, as often as you drink it, in remembrance of me." (I Corinthians 11: 24-25)

These instructions are followed in the Christian sacrament of Holy Communion in which bread and wine are consumed. Though most Christians repeat these actions, the practice has different meanings to different denominations.

When the meal was over, Jesus told his disciples that he would soon be gone. He gave his final commandment, the bedrock of his teachings: love one another (John 13: 34-35).

Later that night, in the Garden of Gethsemane on the Mount of Olives, Jesus was arrested. He was taken before Pontius Pilate, the Roman ruler, and charged with blasphemy and with organizing a revolt against Rome. Jesus was sentenced to death by crucifixion, the common form of punishment for revolutionaries. It meant that the sentenced person would be tied or nailed to a cross and left to die.

Jesus was whipped and a crown of thorns was placed on this head to mock him as a king. Then, he was led to Golgotha, a hill outside of Jerusalem. On his back he carried the wooden cross on which he was to be executed. A crowd of people followed, weeping for Jesus. This route toward death is called *Via Dolorosa*, the Way of Sorrows. On the next page, you will find a detailed account.

Jesus' hands and feet were nailed to the cross. When he was mocked and taunted by the soldiers and the mob, the dying Jesus said these now famous words: "Father, forgive them for they know not what they do." And hours later, in utter pain, Jesus cried out, "My God, my God, why hast thou forsaken me?"

After Jesus died, his body was wrapped in a linen shroud and placed in a tomb that was sealed with a rock. The tomb was offered by a rich man, for Jesus' family would not have been able to afford such a burial.

The story continues with the resurrection (page 61).

Extensions:

1. Research to find out the communion practices of three different denominations. Make a chart listing their similarities and differences.

2. Find some pictures of the crucifixion. Write about the differences you see in them.

The Stations of the Cross and the Via Dolorosa

The Stations of the Cross mark the series of events leading to the death of Jesus. The Via Dolorosa, or the Way of Sorrows, is the actual route in Jerusalem leading to Golgotha. If you visit Jerusalem, you can find these "stations" marked on this road. The final five stations, however, are within the Church of the Holy Sepulchre. This church, shared by several different denominations, is said to contain the actual tomb where Jesus was laid to rest before the resurrection.

Many churches contain artistic representations of The Stations of the Cross. Some have woodcuts while others have paintings or stained-glass windows. Below you will find a typical arrangement of the Stations and what each means.

1. Pilate sentences Jesus to death.

14. Jesus' body is entombed.

2. Jesus receives his cross.

3. Jesus falls to the ground.

13. Jesus' body is taken from the cross.

12. Jesus dies on the cross.

4. Jesus meets his fainting mother, Mary.

5. Simon of Cyrene takes the cross.

6. Veronica wipes Jesus' face.

7. Jesus falls again.

11. Jesus is nailed to the cross.

10. Jesus is stripped.

9. Jesus falls for the third time.

8. Jesus tells the women not to weep for him.

Extension:

As a group, make a poster of the Stations of the Cross. Try to present the Stations creatively with pictures and explanations.

Name_____

Questions: The Last Supper and the Crucifixion

1. How many years did Jesus teach before the Last Supper?

   _____

   _____

   _____

2. Why did the Pharisees dislike Jesus? List a few things Jesus did to upset them. (You might need to review earlier stories.)

   _____

   _____

   _____

3. Why was Jesus so upset when he went to visit the Temple in Jerusalem?

   _____

   _____

   _____

4. Explain the communion service and how it relates to the Last Supper.

   _____

   _____

   _____

5. For what crimes was Jesus convicted?

   _____

   _____

   _____

6. Explain what Jesus might have meant when he said, "Father, forgive them for they know not what they do."

   _____

   _____

   _____

Name _____

Questions: The Last Supper and the Crucifixion *(cont.)*

7. What do you think Jesus was feeling when he said, "My God, my God, why hast thou forsaken me?"

_____

_____

_____

_____

8. What was Golgotha?

_____

_____

_____

_____

9. Explain the literal meaning of crucifixion.

_____

_____

_____

_____

10. What do you think the crucifixion could symbolize?

_____

_____

_____

_____

11. What are the Stations of the Cross and the Via Dolorosa?

_____

_____

_____

_____

Name _____

The Resurrection

The most compelling episode in the life of Jesus is considered by many to be the resurrection. The word *resurrection* actually means *rebirth*. For Christians, however, the word has special significance.

According to Matthew's Gospel, three days after the crucifixion, some friends of Jesus went to visit his tomb. An angel spoke to them, saying that Jesus had risen from death. As they departed to share the news, they met Jesus, who instructed them to find his disciples. But when Jesus met with two of his disciples, they did not recognize him. Though he knew all the scriptures and the story of his own life, it was not until they ate bread together that they felt his presence. Finally, the disciples knew that Jesus was resurrected.

Jesus revealed himself again at the Sea of Tiberias where his disciples were fishing. Though they caught nothing all night, he filled their nets with fish just as he had done years before.

Jesus continued to appear to his disciples for forty days, teaching of the kingdom of God. Finally, atop a mountain in Galilee, Jesus said these final words to his disciples:

> "All authority in heaven and on earth has been given to me. Go therefore and make disciples of all nations, baptizing them in the name of the Father and of the Son and of the Holy Spirit, teaching them to observe all that I have commanded of you; and lo, I am with you always, to the close of the age." (Matthew 28: 18-29)

With this final instruction the spread of Christianity began. It started with a handful of disciples but steadily spread throughout the world, shaping history.

As you may know, the Easter holiday commemorates the resurrection.

Questions:

1. What special meaning does the word "resurrection" have for a Christian?

   _____

   _____

   _____

2. Read Jesus' final words again very carefully. What is he saying? What does he mean by "authority," and "the close of the age"?

   _____

   _____

   _____

   _____

   _____

   _____

Name _____

Sayings of Jesus

As Jesus traveled, he gave many sermons. He spoke a great deal about forgiveness, selflessness, repentance, and surrender to God. Many of his sayings have become well known throughout the world. Interpretations of Jesus' sayings vary, however. Some people take them quite literally. Others understand them symbolically or metaphysically.

Here is a list of some of Jesus' sayings. Below each one, write what it means to you.

1. "You have heard that it was said, 'An eye for an eye and a tooth for a tooth.' But I say to you, do not resist one who is evil. But if any one strikes you on the right cheek, turn to him the other also . . ." (Matthew 5: 38-39)

    _____

    _____

    _____

2. "You have heard that it was said, 'You shall love your neighbor and hate your enemy.' But I say to you, love your enemies and pray for those who persecute you . . ." (Matthew 5: 43-44)

    _____

    _____

    _____

3. "For what will it profit a man, if he gains the whole world and forfeits his life?" (Matthew 16:26)

    _____

    _____

    _____

4. "Truly, I say to you, unless you turn and become like children, you will never enter the kingdom of heaven." (Matthew 18: 3)

    _____

    _____

    _____

5. "Judge not, that you be not judged." (Matthew 7: 1)

    _____

    _____

    _____

Name _____

Sayings of Jesus *(cont.)*

6. "Ask, and it will be given you; seek, and you will find; knock, and it will be opened to you. For everyone who asks receives, and he who seeks finds . . ." (Matthew 7: 7-8)

   _____

   _____

   _____

   _____

7. "So whatever you wish that men would do to you, do so to them; for this is the law . . . ." (Matthew 7: 12)

   _____

   _____

   _____

   _____

8. "Again I tell you, it is easier for a camel to go through the eye of a needle than a rich man to enter the kingdom of heaven." (Matthew 19: 24)

   _____

   _____

   _____

   _____

9. "If any one would be first, he must be last of all and servant of all." (Mark 9: 35)

   _____

   _____

   _____

   _____

10. "Beware of false prophets, who come to you in sheep's clothing but inwardly are ravenous wolves. You will know them by their fruits." (Matthew 7: 15-16)

    _____

    _____

    _____

    _____

Name _____

Forgiveness

Forgiveness is central to the teachings of Jesus. He even spoke about forgiving and caring for one's enemies. But what exactly is forgiveness?

In the space below and on additional paper as necessary, begin by defining forgiveness in your own words. Then respond to the following questions:

a) When is it easy to forgive? When is it difficult?
b) Are some people not deserving of forgiveness? Why?
c) Tell about a time you needed forgiveness for something.
d) Is there anyone you would like to forgive?
e) Is there anything you need to forgive yourself for?

_____
_____
_____
_____
_____
_____
_____
_____
_____
_____
_____
_____
_____
_____
_____
_____
_____

Branches of Christianity

Christianity has undergone many changes over the course of history. Though it began in ancient times as one church, it has divided into many separate churches, each with its own set of beliefs and practices. For non-Christians, understanding the differences among Christian churches can be difficult.

The most significant division within Christianity occurred in 1054 CE when the Eastern and Western churches separated. The Eastern church, as seen on the map below, was composed of the churches of Greece, Russia, Eastern Europe, and Western Asia. The capital of the Western church was Rome, and the Roman Pope, or Bishop of Rome, claimed authority over both churches. The Western church believed that the Pope was the person closest to God and, therefore, most capable of leading Christians. But the Eastern church did not believe the Pope should have power over them. This conflict, when added to the disputes of the past, finally caused the churches to split. From then on, the Roman Catholic Church has been led by the Patriarch of Constantinople, or the Pope.

In the 16th century, a movement called the Reformation caused a split which divided the Roman Catholic Church. At that time, there were many independent Christian groups. Although they did not all share the same beliefs, they each rejected the central authority of the Pope and came to be known as Protestants. It is difficult to speak about Protestantism as one religion since it has divided itself into hundreds of separate sects. They include such groups as the Quakers, Baptists, Methodists, and Presbyterians.

Each of these branches of Christianity maintains different beliefs and practices in different ways. The chart on page 66 will help you follow the branching of Christian churches. Use your encyclopedia to find out more about the denominations listed on page 66.

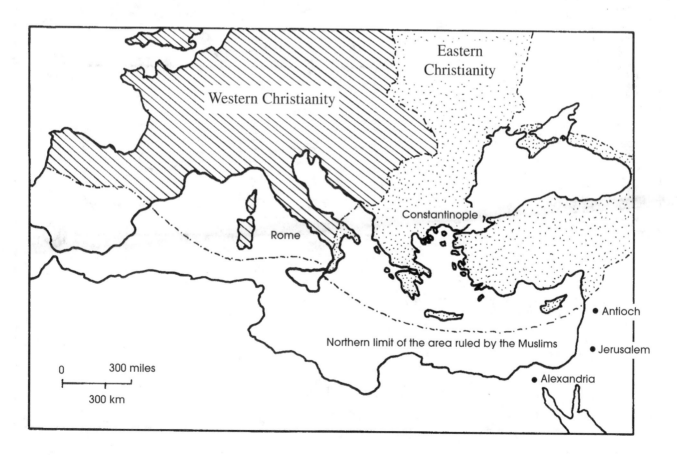

Primary Christian Denominations

The Early Christian Church

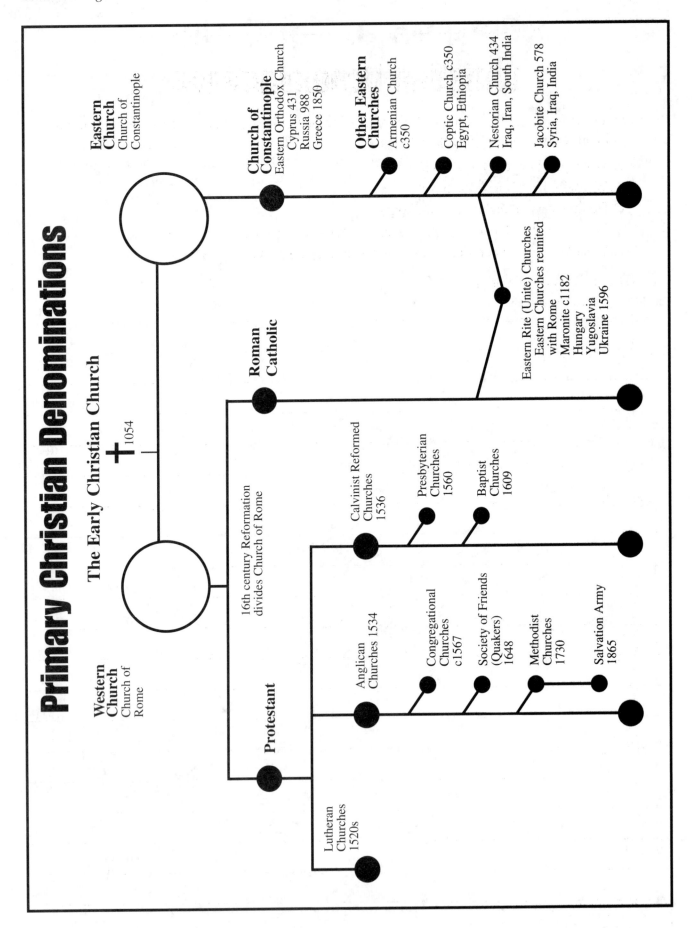

Eastern Church
Church of Constantinople

Church of Constantinople
Eastern Orthodox Church
Cyprus 431
Russia 988
Greece 1850

Other Eastern Churches

Armenian Church
c350

Coptic Church c350
Egypt, Ethiopia

Nestorian Church 434
Iraq, Iran, South India

Jacobite Church 578
Syria, Iraq, India

Eastern Rite (Unite) Churches
Eastern Churches reunited
with Rome
Maronite c1182
Hungary
Yugoslavia
Ukraine 1596

Roman Catholic

1054

16th century Reformation
divides Church of Rome

Western Church
Church of Rome

Calvinist Reformed
Churches
1536

Presbyterian
Churches
1560

Baptist
Churches
1609

Anglican
Churches 1534

Congregational
Churches
c1567

Society of Friends
(Quakers)
1648

Methodist
Churches
1730

Salvation Army
1865

Protestant

Lutheran
Churches
1520s

Name _____

Christian Denominations

Research and write about each of these Christian denominations, or branches, of worship. You might use the following questions as guidelines:

      a. When and how did the church begin?

      b. What do the followers believe?

      c. Do they have a leader or an authority?

      d. Where are they located geographically? How many members are there?

      e. What kinds of celebrations and holidays do they observe?

1. Eastern Orthodox Church

_____

_____

_____

_____

_____

_____

_____

_____

_____

_____

_____

_____

_____

_____

_____

_____

_____

Name _____

Christian Denominations *(cont.)*

2. Roman Catholic Church

_____
_____
_____
_____
_____
_____
_____
_____
_____
_____
_____
_____
_____
_____
_____
_____
_____
_____
_____
_____
_____
_____
_____
_____
_____

Name _____

Christian Denominations *(cont.)*

3. Protestantism

_____

_____

_____

_____

_____

_____

_____

_____

_____

_____

_____

_____

_____

_____

_____

_____

_____

_____

_____

_____

_____

_____

_____

_____

_____

Name _____

Christian Denominations *(cont.)*

4. Lutheran or Presbyterian (Choose one.)

_____

_____

_____

_____

_____

_____

_____

_____

_____

_____

_____

_____

_____

_____

_____

_____

_____

_____

_____

_____

_____

_____

_____

Extensions:

1. Write about another denomination. Can you find another less popular one?

2. Interview people from different denominations. How do they feel about each others' beliefs?

The Holy Trinity

Catholics believe that there is only one God. This God, however, contains three persons or aspects: the Father, the Son, and the Holy Spirit. This is what is known as the Holy Trinity. Though they are united as one, each part contains a special purpose. To Catholics, faith in the Holy Trinity is the pathway to salvation. This belief is summed up in the Athanasian Creed (written between 434 and 440 CE):

"And in this Trinity none is before or after the other; none is greater or less than another; but the whole three Persons are co-eternal together, and co-equal; so that in all things the Unity in Trinity, and the Trinity Unity is to be worshipped. He therefore that will be saved must think of the Trinity."

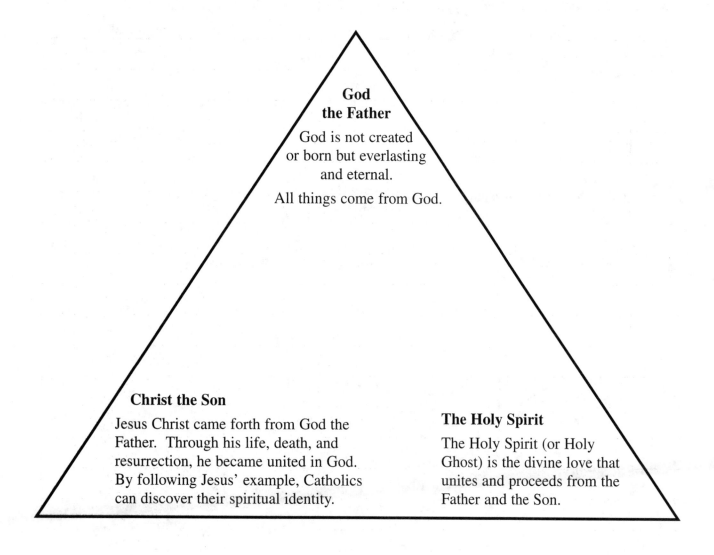

Extension:

Compare the Holy Trinity to the Hindu Trinity on pages 136-139.

The Spread of Christianity

Interestingly, the first community of Christians was Jews. This group believed that Christ, by example of his teachings and through resurrection, had brought a new vision and spoke as an equal to God. As converts to Christianity increased, the religion spread. The most influential early missionary was Paul. A missionary is someone who does religious work in foreign lands.

Before conversion, Paul was actually fervently rooted in the Jewish faith. He was called Saul of Tarsus and even witnessed the persecution of Christians. However, he claimed to have been dramatically converted by God, whereupon he began preaching. This is why he changed his name to Paul, the Apostle to the Gentiles. Gentile means a Christian as opposed to a Jew.

As can be seen on the map below, Paul journeyed tirelessly. He preached that the Old Law, or the Laws of Moses, should be replaced by faith in Christ. Only through Christ, said Paul, can a person live a life of kindness and joy, ultimately being saved and reaching Heaven.

Of course, tensions arose between Jews and Christians. Some Jews wanted to preserve Jewish ways within Christianity. Ultimately, Paul succeeded in separating the two religions and spreading the Christian faith. But this success was hard won. At first, Christianity was declared illegal by the Romans, and for 300 years Christians suffered persecution. Around 64 CE, both Paul and the chief apostle, Peter, were martyred at the hands of the Roman emperor, Nero. It was not until the early 4th century that Christianity was legalized by Constantine the Great. By 300 CE, Christianity became the accepted religion of Rome, spreading throughout the empire.

Paul's journeys are recounted in the New Testament, Acts of the Apostles chapters 13–28. The Letters of Paul, also part of the New Testament, consist of thirteen letters Paul wrote on his journeys.

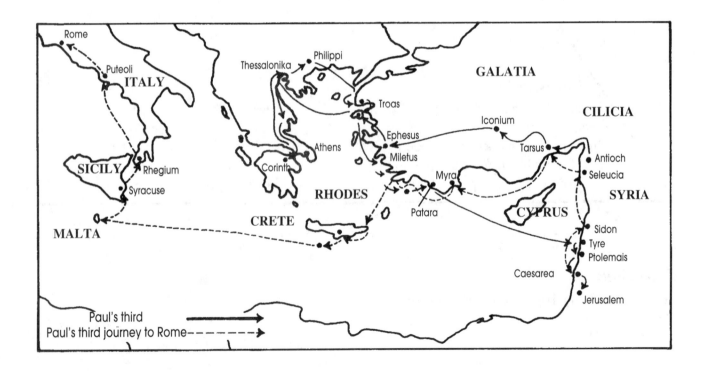

The Spread of Christianity *(cont.)*

With the founding of the New World, Christianity began to spread beyond Europe and Asia. Among the early missionaries were Catholics who journeyed to Central and South America, seeking to convert native peoples. Protestants escaping persecution traveled to North America, bringing with them their beliefs.

As European powers raced to secure lands of North America, they sent missionaries to begin the work. In California, for example, a Spanish monk named Junipero Serra built a string of missions along the coast. These missions served both as places of worship and living quarters for the monks and Native Americans who were converted. Of course, only some Native Americans chose to be converted. Having their own spiritual beliefs and way of life, they did not always welcome European missionaries.

By 1900, Christianity had spread onto every continent. It was a major world religion. Christian missionaries took advantage of the European colonization of India and Africa as well, as can be seen on the map below. Of course, missionary work is not solely a thing of the past. It continues most fervently today.

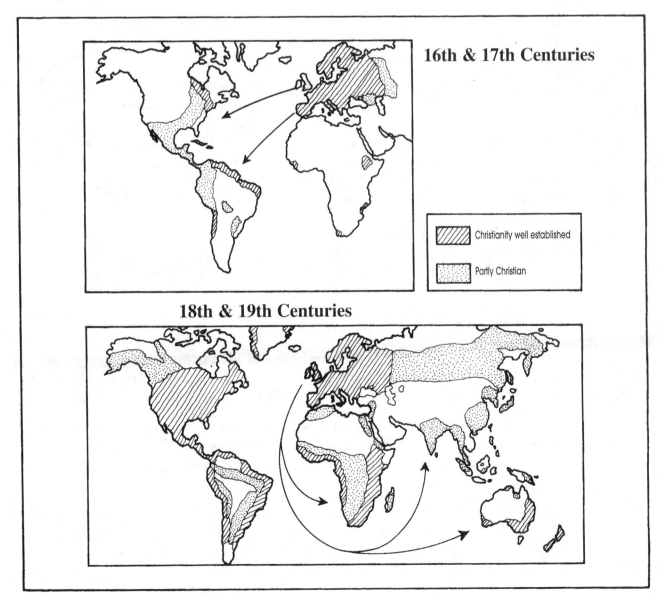

Rites of Passage

Like Judaism, Christianity contains religious ceremonies which mark dramatic changes or transitions in life. Many Christians call these rites of passage *sacraments* since they provide the spiritual guidance to live a religious life.

Although they differ in form, the three most common sacraments in the Christian faith concern baptism, marriage, and death.

Baptism

"No one can enter into God's Kingdom without being begotten of water and spirit."

— (John 3: 5)

As you might recall, baptism began with John the Baptist, the prophet who knew of Christ's coming. For many Christians, baptism occurs a few days after birth, although adults are also baptized. The ceremony is an induction into Christian society and Christian faith.

Although the practice differs with each Christian group, the common factor is the use of water, a symbol of spiritual purification and cleansing. For example, Eastern Orthodox Christians immerse the baby in water, while Roman Catholics pour water over the infant's head. Some Protestant groups, such as Quakers and Christian Scientists, do not practice baptism.

According to Roman Catholic law, godparents are required to attend the baptism ceremony. Godparents agree that they will be responsible for the child's religious upbringing if the parents are unable to do so.

An infant is often given a name during baptism. This is called christening. Many parents choose to name their child after a saint in the hope that the newborn might adopt the saint's characteristics.

Marriage

In a Christian marriage, the man and woman devote themselves to one another for life. This is the sacrament of Holy Matrimony, in which the couple agree to mirror the union of Christ and his church. The marriage should be an active symbol of self-sacrifice and devotion, imitating the qualities of Christ.

The traditional wedding ceremony, which usually takes place in a church, is probably familiar. The bride is escorted down the aisle by her parents and entrusted to the groom. At the altar, the bride and groom exchange wedding vows and rings. After they kiss, the couple is followed down the aisle by the wedding party.

There are many variations on the traditional ceremony. Depending on the couple's denomination and personal taste, they may include music or poetry during their service. Flower girls and ring bearers are also common. Since many Roman Catholic weddings take place during Mass, those present receive Holy Communion. Most weddings are followed by a celebration or party.

Name _____

Rites of Passage *(cont.)*

Death

Before describing the final passage of life, we must understand some fundamental Christian beliefs about death.

To begin with, Christ's resurrection is proof that death can be a passage to life eternal. For Catholics, at the moment of death, people are judged according to how they led their lives. Either heaven, hell, or purgatory awaits them. Those who have repented their sins and lived justly go to heaven. The unrepentant and sinful will suffer in hell, while those somewhere in between wait in purgatory where their souls are cleansed and made ready for union with God. Although not all Christians share the belief in heaven, hell, and purgatory, the belief in eternal life is common to all.

A sacrament once called *Extreme Unction*, and now called the Last Rites or the Anointing of the Sick, is often given to gravely ill people. The sick individual asks forgiveness for his or her sins, or if unable to do so, the minister does in his or her stead.

Christian funeral customs vary throughout the world. In some countries, a wake, or period of mourning and prayer, precedes the funeral. The funeral ceremony usually includes prayers and speeches. Sometimes, the body is displayed before burial or cremation. Roman Catholics pray the rosary over the body on the evening before the funeral. After the funeral, mourners of all Christian faiths often gather at the family's home.

Extension:

Define the following words associated with Christian sacraments:

1. Holy Matrimony _____

   _____

2. Baptism _____

   _____

3. Anointing of the Sick _____

   _____

4. Godparents _____

   _____

5. Wake _____

   _____

6. Christening _____

   _____

Name _____

Personal Rite of Passage

Not all rites of passage have religious significance. Below, describe a rite of passage that you or someone you know has experienced. Remember, it does not have to be a religious event. Describe the process in detail. Here are some possibilities:

    a. school graduation

    b. birthday

    c. becoming a Boy Scout or Girl Scout

    d. receiving a new belt in karate

    e. joining a club

_____

_____

_____

_____

_____

_____

_____

_____

_____

_____

_____

_____

_____

_____

_____

_____

_____

_____

_____

Name _____

Lent, Ash Wednesday, and Holy Week

Lent, which takes place during February or March, stands for the forty days before Easter, not counting Sundays. It is a time of repentance for one's sins and mistakes. The season of Lent was once strictly observed through fasting, emulating the forty days Jesus spent in the wilderness. Now, many people choose to be of service during Lent, to give to others rather than bring sacrifice upon themselves.

Ash Wednesday is the first day of Lent. On this day, Catholics and other Christians have a cross made of ashes brushed on their foreheads. This is symbolic of their mortality and need for purification.

Holy Week is the week preceding Easter. Four of these days have special significance:

- **Palm Sunday** (one week before Easter Sunday) commemorates the day Jesus entered Jerusalem. People celebrated his coming by lining the streets and waving palm branches. Many churches distribute palm leaves on this day.

- **Holy Thursday** commemorates the Last Supper.

- **Good Friday** commemorates the day of the crucifixion. In Jerusalem, Christians walk the Way of the Cross on Good Friday.

- **Holy Saturday** is symbolic of the day Jesus rested in the tomb before his resurrection on Easter Sunday.

Question:

If you needed to be of service for forty days, what kinds of things would you choose to do?

_____

_____

_____

_____

_____

_____

_____

_____

Extensions:

1. Research the Christian period of Advent, beginning the fourth Sunday before Christmas. Compare Advent to Lent.

2. Compare the Christian season of Lent with the Muslim month of Ramaden.

3. Using a poster board, make your own Lenten calendar, including all the days of Holy Week and Ash Wednesday.

Christmas

Christmas, which celebrates the birth of Jesus, is the most popular religious holiday in Christian nations. There are weeks of anticipation and traditions before the formal holiday actually begins on Christmas Eve, December 24.

Whether or not you are Christian, you are probably familiar with many Christmas traditions like gift giving, Christmas trees, caroling, and Nativity scenes. But how did these traditions begin? Here are explanations for a few.

Gift Giving

The tradition of gift giving began with the birth of Jesus himself. When the three wise men found Jesus and Mary in a stable, they offered gifts of gold, frankincense, and myrrh.

In early days, gifts were usually handmade. Parents worked hard sewing rag dolls and carving wooden toys. Today, toy stores and malls are packed throughout the Christmas season as holiday celebrators buy gifts galore.

Christmas Trees

For centuries, evergreen trees have been part of European winter celebrations. The trees are symbols of everlasting life. The custom of decorating trees for Christmas began in eighth century Germany when a monk named Boniface wanted people to stop worshipping the sacred oak. Instead, they began decorating a fir tree in honor of Christ. By the 1500s, Christmas trees were popular throughout Europe.

German settlers brought the Christmas tree to America, beginning with the simple decorations of popcorn, cranberries, stars, and candles in tin holders. In 1895, a telephone operator named Ralph Morris came up with the idea to add electric Christmas lights.

Carols

On the first Christmas night, the Bible tells of the angels' song over Bethlehem. By the fifth century, Christmas hymns were being written in Latin, and by the Middle Ages, costumed troupes traveled through villages presenting Christmas stories in song.

The true Christmas carol has its roots in Italy with Saint Francis of Assisi. These folk songs and lullabies to baby Jesus spread quickly throughout Europe.

Nativity Scenes

Saint Francis also originated Nativity scenes, or a set of figures representing the first Christmas Day. It began, however, with a live donkey and ox and his students playing the parts of Joseph and Mary.

You can enjoy creating a Nativity scene as well buy fashioning one from clay, wood, or some other material.

There are many other important Christmas symbols and events with interesting explanations. Research the two named on the next page. Use an encyclopedia to help you and then share your findings with the class.

Name _____

Christmas *(cont.)*

Santa Claus

_____
_____
_____
_____
_____
_____
_____
_____
_____
_____

Las Posadas

_____
_____
_____
_____
_____
_____
_____
_____
_____
_____

The Cross

The cross, symbolic of the crucifixion and resurrection of Jesus, is the principal symbol in Christianity. Crosses are found atop almost every church in the world. When a Christian dies, a cross is often placed over the person's grave.

Holly oak was the wood of the original cross, though today crosses are fashioned from many different materials. Throughout history, there have been many variations of the cross. They reflect different time periods, positions of authority, and Christian beliefs. Here are several of them.

1. Plain Latin

2. Russian Orthodox

3. Papal, or pertaining to the Pope

4. Cross of Jerusalem

5. Five fold cross

6. Maltese cross

7. Cross with lilies, symbolic of death

8. Cross with 3 steps: faith, hope, and charity

9. Crucifix of Christ dying

Christian Symbols

There are many important Christian symbols in addition to the cross. You may be familiar with some of them.

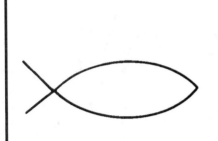

Icthus

In Greek, the word for fish, *icthus*, contains the first letters of Jesus Christ, thus, the symbol of the fish. Early Christians, fearful of persecution, identified themselves to one another with this secret symbol from the late 2nd century.

INRI

INRI is the Latin inscription over the cross. The letters stand for "Jesus Nazarenus Rex Iudaiorum," which translates to "Jesus of Nazareth, King of the Jews."

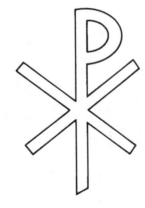

Chi Rho

In Greek, Chi and Rho are the first two letters of Christ superimposed upon one another.

Linked Circles

Three linked circles stand for the unity of God.

Dove of Peace

The Dove of Peace symbolizes God's spirit at the baptism of Jesus.

Palm Leaves

The palm leaves are symbolic of Palm Sunday.

Christian Symbols *(cont.)*

Crown of Thorns

The Crown of Thorns is symbolic of Christ's suffering on the cross.

Scallop Shell

The scallop shell is the pilgrim symbol for St. James of Compostella.

Tongues of Flame

Flames of fire represent the Holy Spirit.

Lamb of God

The Lamb of God has two meanings. One comes from John the Baptist's description of Jesus. The other recalls the Passover lamb and the resurrection of Jesus.

Cross Keys

The cross keys of St. Peter symbolize the keys to Heaven.

Alpha and Omega

Alpha and Omega are the first and last letters of the Greek alphabet. They represent the beginning and the end, meaning that God is all.

Inside a Greek Orthodox Church

1. pantocrator (Christ, Ruler of the Universe)
2. iconostasis (screen)
3. incense
4. altar behind royal door and curtain
5. icons of saints
6. choir
7. pulpit
8. bishop's chair/throne
9. pews (men)
10. pews (women)
11. aisle
12. icons
13. candles
14. side door

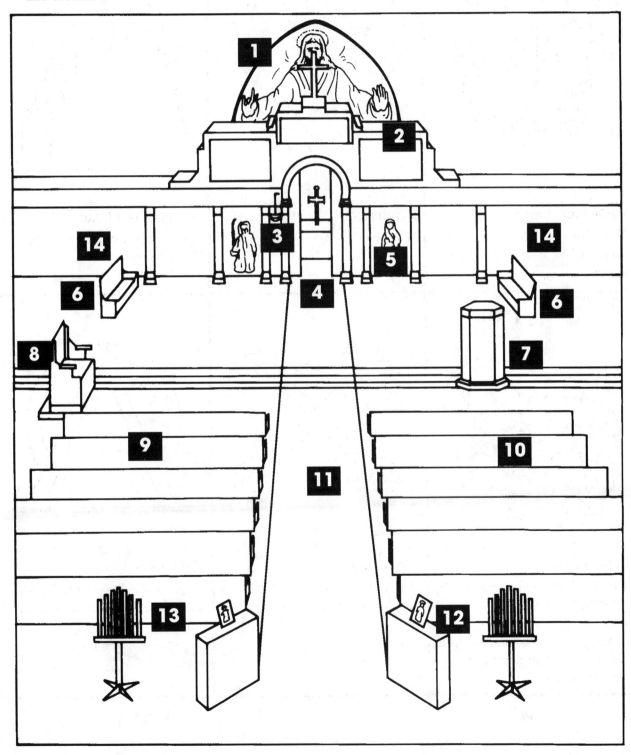

Inside an Episcopalian Church

1. stained glass window
2. statues
3. organ pipes
4. hymn board
5. organ
6. altar table

7. candles
8. chalice
9. chancel
10. pulpit
11. lectern
12. transept

13. pews
14. kneelers
15. font
16. hymn books
17. nave

Inside a Roman Catholic Church

1. altar
2. Bible
3. tabernacle
4. pews
5. stained glass window

6. crucifix
7. baptismal font
8. sacristy
9. lectern
10. statue of a saint

11. chalice
12. organ
13. Stations of the Cross
14. votive candles

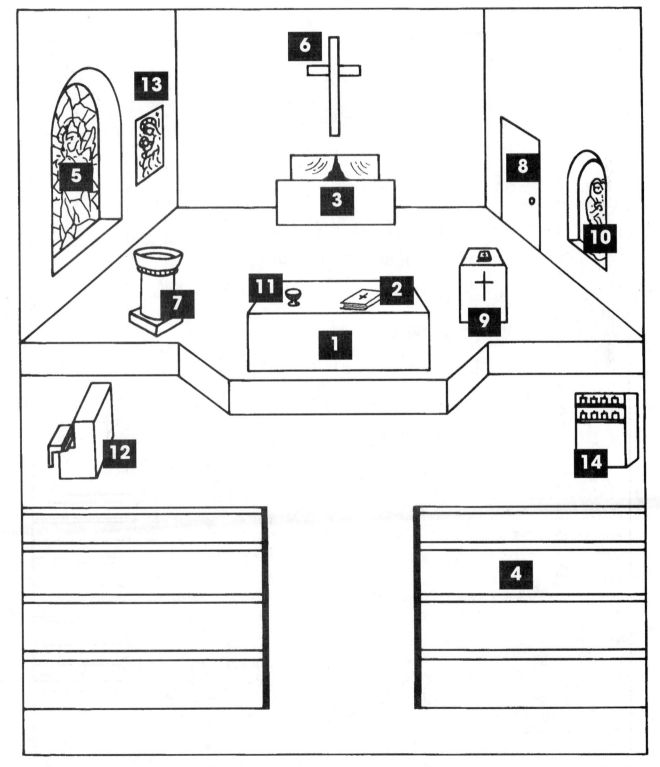

The Lord's Prayer

The Lord's Prayer, from Matthew 7, is the principal prayer for all Christians. Jesus taught it to his disciples when they asked him how they should pray. It is also called *Pater Noster*, which means "Our Father" in Latin.

Our Father who art in heaven,

Hallowed be thy name.

Thy kingdom come,

Thy will be done,

On earth as it is in heaven.

Give us this day our daily bread;

And forgive us out debts,

As we forgive our debtors;

And lead us not into temptation,

But deliver us from evil:

For thine is the kingdom, and the power,

And the glory, forever, Amen.

Extensions:

1. Jesus originally spoke this prayer in the ancient language of Aramaic. Some argue that the above translation of the prayer is not completely true to the original language. Research to find what other translations might be. How do they differ? How are they the same?

2. Research to find the meaning of "Amen."

Name _____

Vocabulary Crossword Puzzle

Across

1. The principal symbol of Christianity.
2. _____ , Apostle of the Gentiles
3. The 40 days before Easter.
4. Jesus was born here.
5. Jesus performed many.
6. Roman Church.
7. A place for souls not yet worthy of heaven but not meant for hell.
8. The Holy.
9. A branch of Christians which protested against the stablished church.
10. Jesus had twelve of these.
11. Jesus lived during the _____ Empire.
12. She gave birth to Jesus.
13. The Last _____ took place on Passover.
14. A sacrament is sometimes a _____ of passage.
15. This is the man who baptized Jesus.
16. The holiday commemorating the resurrection.
17. The three aspects of God.
18. The area of land where Jesus lived.
19. The holiday celebrating Jesus' birth.

Down

1. Jesus was crucified in this city.
2. Another name for the Sermon on the Mount.
3. A common form of punishment for revolutionaries.
4. The sacrament of eating bread and drinking wine.
5. The sacrament using water for purification.
6. Jesus' father.
8. This word means "rising from the dead."
9. Roman Catholics give authority to the

   _____ .

10. The minister of some Christian churches, particularly Catholic.
18. The Lord's _____ begins, "Our Father, who art in Heaven,"

Name _____

Quiz and Review

Part One: Fill in the spaces with the correct answer.

1. _____ was named King of the Jews in 30 BCE.

2. Israel is bordered by the _____ Sea.

3. The three wise men followed the _____ to find baby Jesus.

4. John the Baptist spoke of the coming of the _____ .

5. Alone in the wilderness, Jesus was tempted by _____ .

6. "Blessed are the meek, for they shall _____ the earth."

7. The Pharisees were offended when Jesus healed on the _____ .

8. On the evening of the Last _____, Jesus was arrested and charged with _____ .

9. "It is easier for a camel to go through the eye of a needle than for a _____ man to enter the kingdom of heaven."

10. During the _____ , there was a split in the Catholic Church.

11. Paul was the most influential early _____ .

12. _____ is the first day of Lent.

13. Holy Week is the week before _____ .

14. Nativity scenes originated with Saint _____ .

15. The story of Jesus is told in the _____ Testament.

Part Two: Respond to the following questions in full sentences. Be sure to use details to support your answers.

1. Explain in your own words why Jesus was so threatening to the Roman and Jewish authorities in Jerusalem.

   _____

   _____

2. Describe one of Jesus' miracles and discuss its nature. Why did he perform it? What was its message?

   _____

   _____

Name _____

Quiz and Review *(cont.)*

3. Explain how a few Christian symbols and rituals came to be. Why did they become rituals and symbols? What purpose do they serve?

_____

_____

_____

_____

_____

_____

4. Look through an art book and find at least five different depictions of Jesus. How are they different? How are they the same?

_____

_____

_____

_____

_____

_____

5. Imagine that you have to explain the basic message of Christianity to someone who knows absolutely nothing of the religion. What would you say?

_____

_____

_____

_____

_____

_____

Name _____

Quiz and Review *(cont.)*

6. Even though Catholics believe in the Holy Trinity, they consider their religion monotheistic. Explain this seeming paradox.

_____

_____

_____

_____

_____

_____

_____

_____

_____

_____

7. "You shall love your neighbor as yourself " was Jesus' instruction to his disciples after the Last Supper. What does this mean? Have you met anyone who does this? Is it possible? How are you encouraged to do this? How are you encouraged not to feel this way? Does the word "neighbor" include all people of all races and religions? Feel free to expand on this topic.

_____

_____

_____

_____

_____

_____

_____

_____

_____

_____

Origins of Islam: Abraham and the Ka'bah

Islam is the youngest of the Semitic religions. It was founded by the prophet Muhammad who was born in 570 CE. By 630 CE, Islam was an established faith spreading throughout Arabia. Followers of Islam are called Muslims, which means "one who submits (to) Allah." Allah is the Arabic name for God. Islam means "submission to God." The map on page 94 shows the spread of Islam during Muhammad's lifetime.

The roots of Islam, however, go all the way back to Abraham around 2000 BCE. You may remember Abraham as the father of the Jewish religion. Interestingly, Muslims also regard Abraham as the forefather of their religion.

According to both the Tanakh (the Hebrew Bible) and the Koran (the Islamic holy scripture), Abraham had fathered a son before the birth of Isaac. The boy was Ishmael, whose mother was Abraham's servant, Hagar. Abraham's wife, Sarah, was childless and became jealous. So God told Abraham to bless the child and to send him and his mother south into the desert.

They wandered the desert until they ran out of water. Hagar rested Ishmael on the sand and then searched desperately between two high rocks. She ran back and forth seven times. Finally, resting on one of the rocks, she heard an angel's voice tell her not to be afraid. Miraculously, water spouted from where Ishmael's heels touched the sand. This became the famous well, Zamzam, where the city of Mecca was born.

Toward the end of his life, Abraham traveled into Arabia to visit Ishmael. Muslims believe that God told Abraham to build a holy sanctuary at Zamzam. This site was called the Ka'bah, meaning "cube." It is also known as the House of God. The Ka'bah is about forty feet (12 m) in height, width, and length. The door is seven feet (2.1 m) from the ground and must be entered by a moveable staircase. Curtains and carpets cover most of the outside of the Ka'bah.

Inside the sanctuary are some silver and gold lamps. But the most important object is an oval black stone about seven inches (18 cm) in size. Muslims believe that this stone was given to Abraham by an angel. They say the stone was white but turned black with the kisses of worshippers seeking forgiveness. According to the Koran, God instructed Abraham to tell all worshippers of Allah to make a pilgrimage to the Ka'bah.

As you will see, the Ka'bah plays a central role in the history of Islam. You will learn more about its significance later in this chapter on Islam.

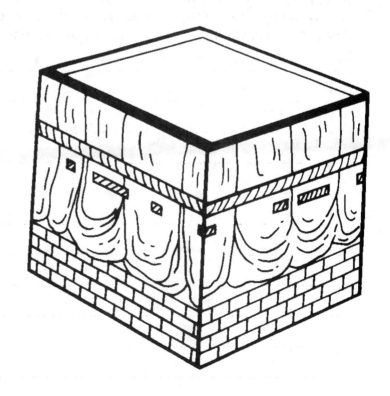

The Life of Muhammad and the Birth of Islam

Early Years

Muhammad ibn Abd Allah, commonly known as Muhammad, was born in the city of Mecca in 570 CE. At the time, Mecca was a busy marketplace crowded with residents and nomads buying and selling goods. Not a great deal is known of Muhammad's early life. Both his mother and father were dead by the time he turned six. He was first cared for by his grandfather, but when he passed away, Muhammad's uncle, Abu Talib, adopted him. Abu Talib was the head of the Hashim clan, one of many clans making up separate Arabic tribes.

It is believed that as a young adult Muhammad worked as a camel driver. He traveled the Arabian Peninsula with his uncle, making contact with various cultures and religions, including Judaism and Christianity. Because idol worship had come to dominate Mecca, this contact was important. The Ka'bah itself housed many idols, including those representing the three main goddesses.

At the age of twenty-five, Muhammad was working for a widow named Khadijah who was a wealthy merchant. Though he was much younger, she admired his intelligence and maturity so much that she proposed to him. They married, and in the fifteen years which followed, Muhammad lived in affluence. He continued traveling, encountering different faiths and customs.

But riches did not satisfy Muhammad. In Mecca, powerful merchants controlled both the flow of goods and the religious life. As the gap between the rich and the poor widened, Muhammad began to question his life and the world around him.

Muhammad's Revelation

By the time he was forty, Muhammad had begun to spend time in solitude, preoccupied with the questions that troubled him. He spent some nights alone in a small cave near Mecca. During one such night, Muslims believe that the angel Gabriel appeared before him. Gabriel grabbed hold of Muhammad and ordered him to recite some words. He did so, and as he fled the cave in fear, he heard the angel say, "Oh, Muhammad, you are the messenger of God, and I am Gabriel."

At first, Muhammad thought he was going insane. But Khadijah, his wife, believed the vision to be true. And as similar encounters continued, Muhammad slowly began to accept his role as a prophet of God. He started to preach in Mecca, though it took him some time to overcome doubts. But after a few years, he gained conviction that he was one of a lineage of prophets that included Abraham, Moses, and Jesus. According to historians, Muhammad continued to receive revelations for the next twenty years.

Muhammad openly declared that there was only one God. He called on Meccans to reject their idols. Though monotheism was shared by Jews and Christians, its introduction into Mecca troubled the ruling class. As Muhammad's followers increased, so did the unease among his opposition.

The Life of Muhammad and the Birth of Islam
(cont.)

Flight to Medina

Opposition to Muhammad increased. The ruling families insulted him and threatened violence. Soon Muhammad knew that he and his followers must leave Mecca. In 619 CE, they moved for a short while to Ta'if, a nearby town. But they were not allowed to stay, and so they returned to Mecca.

Things got worse for Muhammad when death claimed both his wife, Khadijah, and his uncle, Abu Talib. They had represented support and protection for the young Muslim community. However, it was also during this period, in 619 CE, that Muhammad was believed to have experienced his famous journey to heaven. With Gabriel guiding him, they journeyed first to a rock in Jerusalem, and from there Muhammad rode his faithful horse into heaven. It is claimed that he met other prophets, including Abraham, Moses, and Jesus. Finally, he stood in the presence of Allah.

The course of history changed in 620 CE when some pilgrims from the northern town of Medina came through Mecca. At the time, Medina was being torn apart by the violence of two rival tribes. The pilgrims were moved by Muhammad's teachings and hoped he might settle the raging dispute.

For the next two years, groups of people from Medina came to Mecca and converted to Islam. This inspired Muhammad, who instructed all Muslims to settle in Medina. In 622, Muhammad fled Mecca after hearing of a plot to assassinate him. Legend has it that he and a friend, Abu Bakr, hid in a cave. When his enemies rode by, a giant spider's web covered the mouth of the cave, and seeing the web, they assumed no one could have entered.

From there Muhammad and Abu Bakr traveled safely to Medina. This journey is known as the Hijrah, and it holds special significance to Muslims. Muhammad's arrival into Medina marked the birth of a united Islamic community. The Hijrah signifies the beginning of the Islamic calendar. (See page 117.)

Life in Medina and the Growth of Islam

Muhammad arrived in Medina as the new leader, bearing tremendous responsibilities. While receiving communication from God and teaching his devotees, he had to protect Islam from opposition and find a peaceful solution to the local feuds. Though he was able to unite the feuding clans through his teachings (the Jewish and Muslims prayed together, for example), when Muhammad instructed his followers to pray towards Mecca instead of Jerusalem, tensions grew, and the groups separated completely. Violence erupted, ending in the expulsion of some Jewish tribes from Medina.

With his community established, Muhammad began raiding caravans bound for Mecca. These kinds of raids were not uncommon at the time, and they provided sustenance for the Muslims. This angered the Meccans, and a series of battles followed. Despite a few setbacks, the Muslims gained power and recognition. After destroying or converting his tribal enemies, Muhammad all but controlled the Arabian Peninsula.

Finally, in 629 CE, Mecca submitted to the Muslims. Muhammad entered the city and headed directly to the Ka'bah. After circling it seven times, he smashed the stone idols. He spoke of the oneness of God, or Allah, and proclaimed himself a prophet. From that moment until the present, the Ka'bah became the principal holy place for Muslims.

Muhammad's Last Years

By 630 CE, Islam was the dominant religion in Mecca. Muhammad then set out to conquer the Arabian Peninsula. Some tribes were easily converted while others were met by force. The crusade was successful, and Islam spread to the Arabian Sea to as far north as Syria.

In 632 CE, Muhammad made his last pilgrimage to Mecca. First, he ordered that only Muslims could worship at the Ka'bah. Then, he delivered his last sermon, asking for Islamic unity. He ended with his final revelation from God:

> "The unbelievers have this day abandoned all hope of
> vanquishing your religion. Have no fear of them: fear Me.
>   This day I have perfected your religion for you and completed
> My favor to you. I have chosen Islam to be your faith."
>
> (Koran 5.3)

On his way back from this pilgrimage, Muhammad fell ill. He died in Medina on June 8, 632 CE, at the age of sixty-one (the 12th day of Rabi I in the Islamic calendar). Although he had married two wives since the death of Khadijah, he had yet to father a son, leaving the question of successor in the hands of his followers.

The Spread of Islam During Muhammad's Lifetime

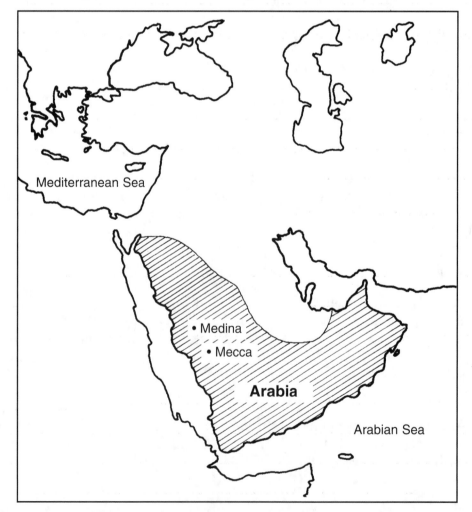

Name _____

The Life of Muhammad in Review

Respond to the following questions and prompts in complete sentences.

1. Briefly explain the connection between Abraham and Islam.

   _____

   _____

   _____

   _____

2. Why was it important that Muhammad traveled a great deal? How did it affect him?

   _____

   _____

   _____

   _____

3. Briefly describe Muhammad's first revelation. Can you think of other prophets who had similar experiences?

   _____

   _____

   _____

   _____

4. Why was Muhammad disliked in Mecca?

   _____

   _____

   _____

   _____

5. Explain the meaning of Hijrah.

   _____

   _____

   _____

   _____

Name _____

The Life of Muhammad in Review *(cont.)*

6. What were some of the challenges Muhammad faced in Medina? What tactic did he use in order to support the community?

_____
_____
_____
_____
_____

7. In what year did Muhammad return triumphantly to Mecca? What did he do when he entered? Why?

_____
_____
_____
_____
_____

8. In what present day country are Mecca and Medina?

_____
_____
_____
_____

9. Define the following words:

    A. Islam _____

    B. Muslim _____

    C. Ka'bah _____

    D. Allah _____

    E. Zamzam _____

The Koran and the Hadith

"He has revealed to you the Book with the truth, confirming the scriptures which preceded it; for He has already revealed the Torah and the Gospel for the guidance of men, and the distinction between right and wrong." *(Koran: 3.1-4)*

The *Koran* is the Islamic holy scripture. Muslims believe it is literally the Word of God as received by Muhammad. They look to the *Koran* for guidance and spiritual sustenance, keeping it close to their hearts throughout life. As children, Muslims begin memorizing verses of the *Koran,* reciting them during prayer. Some people go on to memorize the entire *Koran,* which consists of 114 chapters or *surahs*. Within each surah are verses, each varying in number. The writing is half poetry and half prose. The *Koran* is written in Arabic, the language in which Muhammad is believed to have received the revelations from God.

Muslims believe the *Koran* follows the Torah and the Gospels of the New Testament in a series of holy books. This is why Muslims have reverence for the prophets who preceded Muhammad. However, they believe that the earlier scriptures have been corrupted by false interpreters. Hence, Muslims take the Koran to be the most accurate scripture.

Like the Bible, the *Koran* speaks of a compassionate, loving God, but also warns of a Day of Judgment. Thus, the scripture begins,

"Praise be to God, Lord of the Universe,
The Compassionate, the Merciful,
Sovereign of the Day of Judgement!
You alone we worship, and to You alone we turn for help.
Guide us to the straight path,
The path of those whom You have favored,
Not of those who have incurred your wrath,
Nor those who have gone astray."

(Koran: 1.1-7)

According to the *Koran,* either heaven or hell awaits after death. Both places are described in detail. Therefore, the sincere Muslim tries to follow the rituals of Islam and lead a pure religious life.

But the *Koran,* like the Torah, also has instructions for domestic life. Besides daily religious activities, it attends to issues such as marriage and inheritance.

In addition to the *Koran,* Muslims turn to the *Hadith* for wisdom and support. The *Hadith* consists of the life and teachings of Muhammad. Because Muhammad is regarded so highly, his life and words are models by which the Muslims can live. Originally, the accounts were circulated by word of mouth until there were thousands of versions in existence. Eventually, they were trimmed to six volumes, joining the *Koran* as an Islamic holy book.

Reading from the Koran

The following are two different excerpts from the *Koran*. A *surah* is a chapter.

From Surah 35, The Creator:

"In the Name of Allah, the Compassionate, the Merciful

35:1 Praise be to God, Creator of the heavens and the earth! He sends forth the angels as His messengers, with two, three or four pairs of wings. He multiplies His creatures according to His will. God has power over all things.

35:2 The blessings God bestows on men none can withhold; and what He withholds none can bestow, apart from Him. He is mighty, the Wise One.

Men, bear in mind God's goodness towards you. Is there any other creature who provides for you from heaven and earth? There is no god but Him. How then can you turn away?

If they deny you, other apostles have been denied before you. To God shall all things return.

Men, the promise of God is true. Let the life of this world not deceive you, nor let the Dissembler trick you about God. Satan is your enemy: therefore treat him as an enemy. He tempts his followers so that they may become the heirs of Hell.

The unbelievers shall be sternly punished, but those that accept the true Faith and perform good works shall be forgiven and richly rewarded."

From Surah 55, The Merciful

"In the Name of Allah, the Compassionate, the Merciful

55:1 It is the Merciful who has taught the Koran.

He created man and taught him articulate speech.

The sun and the moon pursue their ordered course. The plants and the trees bow down in adoration.

He raised the heaven on high and set the balance of all things, that you might not transgress it. Give just weight and full measure.

He laid the earth for His creatures, with all its fruits and blossom-bearing palm, chaff-covered grain and scented herbs. Which of your Lord's blessing would you deny?"

Name _____

Reading from the Koran *(cont.)*

1. Copy the phrase which begins each Surah.

   _____

2. In Surah 35, what is the nature of the Creator, or God? What instructions are given to the person reading?

   _____
   _____
   _____

3. Who is the "Dissembler" in Surah 35?

   _____

4. Discuss the similarities between Surah 35 and your readings from the New Testament. What do they have in common? How are they different?

   _____
   _____
   _____
   _____

5. Read the first section of Psalm 136 from the Old Testament. Compare it to the excerpt from Surah 55. Remember to use details in your comparison.

   _____
   _____
   _____
   _____

Extension:

Find a surah in the *Koran* which refers to something from the Bible and write a brief report comparing the two accounts.

The Five Pillars of Islam

The Five Pillars of Islam represent the duties of a Muslim. Like the Ten Commandments, they provide a spiritual foundation and function. These duties will be explained in detail in the following pages.

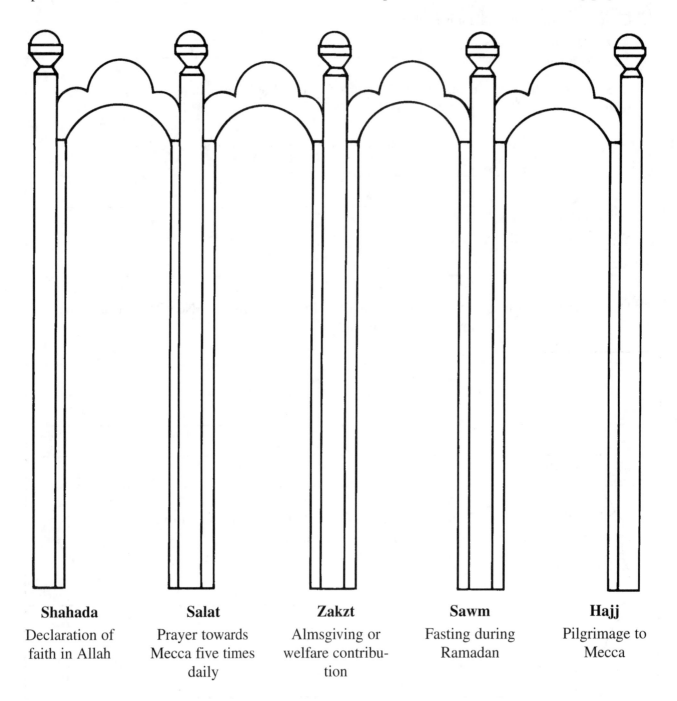

Shahada	**Salat**	**Zakzt**	**Sawm**	**Hajj**
Declaration of faith in Allah	Prayer towards Mecca five times daily	Almsgiving or welfare contribution	Fasting during Ramadan	Pilgrimage to Mecca

The First Pillar: Shahada

The first Pillar of Islam is called *shahada*. It is a brief prayer proclaiming the oneness of God and faith in Islam. Children memorize the shahada, an action which introduces them into the Islamic community. The shahada simply states:

> "There is no God but Allah,
> and Muhammad is the messenger of Allah."

Here is the shahada written in Arabic. (Like Hebrew, Arabic is written from right to left.)

Arabic was Muhammad's native tongue, the language in which he claimed to have received the *Koran*. Many devout Muslims from outside Arabic-speaking countries will learn the language in order to read the *Koran* in its original form. In fact, some Muslims consider any translation of the scripture totally unacceptable. Here is a map of Arabic-speaking countries.

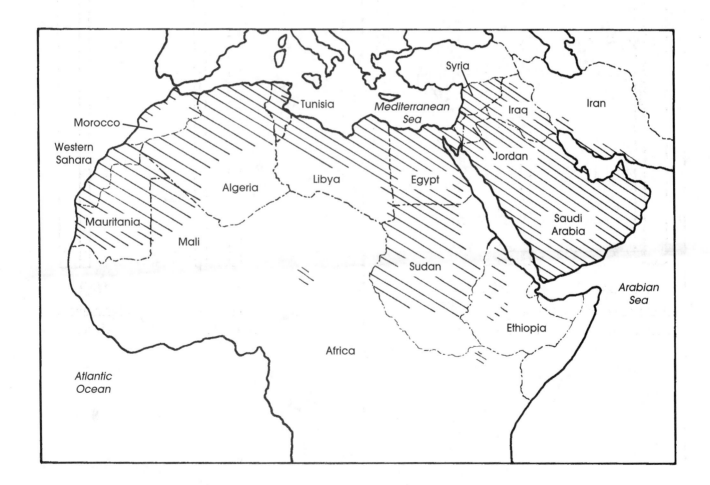

The Second Pillar: Salat

The second pillar is called *salat*. It requires Muslims to pray five times a day toward Mecca. They must pray at sunset, in the evening, at dawn, at noon, and in the afternoon. In Muslim countries, the call to prayer is announced from a minaret atop a mosque. A mosque is where Muslims gather to pray, although it is acceptable to pray alone. In many Islamic countries, women pray at home. If they pray with the men, they do so from behind them or in a separate group. The leader of a mosque is called an *imam*, which means "one who walks before." The imam leads the prayer and gives sermons. However, unlike a priest or rabbi, the imam does not hold special authority. Instead, he is chosen by virtue of his dedication and sincerity. (As you will see, the title of imam holds a very different meaning for the Shiah sect of Muslims.)

Each prayer involves different bowing positions, or *rakahs*. In the morning prayer, for example, after laying out his prayer mat, the devotee raises his hands, touches his earlobes, and proclaims, "*Allahu akbar!*" meaning "God is great!" Next, he rests his hands at his waist and recites the first verse of the *Koran*. The prayer continues when the worshipper bows, prostrates himself, and sits back, each time declaring faith in Muhammad and Allah. If the person is in a mosque, he will turn to either side and wish another person peace and blessings.

The Bowing Positions of Salat

The Third Pillar: Zakat

Almsgiving, or *zakat*, is the third basic requirement. Muslims are expected to give to the poor and sick. Although the zakat is not regulated by the government, sincere Muslims regard it as an important religious duty. In fact, the *Koran* addresses almsgiving as an essential quality of an honest Muslim, a gateway into heaven.

Response:

What are your feelings about almsgiving. Do you think it is the duty of all people who wish to lead a good life? Is it a choice?

_____

_____

_____

_____

_____

_____

_____

_____

_____

_____

_____

_____

_____

_____

_____

_____

_____

_____

_____

_____

_____

Name _____

The Fourth Pillar: Sawm

Sawm is perhaps the most demanding of the Five Pillars. It requires that Muslims fast during the month of Ramadan. Ramadan is the ninth month of the Islamic calendar. During this period, food and drink are not allowed between dawn and sunset. After sunset, only light snacks are allowed.

The fast represents a special time of purification and religious devotion. Stronger ties are made with family and community. Alcohol and tobacco are prohibited the entire month. Both the elderly and children are exempt from the fast.

The Festival of Eid-Al-Fitr

When the month of Ramadan ends, the festival *Eid-al-fitr* is celebrated. The rejoicing begins on the first day of the tenth month of the Islamic calendar. Although the month of Ramadan is spent fasting, families begin preparing for the celebration far in advance, sending cards to relatives and preparing gifts.

When the day finally arrives, Muslims attend special morning prayers in the local courtyard or park. In western countries, the faithful usually take the day off from work or school. In Muslim countries, Eid-al-fitr is considered a three-day national holiday! Throughout the celebration, presents are shared and families gather to rejoice. It is also a time to share food and money with those less fortunate.

Extension:

With parental permission, try fasting one day. Give any lunch money and food to a food bank for the homeless. Then, write a response explaining how you felt during the fast.

_____

_____

_____

_____

_____

_____

_____

_____

_____

_____

_____

_____

_____

The Fifth Pillar: Hajj

Exhort all men to make the pilgrimage. They will come to you on foot and on the backs of swift camels from every distant quarter . . .

Then let the pilgrims spruce themselves, make their vows, and circle the Ancient House. Such is Allah's commandment.

— (*Koran*, Surah 22, The Pilgrimage)

Hajj is the pilgrimage to Mecca which every Muslim is expected to make at least once. A pilgrimage is a journey to a sacred place or shrine. Unlike the other four Pillars, the Hajj can be skipped if it involves great hardships.

Over two million Muslims journey to Mecca each year, and each worshipper must follow certain guidelines. First, the men are expected to shave their heads and wear a piece of white garment around the waist and over the shoulder. Women wear the clothing of their native countries, though they must keep their heads covered at all times.

First, the pilgrims walk counter-clockwise seven times around the Ka'bah, either kissing or touching the stone. Next, they run seven times between the hills of As-Safa and Al-Marwah. This action is symbolic of Hagar's search for water and the miracle of the well, Zamzam.

After spending the night at the village of Mina, pilgrims take the next step, the *wukuf*, together. They meet at the plain of Arafat, about six miles from Mecca. From noon to sunset, they pray quietly. Next, they climb a small mountain called the Mount of Mercy, and they ask God's forgiveness for their sins. They spend the night at Muzdalifah.

Afterwards, they return to the village of Mina where the ritual of "stoning the devil" takes place. Followers gather pebbles which they throw at three pillars. This is symbolic of Abraham throwing stones at the Devil who had disturbed his prayers. On the tenth day, animal sacrifices—sheep or goat— are carried out. Finally, the pilgrimage again goes seven times around the Ka'bah.

Muslims conduct a four-day celebration upon returning home from Mecca. The *Eid al-Adha*, or Festival of Sacrifice, marks the end of the pilgrimage and acknowledges the great accomplishment. Now the male pilgrim has the right to call himself a *hajji* while the woman is called a *hajjah*.

Following the Route of the Hajj

Here is a list of the seven stages of the Hajj. On the following page, identify the correct stage in the diagram by writing in the corresponding number.

1. Walk counter-clockwise seven times around the Ka'bah.

2. Run seven times between the hills of As-Safa and Al-Marwah.

3. Stay overnight at the village of Mina.

4. Hold all-day prayer at the Plain of Arafat.

5. Spend the night at Muzdalifah.

6. Return to Mina for ritual of "stoning the devil".

7. Complete seven more circuits around the Ka'bah.

Name _____

The Fifth Pillar: Hajj *(cont.)*

The route of the Hajj

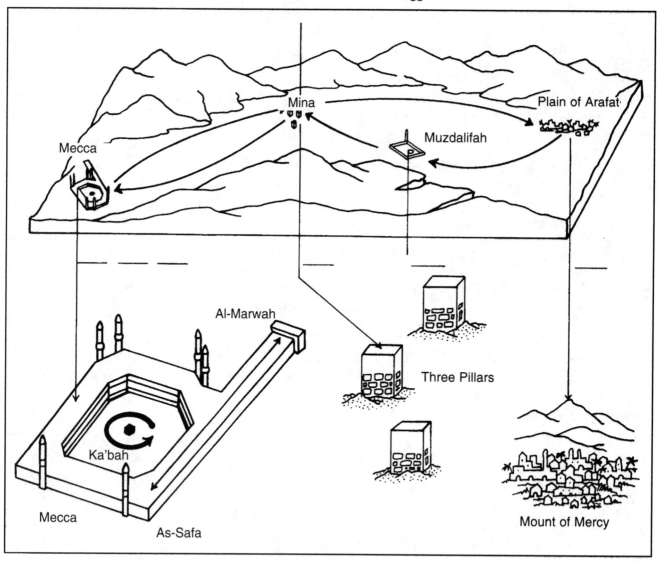

The Caliphs and the Spread of Islam

With Muhammad's death on June 8, 632 CE, Islam faced a crisis. Since Muhammad had left no explicit instructions about a successor, and since he had not fathered a son, how would they decide?

After some debate between the Meccans and Medinans, it was finally decided that Abu Bakr, Muhammad's loyal friend and supporter, should be the new leader of Islam. Not only was Abu Bakr Muhammad's father-in-law (father of Ayesha), but he also gave up his business to make the *hijrah* to Medina. Thus, he was named *First Caliph*. A *caliph* is a successor.

Under Abu Bakr's leadership, and with the help of his first lieutenant, Umar ibn al-Khattab, rebellious tribes were defeated and the Arab world united. Still, the new rulers felt threatened by the political situation in Arabia. They led a series of *jihads*, or holy wars, against neighboring empires. They began by attacking the area of Syria, controlled by the Byzantine Empire, as well as the area of Iraq, ruled by the Persian Sasanians.

Abu Bakr died in 634 CE, and Umar was elected Second Caliph. For a decade, Umar led his armies, victoriously capturing both Damascus and Jerusalem, strongholds of the Byzantine Empire. As seen on the map below, by 644 CE Muslims also controlled all the Persian area of Iraq and most of Iran.

Spread of Islam: 632-644 CE

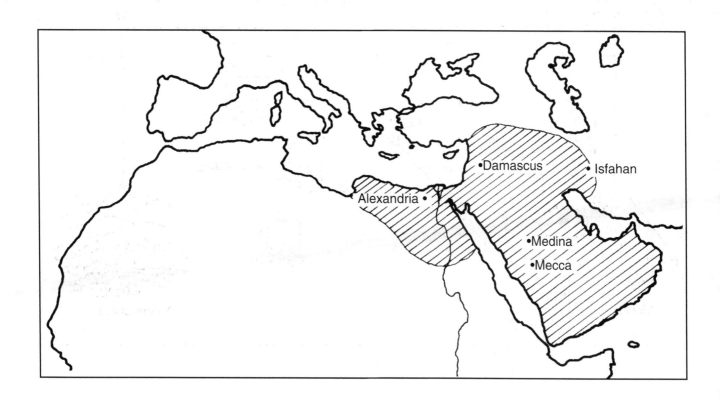

The Third and Fourth Caliphs

With the election of the third caliph, Uthman ibn Affan, came the first serious tensions within the Islamic community. Although a Muslim, Uthman's family, the Umayyads, had initially opposed Muhammad, and some followers resented his leadership. Despite spreading the forces of Islam through Egypt and into Northern Africa, (see map below) opposition to Uthman grew. Finally, in 659 CE Uthman was assassinated, slain by the sword of an enemy.

The Fourth Caliph was Ali ibn Abi Talib, the son of Muhammad's uncle, Abu Talib. Ali was the second convert to Islam and had waited forty-six years to succeed Muhammad, a position he felt he deserved. In fact, Ali's followers believed it was God's will that only those belonging to the lineage of Muhammad should rule the Muslim community. Soon civil strife began between Ali and Uthman's remaining family, led by Mu'awiyah, Muslim governor of Syria. Rather than destroy his enemies, Ali chose negotiations, a decision which infuriated his fundamentalist followers. They formed a group, the Kharijites, who were responsible for the stabbing death of Ali in 661 CE. Ali was the last caliph who knew Muhammad personally.

The Orthodox Caliphs		
Islamic Calendar	**Caliphs**	**Gregorian Calendar**
11-13 AH	Abu Bakr	632-634 Ce
13-23	Umar	634-644
23-35	Uthman	644-656
35-41	Ali	656-661

The Spread of Islam 644-661 CE

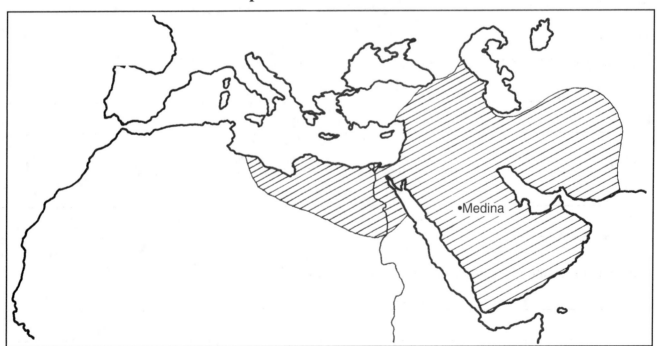

Name _____

The Shi'ah and Sunni Sects

Now it was Mu'awiyah's turn to assume leadership. He moved the capital of the Islamic empire to Damascus and began the Umayyad Dynasty. Although they still faced opposition from the Kharijite, more threatening were the followers of Ali, or the Shi'at Ali. This group come to be known as the Shi'ah (or Shiite) and believed only descendants of Ali should lead the nation of Islam. For years, the Shi'ah led revolts against the Umayyads in an attempt to restore their leadership to the caliphate. Though they failed, their presence in the Islamic world was, and continues to be, influential.

In fact, the lineage of Ali continued in the Successions of Imams, or leaders of the Shíah community. Interestingly, for political reasons the identity of the Twelfth Imam was not revealed. He came to be called the Hidden Imam, or al-Mahdi, "the one guided by God." Scholars of the Imams believe that the Hidden Imam will appear at the end of time to judge the faithful and unfaithful.

The largest group of Muslims, however, are the Sunnis, the orthodox Muslims. They follow the traditional path shown by Muhammad directly from Allah. They differ in many fundamental ways from the Shi'ah. First, they do not believe the Islamic leader must be a direct heir of Muhammad. Although they respect the Imams, they do not believe that the lineage holds special religious inspiration. Instead, the Sunnis elect caliphs by merit of their character and ability to lead the world's Islamic community.

The other basic argument between the sects concerns salvation. While the Sunnis believe that the total Muslim community will be judged on the Day of Judgment, the Shia'h focus their fate on the Imams— only the Imams can guide Muslims to salvation.

In Islam, like Christianity, many branches, or sects, began to form after the initial division. The most significant of these is *Sufism*, or Islamic mysticism. Although it began quietly, by the 15th century Sufism was worldwide and politically powerful.

Questions:

1. To the Shíah, what is an Imam? What is special about him?

   _____

   _____

2. Over what issues are the Sunni and Shi'ah most in disagreement?

   _____

   _____

3. On a separate piece of paper, write a short report on Sufism.

   _____

   _____

More on the Spread of Islam

The map below shows the area conquered by the Umayyad Dynasty, from 661-750 CE. The powerful Islamic Empire moved across North Africa to the Atlantic Ocean, finally conquering and holding Spain for 750 years. For a short span, they held the southwest of France. Eventually, the Empire spread as far eastward as the River Indus, threatening the Indian subcontinent.

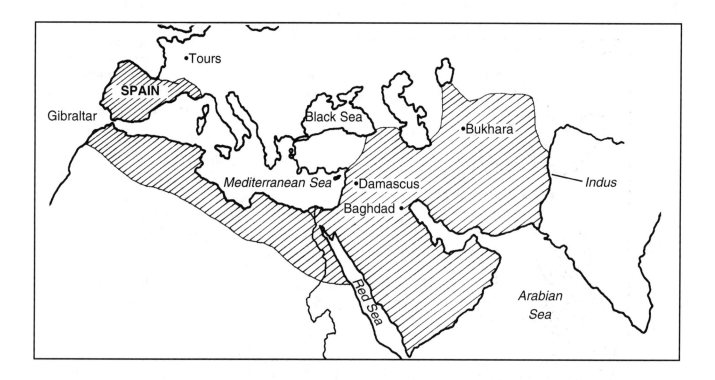

The Ottoman Empire

For the next 500 years, until 1258 CE, the Abbasid Dynasty ruled, continuing the fast-paced spread of the Islamic Empire. Their leadership fostered a cultural and intellectual explosion; the result was dazzling architecture, lasting literature, and advances in fields of mathematics, medicine, and law.

After the Abbasid Dynasty, Muslim empires split. In 1453, the most powerful of these empires, the Ottomans, captured Constantinople. They renamed the city Istanbul and declared it the Muslim capital. The map on the next page shows the extent of the Ottoman Empire at the end of the 17th century. Using an atlas, fill in the countries and bodies of water which currently occupy the area.

Name _____

The Ottoman Empire

This is a map of the Ottoman Empire at its greatest extent at the end of the 17th century CE. Fill in the
modern countries and bodies of water. Use an atlas to help you.

Istanbul

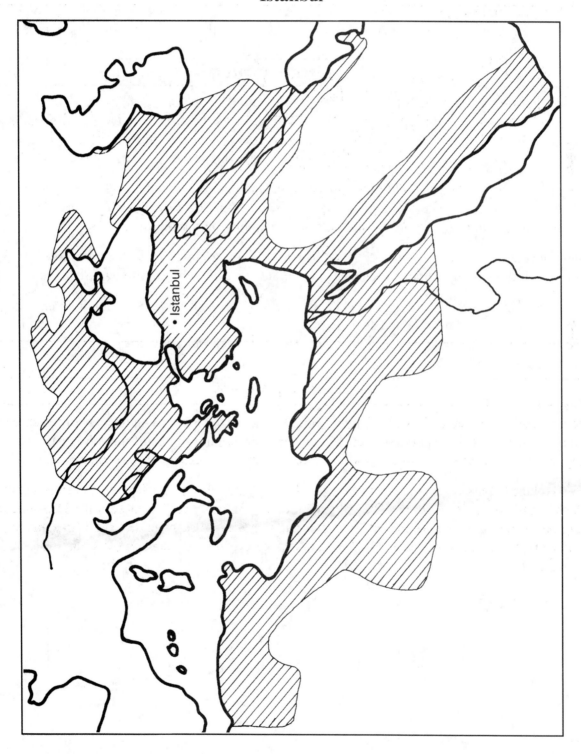

The Mosque

The mosque is the place of worship for Muslims. Like the synagogue for Jews and the church for Christians, Muslims gather at the mosque to pray in union. The most important gathering occurs each Friday, the Muslim Sabbath, when a sermon is given by a preacher, or imam. Unlike the priest or rabbi, the imam does not hold special status apart from other followers. Rather, he is elected by merit of his scholarship and dedication to Islam.

Most mosques are quite small, serving local populations. These are called *masjids*. Friday sermons are delivered at a larger, central mosque called a *jami'*. But a Muslim need not be at a mosque to pray. He or she can pray at home or at work. After all, it would be difficult to visit the mosque five times a day.

The Features of a Mosque

Traditional mosques are built around a large dome. The interior is plainly furnished and the floor is covered with prayer rugs. This allows the followers to prostrate themselves in prayer. Most mosques also provide either running water or pools used for abslutions (ritual washing). Interestingly, nomadic Muslims who wander the desert are permitted to wash with sand.

When Muslims pray in a mosque, they face a *mihrab*, a small alcove or niche, marking the direction of Mecca. Another common feature of a mosque is a *minbar*, a pulpit for the imam who preaches the Friday sermon. The minbar vary in size and stature, depending on the mosque.

Although mosques are plainly furnished, the walls and ceilings are often inlaid with beautifully designed inscriptions of the Koran. The designs are done in calligraphy, a prominent Islamic art form.

Another important feature of a mosque is a tall, slender tower called a *minaret* or a *ma'dhana*. Minarets vary in their architecture and size. Each morning, the *adhan*, call to prayer, is chanted from atop the minaret by a person known as a *muezzin*. The call is repeated five times daily. In most large cities, the muezzin's voice comes through a loudspeaker, filtering through the streets.

Extension:

The following is a list of five famous mosques around the world. Using an encyclopedia or other resource book, write a brief report about the history and architecture of one of the mosques.

1. Blue Mosque (Turkey)

2. Masjid-i-Shah (Iran)

3. The Great Mosque (Iraq)

4. Central Mosque (London)

5. Cano Mosque (Nigeria)

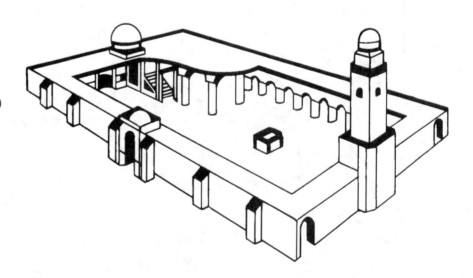

Name _____

The Mosque *(cont.)*

Using the information on the previous page, identify the following parts of the mosque below:

1. minbar   2. dome   3. mihrab   4. fountain   5. minaret

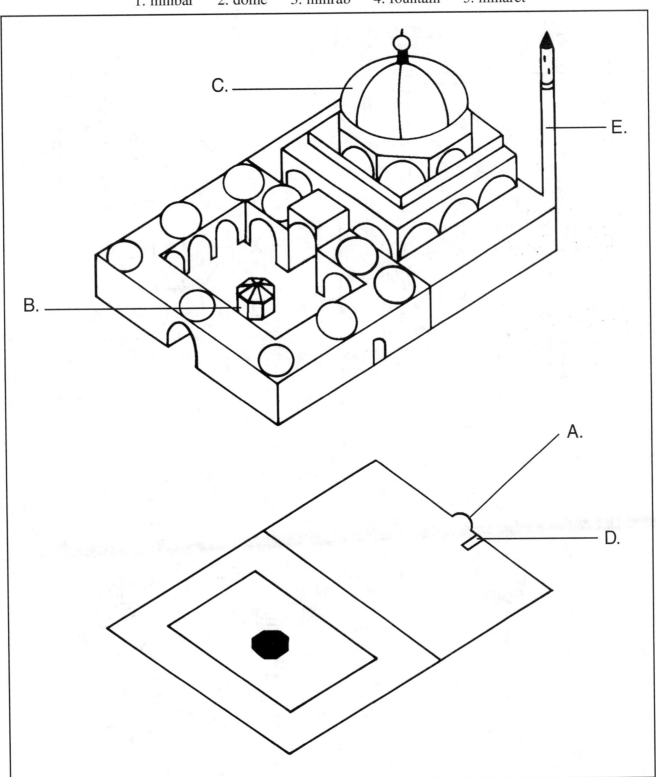

Name _____

The Mosque *(cont.)*

Use the following illustrations as models to construct a mosque. Research to determine appropriate colors.

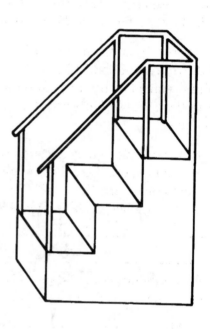

Rites of Passage

Birth and Childhood

The first words a Muslim baby hears is the *shahada*, the first pillar of Islam:

"There is no God but Allah, and Muhammad is the messenger of Allah."

Although circumcision is not mentioned in the *Koran*, it usually takes place—along with a celebration—shortly after birth. In some Muslim countries, it occurs either around the age of ten or when the boy can recite the *Koran* by memory.

It is customary to name the newborn seven days after birth. Devout Muslims observe a ceremony called the *Aqiqa*. A child's head is shaved, and he or she is given a Muslim name. Most commonly, the child is named after a revered figure. Many boys, of course, are named Muhammad. Others adopt names of the caliphs. Girls are often named Khadijah, after Muhammad's first wife, or Fatimah, one of his daughters.

The Koran is central to the education of a Muslim. At an early age they begin reciting from the scripture and memorizing common prayers. The most popular phrase translates, "in the name of Allah, the Compassionate, the Merciful." These words are used as daily prayers, when entering structures, and before meals. In fact, each chapter of the *Koran* begins with this phrase.

Marriage

As in most religious communities, marriage and family are an essential part of Islam. Moreover, marriage is viewed as the union of both families as well as the individuals.

Traditionally, marriages were arranged by families, although more contemporary Muslims are choosing their own mates. Another traditional practice that is being questioned is polygamy, or the practice of a man marrying more than one wife. According to the *Koran*, a man may marry up to four wives as long as he can treat them equally. (Muhammad himself had four wives). However, polygamy is a subject of much debate.

Though the marriage ceremony is simple, the celebrations are elaborate and joyous. Families extend themselves to provide the proper environment, often including the local Muslim community and extending through the night. It is still common, however, for men and women to celebrate separately.

Death

"Has He who created the heavens and the earth no power to create their like? That He surely has. He is the all-knowing Creator. When He decrees a thing He need only say: 'Be,' and it is." (36.81-83)

Passages such as these, from the 36th surah of the *Koran*, are recited in the final hours of a Muslim's life. For Muslims, death is regarded as a release from the suffering of life until the Last Judgment. Thus, recitations such as these comfort and inspire the dying.

Following a death, the corpse is prepared for burial by a ritual washing and being wrapped in a white sheet. The funeral service consists of some simple prayers, and the Muslim burial takes place quickly and without extravagance. A coffin is not required, and a procession carries the deceased to the grave. As expected, it is essential that the head of the deceased point in the direction of the Ka'bah in Mecca. Normally, the grave has no marker or headstone.

Name _____

Rites of Passage *(cont.)*

In the space provided below, choose one of the three areas described on the previous page and compare it to your own experiences. How is the Muslim treatment of birth, marriage, or death different and the same from your own?

_____

_____

_____

_____

_____

_____

_____

_____

_____

_____

_____

_____

_____

_____

_____

_____

_____

_____

_____

_____

_____

The Islamic Calendar

The Islamic calendar dates from 622 CE, the time of the Hijrah, Muhammad's famous journey to Medina. It is also a lunar calendar, meaning each month begins with the appearance of the new moon. Therefore, Islamic celebrations and holidays happen eleven days earlier each solar year, giving them no particular connection to the seasons.

Here are the months of the Islamic calendar. Below, you will find the dates of significant Islamic festivals.

The Islamic Calendar

1. Muharram	2. Safar	3. Rabi 1
4. Rabi 2	5. Jumad 1	6. Jumad 2
7. Rajab	8. Sha' Ban	9. Ramadan
10. Shawwal	11. Dhul-Quada	12. Dhul-Hijjah

Significant Festivals and Holidays

1 Muharram: New Year's Day (celebrates the Hijrah)

12 Rabi 1: *Mawlid-al-Nabi*, Muhammad's birthday celebration

27 Rajab: *Lailat-al-Miraj*, Nygannad's ascension to Heaven

1-28 Ramadan: the month of fasting

1 Shawwal: *Eid-al-Fitr*, the festival to complete Ramadan

8-13 Dhul-Hijja: *Hajj*, the annual pilgrimage to Mecca

10 Dhul-Hijja: *Eid-ul-Adha*, the feast of sacrifice

Extension:

Explain in detail the happenings during one of these special occasions.

Symbols of Islam

The Crescent and the Star

The crescent and the star is the principal symbol of Islam. It is widely used, often appearing atop minarets and on the flags and stamps of Muslim states.

The crescent and the star—a symbol associated with moon worship—was originally used in Byzantium. But when the Ottoman Turks conquered the Byzantine Empire, they adopted it as a military symbol. Gradually, it became the accepted symbol of Islamic culture.

Some Muslim scholars say the crescent and the star is symbolic of the solace and understanding offered by Islam. Just as the waxing moon increases in light and the star provides direction, Islam steadily guides the faithful toward Allah.

The Ka'bah

The picture of the Ka'bah, the sacred shrine at Mecca, is another popular Muslim symbol. For additional information on the Ka'bah, see page 91.

Name _____

Islam and Stereotypes

Of the major Semitic religions, Westerners know the least about Islam. Very few people, for example, understand the connections between Judaism, Christianity, and Islam. Why is this? First of all, many Westerners have never personally known a Muslim. Though there are millions of Muslims living in the West today, the majority live in the Middle East, Africa, and Indonesia.

Unfortunately, the gulf of ignorance surrounding Islam has led to a great deal of prejudice and stereotypes. The dictionary defines a stereotype as "a conventional and usually oversimplified conception or belief." Here are two of the most widespread misconceptions:

1. **All Muslims are Arabs.**

   This is not true. The Arab-speaking population is made of the countries in the Arabian Peninsula. including Iraq, Syria, Sudan, Egypt, and most of North Africa. Their populations are at least 90% Muslim.

   But if you refer to the map on pages 8-9, you will notice more countries that are homes to major Muslim populations. These countries include several of the former Soviet Republic as well as India, China, Bangladesh, Pakistan, and especially Indonesia.

   With the increasing Muslim population in the United States and throughout the world, you can see that the international Muslim community is rich in cultures and nationalities.

2. **Muslims are violent and promote terrorism.**

   Although there are certain fundamentalist sects which promote terrorism, and although some countries of the West have had several military conflicts with Muslim groups, the vast majority of Muslims are peaceful and consider Islam a religion of peace.

   One of the factors contributing to this stereotype is the media. Violence receives extensive media coverage, causing people to identify Islam solely with terrorism.

Extension

1. List three things you could do to help dispel Muslim stereotypes.

   A. _____

   B. _____

   C. _____

2. Research and write a report on political conflicts which may have led to assumptions about Islam.

3. Keep a notebook by your television set. Describe the stereotypical portrayals of both Arabs and Muslims.

Islam in the World Today

The map at the bottom of this page highlights countries with majority Muslim populations and large Muslim populations. These territories, as you can see, are widespread and growing. In fact, the world's current population, which is approximately five and a half billion, claims over twenty percent— more than one billion—as Muslims. Here is a chart of Muslim populations in different world regions:

Region	In Millions
India/Pakistan	250-300
Africa	200
Arab countries	180
Southeast Asia	170
Europe	65
Iran	50
Central Asia	50
China	50
Afghanistan	15
North America	6
Australia	1

The majority of the Shi'ah Muslims live in Pakistan, Iran, Afghanistan, Israel/Palestine, Iraq, and small regions of Saudi Arabia and India.

North America	Morocco	Ethiopia	China
Europe	Algeria	Tanzania	Pacific Ocean
Asia	Libya	Africa	South America
Turkey	Egypt	Indian Ocean	Pacific Ocean
Afghanistan	Saudi Arabia	Australia	Muslim majority
Pakistan	Iran	Indonesia	large Muslim population
Iraq	Nigeria	Bangladesh	
Tunisia	Somalia	India	

Name _____

Islam in the World Today *(cont.)*

Referring to the map and information on the previous page, answer the following questions. (You will also need to refer to earlier pages and consult an atlas.)

1. List the continents containing countries with a majority Muslim population.

   _____

   _____

2. Which continent contains the highest Muslim population? The lowest?

   _____

   _____

3. Do most Muslim countries have warm or cold weather climates? How can you tell?

   _____

   _____

4. About how many countries have Muslim majority populations?

   _____

5. In which country did Islam begin? Locate it on your map.

   _____

6. List five Arabic speaking countries.

   _____ _____ _____ _____ _____

7. Are Shia'h Muslims basically centralized or spread throughout the world?

   _____

8. Which Muslim country is furthest east of Mecca?

   _____

9. Find an up-to-date atlas and list the exact Muslim population of three countries from three different continents.

   _____

   _____

   _____

Name _____

Calligraphy

Calligraphy—the art of writing—is sacred to Muslims. It was born from the Arabic script of the *Koran.*

Since Islam forbids idolatry, mosques are decorated with calligraphy rather than with pictures of human or animal figures. Verses of the Koran, drawn in flowing Arabic, are bordered by complex geometrical and floral designs. Often colorful, the walls and domes of mosques are inspiring works of art in themselves.

Practicing Calligraphy

Here is the *shahada*, the Islamic statement of faith, written in Arabic. In the space below, try copying it by hand. This should give you an idea of the artistic complexity of calligraphy.

Name _____

Calligraphy *(cont.)*

As you know, the art of calligraphy now exists in many languages. Here is one style of letters in English calligraphy. Write an inspiring statement using these letters as models. If you have a calligraphy pen, all the better!

A   B   C   D   E   F   G   H   I   J   K   L   M
N   O   P   Q   R   S   T   U   V   W   X   Y   Z

Name _____

Wordsearch

In the wordsearch puzzle below, find the following words associated with Islam.

- Koran
- Kabah
- caliph
- Islam
- Ottoman
- Hajj

- Muhammad
- Mecca
- Ramadan
- Sunni
- minaret
- pillars

- Medina
- Khadija
- Shi'ah
- imam
- mosque
- calligraphy

- Muslim
- pilgrimage
- Allah

```
N F M F S I E R K U K C D J G H D S P I L G R I M A G E K D J
R F M I N N U S K P J H F S I U Y E R I U W A E Y Q U B D J F
A A S M B Z D K S I J S I N L L A C C E M N F D S C A M O F S
M R E I N S K H A L L A H A F A D F G R E S M M G A S F H H F
A N D S A F K Q K L H F S M D B K L H A B A K M G L K B D D S
D N G L R X C M V A R E S O U G R E T T L H F D D I B D A F G
A L I W O A A B N R B F D T H S R J A S T H F M J P L D N F S
N N B X K M M T R S W F D T N G L J I P O I U O E H G F I N V
J R O A I A D K G P G A J O Q A Z I V B N H P S H J U S D F E
M F G S J M U H A M M A D S K H F G M A K H Q Q T E Y S E L I
M E I A H V O A R W Q Y H P A R G I L L A C B U J H F D M D R
P Q M Z K I K J A S R K C G W K E L E L E L A E S K W F S G L
M R H T K H A D I J A J A S D H L T Q P E Q Z N X S C J S Y E
K F D G K S R H H D J J A H H D X F N A S H M I N A R E T L O
```

Name _____

Quiz and Review

Part One: For questions 1-10, fill in the space with the correct answer.

1. Abraham is important to Muslims because he built the _____ in _____ .

2. Judaism, Christianity, and Islam are all _____ religions.

3. The Islamic calendar dates from Muhammad's journey to Medina, called the _____ .

4. The Islamic holy book is the _____ . It contains chapters called _____ .

5. Today, Mecca and Medina are in _____ .

6. The first pillar of Islam, the _____, proclaims, " _____ ."

7. Muslims pray _____ a day toward _____ .

8. Zakat, or _____ , is the third pillar of Islam.

9. The month of _____ requires fasting. Afterwards, Muslims gather to celebrate the Festival of _____ .

10. The Hajj, or _____ , to Mecca is required at least once in a Muslim's lifetime.

Part Two: Answer the following questions in the spaces provided.

1. Explain the origin and role of the caliph in Islam.

_____

_____

_____

_____

_____

2. By the end of the 17th century, the Ottoman Empire had spread enormously. List the geographical areas the Empire controlled.

_____

_____

_____

_____

_____

Name _____

Quiz and Review *(cont.)*

Part Two *(cont.)*:

3. Explain one basic difference between the Sunni and Shi'ah sects.

4. Write one feature particular to these Muslim rites of passage:

    A. birth _____

    B. marriage _____

    C. death _____

Part Three: Respond to the following with *true* or *false*.

_____ 1. All Muslims speak Arabic.

_____ 2. Muslims believe in one God.

_____ 3. Mosques are decorated with pictures of Muhammad.

_____ 4. The majority of Muslims are peaceful people.

_____ 5. Islam began in Saudi Arabia.

_____ 6. All Muslims live in the Middle East.

_____ 7. Over 20% of the world's population is Muslim.

_____ 8. Islam follows a lunar calendar.

_____ 9. The *Koran* rejects all other religions.

_____10. All Muslims have the same values and beliefs.

Part Four: Write five ideas or facts you have learned about Islam.

1. _____

2. _____

3. _____

4. _____

5. _____

Name _____

The Indian Religions

So far, we have covered the Semitic religions of Judaism, Christianity, and Islam. All three are monotheistic in their beliefs, and all three originated in the Middle East.

We move now to the Indian religions of Hinduism, Buddhism, and Sikhism. They are referred to as Indian religions because all three originated in the subcontinent of India, beginning with Hinduism as early as 2000 BCE. Unlike the shared monotheism of the Semitic faiths, the Indian religions differ in some of their most basic beliefs. Hinduism, for example, is a polytheistic religion, meaning that Hindus may believe in various forms of god. (*Poly* means *many*, while *theism* means *belief in God or gods*.) Buddhists, on the other hand, do not necessarily believe in God at all. Sikhism, youngest of the three faiths, is monotheistic and combines influences from Hinduism and Islam.

Look at the map on the next page of the Indian subcontinent. The Indus valley, nurtured by the Indus River, is the birthplace of Hinduism. The Buddha delivered his first sermon at the city of Sarnath near the sacred Hindu city of Banares. To the north is Amritsar, the spiritual center of the Sikh religion. As you can see, this area of the world contains a rich variety of religions. All together, the Indian religions constitute about 900 million people.

Questions:

1. Why are Hinduism, Buddhism, and Sikhism referred to as Indian religions?

   _____

   _____

2. Which is the oldest of the Indian religions? Which is youngest?

   _____

   _____

3. What does polytheism mean?

   _____

   _____

4. What fundamental difference is there between the Semitic and Indian religions?

   _____

   _____

The Indian Religions *(cont.)*

Name _____

Origins of Hinduism: The Indus Valley Civilization

Hinduism, unlike most major religions, does not have a central figure upon whom it is founded. Rather, it is a complex faith with roots stemming back five thousand years to the people of the Indus Valley, now part of Pakistan. When the Aryan tribes of Persia invaded the Indus Valley around 1700 BCE, the groups' beliefs merged and Hinduism began to form.

Most of what we know of the Indus people (also called Dravidians) comes from archaeological findings. Artifacts and relics dating back as early as 2000 BCE tell the story of a civilization flourishing with craftsmanship, agriculture, and religious life. As we will see, many of these early practices and beliefs still shape Hinduism.

For example, the Indus put great importance on cleanliness or ritual bathing. MohenjoDaro, one of the major Indus cities, contained a huge water tank for public bathing. Today, many Hindu temples feature such tanks.

Another lasting legacy of Hinduism is found in the abundance of terra-cotta figurines unearthed in the Indus Valley. Popular among these small ceramic statuettes were depictions of pregnant women, "mother goddesses." The fertility and strength of the goddess and the rebirth and continuity she provides remain central to the Hindu faith.

Ceramic seals also provide insight into the Indus' religious beliefs. Among the most common design was that of the bull. It represented virility, or sexual force, which is still considered sacred to the Hindus. Shiva, among the most revered Hindu gods, is associated with the bull.

The Indus were an agricultural people, growing crops and raising animals. Living on the banks of the Indus River, dependent on its nourishment and renewal, there was deep reverence for water. Water still remains sacred to Hindus.

Questions:

1. How did researchers discover most of the information about the Indus people?

   _____

2. List three findings and briefly explain their links to Hinduism.

   _____

   _____

   _____

   _____

3. How did the Indus people survive? How does it relate to their religious worship?

   _____

   _____

The Indus Valley

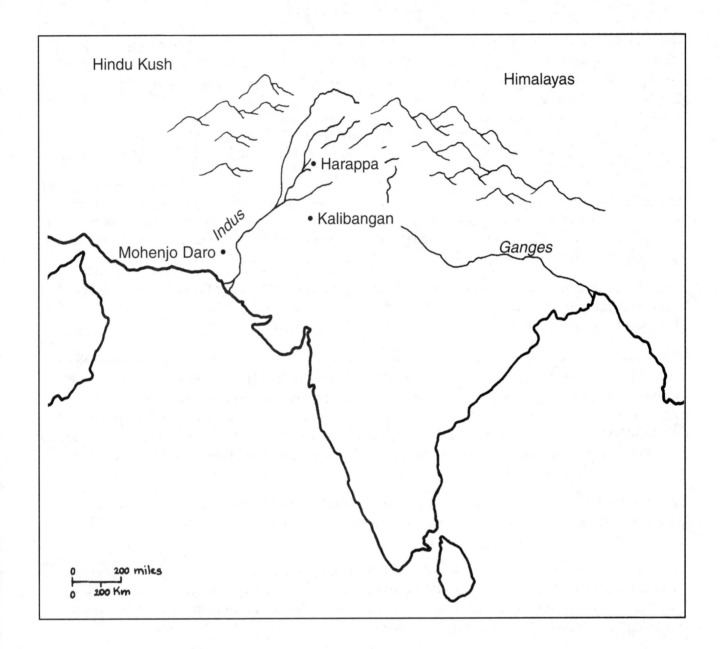

Name _____

Origins of Hinduism:
The Aryan Invasion and the Vedas

The Aryan Invasion

Although there is evidence that the Indus Valley civilization may already have been struggling, its collapse began with the invasion of the Aryan tribes around 1700 BCE. The Aryans, a powerful race, traveled through Europe and Asia, conquering whomever they encountered. When they descended from the Hindu Kush and the Himalayas into the Indus Valley, they brought with them a very different belief system and way of life.

To begin with, the Aryans were not agricultural people. Rather than fertility symbols, they crafted beautiful bronze weaponry. Another major contrast was their religious focus. The Aryans were patriarchal, worshipping only male gods. Their central god was a "sky father," probably an influence of the Greek and Roman gods, Zeus and Jupiter. Their principal deities, such as Agni and Indra, were associated with the sun. Aryan priests composed verses to these gods which were recited during fire sacrifices.

The Aryans settled the lush Indus Valley and maintained their rituals. However, much of the Indus' religious culture remained alive in villages and was adopted by the Aryans. From this mixture of beliefs and practices, Hinduism was born.

The Vedas

With the Aryans arrived the bedrock of the Hindu thought system, the *Vedas*. Considered the world's oldest writings, these scriptures originated before the Aryans migrated to the Indus Valley, later evolving into four scriptures: the *Rig-Veda*, the *Yajur Veda*, the *Sama-Veda*, and the *Atharva-Veda*. The oldest and most popular of these is the *Rig Veda*, a collection of hymns which may date back as early as 5000 BCE. It is important to note, however, that the historical sweep of Vedic writing reflects deep shifts in spiritual interest and ways of worship.

Interestingly, for centuries the *Vedas* were only transmitted orally, through memorization and recital. Eventually, however, they were transcribed into Sanskrit, the sacred Hindu language developed by the Aryans of the Indus Valley.

The *Rig-Veda* tells of thirty-three gods, all of whom are born of one creator, Brahman. Complementing Brahman are Vishnu and Shiva. These three gods form the Hindu trinity. The principal goddesses, Lakshmi, Sarasvati, and Kali are also part of the *Rig-Veda*. This variety of deities—many of whom take on different personalities and names—are very much alive in everyday Hindu life.

Response:
Describe three major differences between the Aryan and Indus people.

_____

_____

Name _____

Origins of Hinduism:
The Ascetics and The Upanishads

The Ascetic

By the 7th century BCE, Aryans, along with people of the Indus Valley, had migrated across India to the Ganges Valley, settling among the native population. Wherever they lived, the Aryans represented the elite of society, and the most elite were the *Brahmins*, priests. These priests determined a class order, or caste system, which they included as a Vedic hymn. To this day, the caste system helps shape Hindu society. (See page 155.)

Although the Brahmins were revered in the early Hindu periods, slowly their role began to be questioned. The Brahmins assumed spiritual authority, overseeing the writings of the Vedas and demanding complicated rituals. These rituals centered around the Brahmins and excluded those from lower classes. As disillusionment rose, a more individualized way of religious life was born, the life of the *ascetic*.

The ascetic was a person dedicated to a life of spiritual austerity and self-discipline. Untouched by the social system, ascetics often chose a hermitage in the forest or gathered with others to live lives of intense devotion and meditation. By example, these individuals inspired people away from dependence on priests, creating a revolution of spiritual thought and practice.

The Upanishads

From this revolution were born *The Upanishads*, authored by ascetics between 700-500 BCE. As the final part of the *Vedas, The Upanishads* contain almost exclusively dialogues of a *guru*, spiritual master. In fact, "Upanishad" literally means "sitting beside" a guru. These texts differ from earlier Vedic writings in that they are intended to inspire and welcome anyone, regardless of status or caste. Although *The Upansihads*, like much of the Vedic writings, are difficult to absorb, what matters is the seeker's depth of sincerity and character.

It follows, then, that the fire rituals so common among Vedic priests were replaced by the deep internal searching of the ascetics. To the students of *The Upanishads*, the fire of understanding burns within. The fire rituals are metaphors for an inner revelation.

Central to Upanishadic belief is that of the *atman*, higher self. The atman is a person's soul which must return to Brahman, the universal soul. Through meditation and self-sacrifice, an individual may come to realize fully that he is not separate from the universal soul, he is not a body or an isolated identity.

Response:

Briefly explain the importance of the ascetics in Hindu life.

_____

_____

Reading from the Rig-Veda

The following passage is from the creation hymn, "The Unknown God, the Golden Embryo." The word *oblation* means "an offering to a god."

[1] In the beginning the Golden Embryo arose. Once he was born, he was the one lord of creation. He held in place the earth and this sky. Who is the god whom we should worship with the oblation?

[2] He who gives life, who gives strength, whose command all the gods, his own, obey; his shadow is immortality—and death. Who is the god whom we should worship with the oblation?

[3] He who by his greatness became as one king of the world that breathes and blinks, who rules over his two-footed and four-footed creatures—who is the god whom we should worship with the oblation?

[4] He who through his power owns these snowy mountains, and the ocean together with the river Rasa, they say; who has the quarters of the sky as his two arms—who is the god whom we should worship with the oblation? (Rig-Veda 10.121 1,2,3,4)

The next passage is from the hymn, "The Killing of Vrita." It tells of Indra's slaying of the dragon, Vrita. Indra is king of the gods. Soma is a nectar of the gods.

[1] Let me now sing the heroic deeds of Indra, the first that the thunderbolt-wielder performed. He killed the dragon and pierced an opening for the waters; he split open the bellies of the mountains.

[2] He killed the dragon who lay upon the mountain; Tvastr fashioned the roaring thunderbolt for him. Like lowing cows, the flowing waters rushed straight down to the sea.

[3] Wildly excited like a bull, he took the Soma for himself and drank the extract from the three bowls in the three-day Soma ceremony. Indra the Generous seized his thunderbolt to hurl it as a weapon; he killed the first-born of the dragons. (Rig-Veda 1.32 1,2,3)

This is a section of the hymn, "In Praise of Generosity."

[1] The gods surely did not ordain hunger alone for slaughter; various deaths reach the man who is well-fed. The riches of the man who gives fully do not run out, but the miser finds no one with sympathy.

[2] The man with food who hardens his heart against the poor man who comes to him suffering and searching for nourishment—though in the past he has made use of him— he surely finds no one with sympathy.

[3] The man who is truly generous gives to the beggar who approaches him and in search of food. He puts himself at the service of the man who calls to him from the road, and makes him a friend for times to come.

[4] That man is no friend who does not give of his own nourishment to his friend, the companion at his side. Let the friend turn away from him; this is not his dwelling-place. Let him find another man who gives freely, even if he be a stranger. (Rig-Veda 10.117 1,2,3,4)

Reading from The Upanishads

The following excerpt is from "Isha," chapter two of *The Upanishads.*

> The Self is one. Unmoving, it moves swifter than thought. The senses do not overtake it, for always it goes before. Remaining still, it outstrips all that run. Without the Self, there is no life.
>
> To the ignorant the Self appears to move—yet it moves not. From the ignorant it is far distant—yet it is near. It is within all, and it is without all.
>
> He who sees all beings in the Self, and the Self in all beings, hates none.
>
> To the illumined soul, the Self is all. For him who sees everywhere oneness, how can there be delusion or grief?
>
> The Self is everywhere. Bright is he, bodiless, without scar of imperfection, without bone, without flesh, pure, untouched by evil. The Seer, the Thinker, the One who is above all, the Self-Existent—he it is that has established perfect order among objects and beings from beginningless time.
>
> To darkness are they doomed who devote themselves only to live in the world, and to a greater darkness they who devote themselves only to mediation.
>
> Life in the world alone leads to one result, meditation alone leads to another. So have we heard from the wise.
>
> They who devote themselves both to life in the world and to meditation, by life in the world overcome death, and by meditation achieve immortality.

This next passage is from chapter 9, "Chandogya."

> One day the boy Satyakama came to his mother and said: "Mother, I want to be a religious student. What is my family name?"
>
> "My son," replied his mother, "I do not know who was your father. I am Jabala, and you are Satyakama. Call yourself Satyakama Jabala."
>
> Thereupon the boy went to Guatama and asked to be accepted as a student. "Of what family are you, my lad?" inquired the sage.
>
> Satyakama replied: "I asked my mother what my family name was, and she answered: 'I do not know. In my youth I was a servant and worked in many places. I do not know who was your father. I am Jabala, and you are Satyakama. Call yourself Satyakama Jabala!' I am therefore Satyakama Jabala, sir."
>
> Then said the sage: "None but a true Brahmin would have spoken thus. Go and fetch fuel, for I will teach you. You have not swerved from the truth."

Name _____

Questions: The Vedas and The Upanishads

1. Compare the Vedic creation hymn, "The Unknown God, the Golden Embryo," to "Isha" from *The Upanishads*. In what ways is their focus the same and in what ways different?

    _____

    _____

    _____

    _____

    _____

2. Describe the tone of the Vedic hymn, "The Killing of Vrita." To whom is the hymn in honor? List a few other stories which contain dragons.

    _____

    _____

    _____

    _____

    _____

3. What is the message of the hymn, "In Praise of Generosity"? Does it echo any other religious material you have studied? Explain.

    _____

    _____

    _____

    _____

    _____

4. How does the passage from "Chandogya" illustrate the difference between the *Vedas* and *The Upanishads?*

    _____

    _____

    _____

    _____

    _____

The Hindu Trinity

As you know, Hinduism is a polytheistic religion, meaning that its followers believe in more than one god. In fact, worshippers commonly devote themselves to one god, their personal deity. Household shrines feature pictures and statues of the chosen gods. Individuals may choose this god for its special attributes. For example, Ganesh, the god with the head of an elephant, is known for overcoming obstacles and bringing success.

Some of these gods appear in the famous Hindu epics, the *Ramayana* and the *Mahabarata*. These poems originated from the storytelling and parables of the Brahmins and ascetics. In present-day India these stories are beloved and more popular than the *Vedas* and *Upanishads*. Accessible and entertaining, rich with heros and villains, they simultaneously provide moral and spiritual instruction.

The *Rig-Veda* introduced the foremost of the Hindu gods: Brahama, Vishnu, and Shiva. Although each of these deities possess special attributes, many Hindus believe they represent three properties of one god. Together they form the Hindu Trinity. This trinity will be explored below and through page 139.

Brahma: The Creator

Brahma is considered the mystical creator, the supreme presence, or God. Many Hindus believe that all other gods originate from Brahma. To the right is a depiction of Brahma. His four faces stand for the four corners of the universe. He holds a sacrificial ladle, the four Vedas, a jar of holy water from the Ganges, and a necklace of prayer beads. Like all Hindu gods, he sits upon a lotus throne.

The Hindu Trinity *(cont.)*

Vishnu: The Preserver

"Whenever the Sacred Law fails, and evil raises its head, I (Vishnu) take embodied birth. To guard the righteous, to root out sinners, and to establish Sacred Law, I am born from age to age." (Bhagavad Gita IV. 6-8)

Followers of Vishnu worship him as the preserver, greatest of the gods. His role is to maintain a balance between good and evil powers in the universe. In order to do this, Vishnu returns to earth in different forms, both animal and human. Tradition holds that there are ten *avatars*, incarnations, linked to Vishnu. However, only Rama and Krishna remain the focus of worship among Hindus. Here are the ten incarnations of Vishnu and the task each performed:

1. **Matsya** (Fish): As a giant fish, Vishnu warned the world of a great flood, rescuing both a famous sage and the Vedas from the flood.

2. **Kurma** (Tortoise): After the flood, Vishnu, in the form of a huge tortoise, retrieved the gods' elixir of immortality, which was lost in the depths of the ocean.

3. **Varah** (Boar): After the demon Hiranyakasipu plunged the earth into the ocean, Vishnu, in the form of boar, hoisted the world above water.

4. **Narasimha** (Man-Lion): In order to destroy another demon, Vishnu became half-man, half-lion. This was because the demon, Hiranyakasipu, could be killed by neither animal nor man alone.

5. **Vamana** (Dwarf): When Vishnu first came as a human avatar, he did so to outwit the ruling demon-king, Bali. As a dwarf, he convinced Bali to give him as much land as he could cover in three steps. Immediately, Vishnu transformed himself into a giant, striding across the universe.

6. **Parashurama** (Rama with an axe): Vishnu returned as Rama with an axe to defeat the ruling warrior class and restore the Brahmins to power.

7. **Rama** (Prince): As prince of Ayodya, Rama is the hero of the epic poem, *The Ramayana*.

The Hindu Trinity *(cont.)*

Vishnu *(cont.)*

8. **Krishna** (Young hero and lover): Krishna is considered by many Hindus to be the most important avatar. Fleeing the King (his evil uncle), he was raised in a forest where he slayed many demons. Eventually, he killed his uncle and restored his kingdom. When he returned to the forest to battle demons, he was accidentally slain by the arrow of a follower. Krishna's charm and power are the subject of many stories in Hindu mythology. Here he is in one of his famous poses, dancing upon the head of a tamed snake.

9. **The Buddha:** The story of Prince Siddhartha, the Buddha, is told in full on pages 170-172.

10. **Kalki:** Yet to come, some Hindus believe Kalki will appear upon a white horse, yielding a flaming sword, at the end of time.

Shiva: The Destroyer

Shiva is worshipped as the destroyer or purifier. Like Vishnu, Shiva appears in many different forms throughout Hindu legends. However, the most widely known is that of Shiva Nataraja, the Lord of the Dance.

Shiva dances in a halo of fire, representing the cycle of birth and death. As he dances, he crushes the dwarf, the demon of ignorance. In his right hand, he keeps rhythm beating a drum, while in his left hand he holds the flame of destruction, purification, and renewal. His other hands are in a position of blessing or refuge. Around his arms and neck he wears deadly snakes. The snakes symbolize Shiva's power over evil forces, while its ability to shed its skin makes it a symbol of fertility as well.

Finally, Shiva Nataraja is a symbol of sexual power and union. This is demonstrated by the female earring on his left ear and the male one on his right.

Name _____

The Hindu Trinity *(cont.)*

Shiva *(cont.)*

Use the information on the previous page to identify parts of Shiva.

Name _____

Hindu Goddesses

The worship of the goddess in Hinduism has its roots in the Indus Valley civilization where the mother was revered as the renewer of life and as a symbol of fertility and strength. Like their male counterparts, each goddess possesses particular attributes, and worshippers adopt each for the personal qualities she brings.

Three of the principal goddesses are directly related to the gods of the Hindu Trinity: Sarasvati, daughter of Brahma; Lakshmi, wife of Vishnu; and Mahadevi Shakti, wife of Shiva. For many, Mahadevi Shakti, like Brahma, is the ultimate reality. She is the "great goddess" from whom all the goddesses are born. While an abundance of minor goddesses are featured in village shrines, Mahadevi is the central figure of goddess worship.

Mahadevi, like many Hindu deities, takes on many forms, some of which are very different in nature. Like her husband, Shiva, her role can either be forceful or self-sacrificing. One of her most popular and feared manifestations is that of Kali.

Kali: Goddess of Destruction

This common depiction of Kali shows her wearing a necklace of human skulls while wielding a sword in one hand and the decapitated head of a giant dripping blood in the other. Her tongue hangs out and a third eye watches from her forehead. Because death cannot touch her, she stands on a corpse and resides in the cremation ground. As the ultimate symbol of death and pain, many Hindus revere Kali, believing that going beyond her will bring enlightenment.

Although Kali leaves behind her bloodshed and death, one legend tells of how she destroyed the terrible oppressor, Raktabija. Each time a drop of Raktabija's blood fell, multitudes of demons came to life. Kali rescued the world by slaying the tyrant and then draining his blood.

Extension:

For each goddess (below and on the next page), research and describe her characteristics. Can you explain her posture, what she is holding, and why?

Kali: Goddess of Destruction

_____

_____

_____

_____

_____

_____

_____

Name _____

Hindu Goddesses *(cont.)*

Lakshmi: Goddess of Wealth

_____

_____

_____

_____

_____

_____

_____

_____

_____

_____

Sarasvati: Goddess of Knowledge

_____

_____

_____

_____

_____

_____

_____

_____

_____

The Ramayana

The epic poem, *Ramayana*, tells the story of the life of Rama, Prince of Ayodya. Rama is the seventh incarnation of Vishnu. This story, combined with the Mahabharata, represents the most celebrated tale in all of Hinduism. In fact, Hindus are often named after the colorful and profound characters of these epics. It is also common to see these deities worshiped in temples and during festivals.

Here is a brief retelling of the cycle of *Ramayana*.

Our story begins in the city of Ayodya, capital of the land of Koshala, to the north of Benares, between the River Ganges and the Himalayas. Here lived Prince Rama and his younger half-brother, Lakshmana. Their father was King Dasharatha, ruler of Ayodya. Rama's mother was Kaushalya.

The brothers grew up happily, excelling in sports while mastering weaponry and horsemanship. But their real adventures began when the famous sage, Vishwamitra, asked for Rama's help in slaying a stronghold of *rakshasas*, forest demons. These demons plagued the forest-dwelling ascetics, ruining their fire sacrifices and defiling their altars. Although only teenagers, the boys accompanied the sage into the depths of the woodlands.

Soon, the brothers had won the hearts of their people by destroying demon after demon. Despite the evil spirits' powers of invisibility and great strength, Rama's arrows pierced them all, even the most terrible.

They returned with the sage to the city of Mithila, where the famous bow of Shiva was kept under the rule of King Janaka. The brothers were anxious to see the bow which no one—not king or sage—could string. Impressed by the brothers' heroism, King Janaka announced that if Rama could string Lord Shiva's bow, then the young prince would marry his daughter, Sita.

Effortlessly, Rama lifted the mighty bow. And as he strung it, it broke in two with a thunderous sound.

Rama and Sita were married. Lakshmana and Sita's sister, Urmila, were also wed. When the couples returned to Ayodya, a festive welcome awaited them. There they lived happily for the next twelve years.

When the aging King Dasharatha had to name a successor, he chose Rama, his eldest son. Throughout the land the inhabitants celebrated, knowing that the Prince would be a wise and brave leader. What they did not know, however, was that a crisis was about to befall Ayodya.

The trouble began when Kaikeyi, Dasharatha's third wife and mother of Bharata, heard the news that Rama was to be crowned. She was overjoyed, feeling as if Rama were her own son. However, her maid, Mantharama, had evil intentions. She worked relentlessly to convince Kaikeyi that Rama would have Bharata sentenced to death, even though Bharata was away in his grandfather's kingdom.

Now, years back, Kaikeyi had saved King Dasharatha's life. He had promised her any two things she wished, and she had saved these boons. Now she demanded that Bharata be made king and that Rama be exiled to the forest for fourteen years. The King, deeply distressed, tried to go back on his word, but Rama would not let him. Instead, he nobly agreed to Kaikeyi's terms, announcing that the most virtuous act was to keep his father's word.

The Ramayana *(cont.)*

Hearing this, Sita said she would join her husband. The dangers of the forest, she proclaimed, would be nothing compared to living without her husband. The loyalty of Lakshmana also compelled him to join his brother. So, without malice or regret, Rama clothed himself in the robe of an ascetic, blessed the throne for Bharata, and left for the forest with Sita and Lakshmana.

Deep into the forest traveled the three companions. But it was not long before they received a visitor, Bharata himself.

Having learned of Rama's exile, Bharata came to his brother in distress, asking Rama to return to Ayodya and assume his role as king. But again Rama stood firm: it was most important that their father's pledge to Kaikeyi remain unbroken. He would remain in exile. Bharata understood, proclaiming that he would rule on Rama's behalf. As a symbol of his elder brother's true authority, Bharata placed Rama's sandals on the throne.

After Bharata departed, Rama, Sita, and Lakshmana found a peaceful spot by a river. There they built a cottage. Living in harmony, the trio was esteemed by the sages of the forest. These ascetics were also thankful for the protection which Rama provided. Since his arrival, many Rakshasas were slain.

As news of Rama's might spread, the demons became angrier. In fury, they gathered an army of fourteen thousand and attacked, swearing to defeat their nemesis. At once, Rama ordered Lakshmana and Sita to take refuge in a nearby cave. Then, single-handedly, he defeated the massive demon army. However, the evil Akampana escaped Rama's arrow and flew in his carriage back to his ruler, Ravana. King of the Rakshasas, the demon Ravana had ten heads and twenty arms, standing giant and powerful.

Learning that Rama had slain his two brothers and thousands of other demons, Ravana swore vengeance. Aware of Rama's physical prowess, he plotted the kidnaping of Sita, for without his beloved wife, his source of love and devotion, the Prince would surely die of a broken heart.

And so it was that Ravana, disguised as an ascetic, arrived at the forest home of the royal family. There he managed to lure Rama away in pursuit of a demon appearing as a beautiful deer. As the deer led Rama deeper into the woods, Sita worried and pleaded with Lakshmana to find her husband. It was then that Ravana appeared at the cottage.

Although she did not recognize Ravana, Sita sensed danger. At once, Ravana assumed his true form and abducted Sita. As they flew southward to the land of Lanka, he promised her riches and power if she would be his queen. Sita scoffed at his offer, warning that he would be destroyed by Rama.

Meanwhile, Rama and Lakshmana despaired. After discovering the deer's true identity, they returned to find Sita missing. Rama plunged into sorrow, vowing to destroy the world unless the gods restored Sita to his side. Just then, Jatayu, an aged vulture loyal to King Dasharatha, spoke to the brothers. Wounded and breathing his last breaths, the faithful bird had tried but failed to rescue Sita. Now the vulture told Rama that his wife was not dead, but kidnaped by Ravana. As the brothers buried Jatayu, they vowed to rescue Sita.

The Ramayana *(cont.)*

Knowing they would need help, Rama and Lakshmana sought out the well-known monkey, Hanuman. A strong bond grew between them, and soon Hanuman had gathered together an army of monkeys, promising to liberate Sita. Indeed, they already had some jewelry the Princess had dropped from Ravana's carriage. The legion searched and searched in all directions until they learned that Sita had been carried to the land of Lanka, in the southern ocean.

Although the monkeys were powerful animals, able to leap great distances, the vast stretch of ocean between the lands was disheartening. Only the mighty Hanuman, son of the wind god, possessed the divine energy to jump the great waters. They watched as Hanuman changed into a huge form and soared above the ocean at great speed.

When Hanuman finally reached Lanka, he leapt the city walls and began to search for Sita. He sneaked through the palace, but nowhere could he find the Princess. Finally, wandering the night, he found the captive Sita in a grove of trees. There he witnessed as Ravana tried in vain to lure Sita into marriage. But she would not budge, speaking only of her loyalty to Rama. At last, the demon king threatened to have her killed unless she consented.

When Sita was alone, Hanuman lowered himself from the trees. He gave her one of Rama's rings and offered to carry her home on his back. But Sita refused. She would be rescued, she declared, only by her husband who would destroy Ravana and restore her honor. Nothing short of this would she accept. Handing Hanuman a jewel, she bid the brave messenger return to Rama and deliver it to him.

And so Hanuman crossed the ocean once again to deliver the news of Sita's safety. Rama's heart swelled when he saw the jewel Sita had sent. And when he learned that she would be rescued by him alone, he felt heavenly pride.

Now, led by Rama and Lakshmana, the monkey troops gathered again on the shores of the sea. Suddenly, they saw a group of rakshasas flying toward them. Braced for attack, they were surprised to find that it was Ravana's younger brother, Vibheeshev, come to seek refuge with them, for he would not take part in Ravana's evil scheme.

The newcomers were welcomed by the monkeys, who still faced a serious problem: how were they to cross the sea? They could not find a solution until Rama threatened to dry the waters himself if the ocean gods did not help. But as the enraged Prince lifted his bow, the Lord of the Ocean, Sagara, rose before him. Sagara instructed the army to build a bridge which his powers would support.

The monkeys worked furiously until the bridge was built and they crossed safely to Lanka. Ravana, witnessing their passage, gathered his soldiers for war, vowing to destroy Rama. Thus, the battle began.

All day, the demons and monkeys fought to a standstill. Slowly, though, the monkeys proved mightier. Seeing this, Ravana himself appeared on the battlefield, showering arrows upon his enemies. Rama acted at once, destroying Ravana's chariot, leaving the king defenseless before him. But in his honor Rama would not kill an unarmed enemy, and Ravana retreated, ashamed, to his palace.

The Ramayana *(cont.)*

It was not long, however, before the demon King returned fully armed for war. Now he raged and took deadly aim at Lakshmana. Ravana's arrow pierced the young man's heart. Rama, stricken with grief, lay by his dying brother's side. But a voice consoled him. The wise monkey, Sushena, knew of an herb from the distant mountain, Mahodaya. This herb would heal Lakshmana's wounds.

At once, Hanuman flew to the Himalayas. But when he reached the mountain, he did not know which herb to bring. So he gathered his strength and lifted the entire mountain back to Lanka! The monkeys watched in awe as Hanuman delivered the mountain. They found the correct herb and celebrated as Lakshmana was healed.

Just then, a war cry rent the air. Aboard a new chariot, Ravana attacked. Rama mounted his chariot and charged. The Prince of Ayodya and the king of the rakshasas battled fiercely. For a long time, the clanging of steel was all that was heard. Finally, Rama, invoking help from the gods, fired an arrow into Ravana's heart. The demon fell dead.

Lanka was captured and Sita set free. But as Rama approached her, he looked forlorn. He told Sita that they must part, that a husband cannot take back a wife who has lived in another man's house. But Sita had thought only of Rama during her captivity. How, she wondered tearfully, could he doubt her purity?

Boldly, she proclaimed that she would prove her purity. Sita ordered the monkeys to build a funeral pyre. When the wood was piled and set aflame, she walked three times around the pyre. Proudly, she bid farewell to the world and leapt into the fire.

But no harm came to Queen of Ayodya. Agni, the fire god, appeared before her and, leading her safely out of the flames, announced to Rama that she was indeed virtuous.

Rama, deeply moved, accepted his Queen. Indeed, in truth he had never doubted her. If they were to rule the people of Ayodya, he knew, all suspicion must be removed.

Together, the royal pair returned to their kingdom, where they ruled for many years. Virtuous and wise, they brought order and happiness to the people of Ayodya and beyond.

The Ramayana: Comprehension

Below is a list of questions and prompts focusing on comprehension of the story you just read. Some questions require that you refer to the map of India on page 128. On a separate sheet of paper, write your responses in full sentences. Feel free to review the story if you need.

1. On the map of India, circle where Ayodya may have been located.

2. Write the names of Rama's mother, father, and brother.

3. How did Rama first win his reputation?

4. How did Rama win Sita's hand in marriage?

5. Why does Kaikeyi have Rama exiled?

6. Why does Rama agree to be in exile? Is he angry about it?

7. How does Bharata feel about Rama's exile? What does Rama say to him?

8. Knowing of the danger, why does Sita join her husband?

9. Describe Ravana's physical appearance.

10. Why does Ravana choose to kidnap Sita? How does he succeed?

11. Who tells Rama and Lakshmana about Sita's abduction?

12. Look on your map. Where is the land of Lanka?

13. Who is Hanuman? Why is he able to jump so far and change forms?

14. Why does Sita refuse to be rescued by Hanuman?

15. Why does Vibheesheva seek refuge with Rama?

16. What happens when Rama lifts his bow to dry the ocean?

17. Why won't Rama kill Ravana when they first battle?

18. On your map, chart the route Hanuman may have taken to retrieve the mountain of herbs.

19. For what reason does Rama separate himself from Sita after her rescue?

20. How does Sita feel about this?

21. What action does Sita take? Why? What happens?

22. How does the story end?

Name _____

The Ramayana: Critical Thinking

The Ramayana is an adventure rich in meaning. Although there is a great deal of action, this epic is meant to be instructive as well as entertaining. In the section below, write about each topic listed. Review the story and give detailed examples to support your findings.

1. Write about the role of virtue, or honor, in the story.

    _____

    _____

    _____

    _____

    _____

    _____

    _____

2. What role do the gods play in the story?

    _____

    _____

    _____

    _____

    _____

    _____

    _____

3. What role do animals play in the story?

    _____

    _____

    _____

    _____

    _____

    _____

Name _____

The Ramayana: Essay Response

Although thousands of years old, the *Ramayana* involves many plot elements which remain popular to this day. For example, how many stories do you know where a princess is kidnapped and then rescued? Have you ever seen a movie starring a "demon king"? What about gods who intervene, or characters who change forms, or animals who speak and have special powers?

In the page below, compare a movie or book with such plot conventions to the *Ramayana*. How are they similar? How are they different?

_____
_____
_____
_____
_____
_____
_____
_____
_____
_____
_____
_____
_____
_____
_____
_____
_____
_____
_____
_____

Hindu Beliefs

In order to understand Hinduism, we must learn about a few basic beliefs which form the foundation of the religion. These beliefs are rooted in both *The Vedas* and *The Upanishads*. Some of these ideas may be new to you, although some have become quite popular, such as the idea of reincarnation. Besides defining a belief system, these ideas also carry into Hindu law and rites of passage.

Dharma

Dharma stands for the ultimate moral balance of all things. Dharma belongs to the universe and to the individual as well. So, just as there is a divine order of the natural and cosmic realms, there is the same order within a personal life. However, each one has the responsibility to balance his or her own dharma.

A Hindu's dharma is played out in all areas of life: religious, social, and familial. If a person makes a promise, the promise must be kept at all costs. Likewise, the faithful maintain their religious rituals while attending to their family's needs.

But what if an individual goes astray? This leads to the next major Hindu belief, karma.

Karma

Have you ever heard someone say, "What goes around comes around"? What about, "You reap what you sow"? Both of these sayings mirror the Hindu concept of *karma*.

Basically, karma stands for the belief that a person experiences the affects of his or her actions—that every act or thought has consequences. Living in a balanced universe, if an individual disturbs this order, he or she will suffer commensurately. But an ethical and moral life, with undisturbed dharma, will lead to happiness. How, then, can a Hindu hope to find redemption from wrongdoing? If the person does not lead a pure and stainless life, what hope is there for happiness? The answer lies in samsara.

Samsara

In the Western world, *samsara* is commonly known as reincarnation. Samsara represents the cycle of life, death, and rebirth in which a person carries his or her own karma. Each life cycle presents an opportunity for balance.

Therefore, an individual may experience effects from past lives, although the circumstances may be totally different. In fact, many Hindus believe that a person's worldly status depends upon actions in a past life. Likewise, good thoughts and actions can liberate a person. Some Hindus believe that certain people meet in more than one life in order to achieve karmic balance. Thus, every relationship and situation becomes meaningful.

What happens, then, when a person becomes purified? Is reincarnation an eternal process, or is there another realm? The answer lies in moksha.

Moksha

Like heaven for the Christian, Hindus strive to reach *moksha*, or a state of changeless bliss. Moksha is achieved by living a life of religious devotion and moral integrity without any interest in worldly things. However, it may be many lifetimes within the wheel of life before moksha is achieved. The ultimate reward is release from samsara and union with God.

Name _____

Hindu Beliefs *(cont.)*

Responses:

1. Do you have a sense of dharma in your own life? Explain.

   _____

   _____

   _____

   _____

   _____

2. Does our society have a sense of dharma? If so, how is it maintained?

   _____

   _____

   _____

   _____

   _____

3. How is the story, "The Boy Who Cried Wolf" an example of karma? Can you think of other examples, even in your own life?

   _____

   _____

   _____

   _____

   _____

4. Describe a book or movie which contains the idea of samsara.

   _____

   _____

   _____

   _____

   _____

Name _____

Hindu Pilgrimages

Like the hajj of Islam, religious pilgrimage plays an important role in Hinduism. There are many holy sites in India, each dedicated to a certain god, a group of gods, or a famous happening. At these centers of worship, the devotee is energized by history, by the meeting of the spiritual and the earthly.

Within India there are four principal places of pilgrimage resting on the four compass points. Hindus visit these sacred spots in a popular all-country route. The pilgrimage normally lasts ten weeks.

Look on the map on the next page. Beginning at Rameshravaram at the southern tip of India, the pilgrims proceed in clockwise order until they encircle the country. If you recall from *The Ramayana*, this is where Rama and Hanuman's troops built a bridge to Sri Lanka in order to rescue Sita. The principal deities worshipped here are Vishnu and Shiva.

Next, the devout journey to Dwarkadheesh in western India where Vishnu is deified. From there, they pilgrim travels to Badrinath in the far north. There, high in the Himalyas, rests another shrine to Lord Vishnu where for centuries Hindus have worshipped. The faithful are then likely to visit the source of the sacred River Ganges at Gangotri. (You will read a myth about the Ganges later in this chapter.)

From the thin air of Badrinath, the sojourners follow the Ganges southward to the populated city of Calcutta, and then they proceed onward to Puri. Thousands of Hindus gather here annually in July for a great temple festival worshipping Krishna as "Lord of the Universe." Joyous crowds follow as a forty-six foot (13.8 m) image of Lord Krishna aboard a massive chariot is paraded through the streets.

Completing this pilgrimage is a difficult task requiring self-discipline and spiritual austerity. Hindus, therefore, place great emphasis on such journeys, whether they include all of India or not. Since Hindus regard life as a pilgrimage toward enlightenment, each holy destination fosters the religious connectedness needed to advance spiritually.

Other Pilgrimage Sites

Beside the four locations mentioned above, India is rich with pilgrimage sites. One such place is Harwar, meaning "Lord's Gate." On the banks of the Ganges, Hindus commit the ashes of the dead into the holy water.

Below is a list of other important places of pilgrimage. Do some research to find out the significance of each area. What took place there? Who is the principal god or form of worship? Respond below and on the back of this paper.

1. Vrindavan _____

2. Ayodya _____

3. Ujjain _____

4. Benares_____

5. Kanchipuram _____

6. Gaya_____

Hindu Pilgrimages *(cont.)*

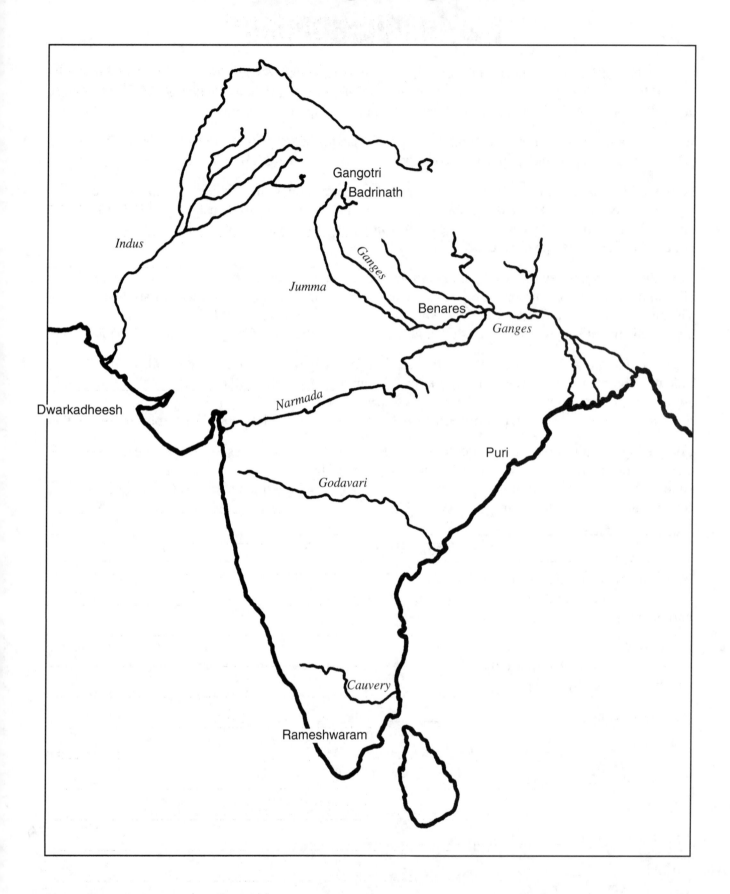

Name _____

Your Own Pilgrimage

Throughout history, people have been making pilgrimages. These journeys are not always tied to a religion, although many are. If you were to go on a pilgrimage, where would you go? Why? What would be required of you?

In the space below, write an essay describing your personal journey. Remember to include lots of details.

_____

_____

_____

_____

_____

_____

_____

_____

_____

_____

_____

_____

_____

_____

_____

_____

_____

_____

_____

_____

_____

_____

The Sacred River Ganges

The people of the Indus Valley considered water sacred, a reverence which seeped its way into their Aryan conquerors. To Hindus, water is both literally and symbolically a source of life, renewal, and hope.

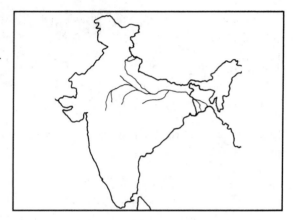

The river Ganges, born in the Himalayas and nourishing the holy city of Varanasi, is the most venerated river in all of India. Countless people visit its banks every year, washing themselves or committing the ashes of a loved one into its waters. In either case, there is the belief that contact with sacred rivers helps balance a person's karma.

There are many stories surrounding the origin of the Ganges. One of the most famous myths tells the story of Ganga, a goddess with the power to purify anything that touched her.

The story tells of the royal family of King Sagara, and his queens, Keshini and Sumati. Sumati alone has 60,000 sons, all regal and enthusiastic. So when the sacred sacrificial horse is stolen from the palace, the princes eagerly quest for its return. They search the entire surface of the earth without luck. Finally, in their haste, they dig into the netherworld. This disturbs the planet's balance, causing a tremendous earthquake.

Oblivious to the harm they have done, the boys discover the sacrificial horse in the presence of the sage, Kapila. They accuse Kapila of stealing the horse, and they prepare to attack him. But the powerful sage, enraged by their accusation, utters one syllable and engulfs the 60,000 in flames, reducing them to ashes.

Later, Amsuman, the nephew of the brothers, meets with Kapila. The sage explains that there is only one way the thoughtless princes can escape suffering in hell forever: Ganga, in all her purity, must descend from heaven and touch the ashes of the cursed uncles.

But neither Amsuman nor his son, Dilipa, is able to bring Ganga to Earth. But when Dilipa's son, Bhagiratha, refuses to take the throne until Ganga descends, Lord Brahma is impressed. The god offers Bhagiratha a boon, and the prince asks that Ganga descend. But Brahma cannot grant the boon. The earth, he explains, would be destroyed by the force of Ganga's current. Only Shiva could withstand it.

So Bhagiratha performs penances until Shiva agrees to receive Ganga's mighty force. But when the goddess tries to sweep Shiva into the netherworld, she is imprisoned in the matted locks of his hair. Again, Bhagiratha worships Shiva, begging for pity. Shiva, moved by the prince's sincerity, releases Ganga, who has been purified by contact with Shiva's hair. Soon, many people rush to Ganga to be cleansed.

But on their way to the netherworld, Ganga disturbs the meditations of sage Jahnu, who consumes her in one swallow. Devastated, Bhagiratha again must beg for release. Finally, Jahnu frees the captured goddess, who is even more pure after her contact with the sage.

At last, Bhagiratha and Ganga flow over the Earth, the ocean, and into the netherworld. The sons of Sagara are redeemed, and Brahma promises that Ganga will continue to flow, offering purification to all the faithful.

Varna: The Hindu Caste System

The Hindu class system, *varna*, is rooted in the traditions of the Aryan people. The Brahmins, or high priests, determined a class order using Vedic hymns as testimony. Take, for example, this excerpt from the famous verse, "The Hymn of Man:"

> [11] When they divided the Man, into how many parts did they apportion him? What do they call his mouth, his two arms and thighs and feet?

> [12] His mouth became the Brahmin; his arms were made into the Warrior, his thighs the People, and from his feet the Servants were born." (Rig-Veda, 10.90 11,12)

> Using the human body as a metaphor, this hymn divides society into four distinct classes, or castes, based on occupation. The mouth is the *Brahmin*, priest. The arms are the *Shatriyas*, warriors and rulers. The thighs are the *Vaishyas*, skilled workers and farmers. The feet are the *Shudras*, servants.

Although people are expected to marry within their own caste, they have not always done so. Because of inter-caste marriages, *jatis*, subdivisions of castes, were established. If a couple within the three higher strata are mixed, their children represent a new caste below the Vaishyas but above the Shudras. But if an individual from one of the three upper classes should wed a Shudra or a non-Hindu, the descendants become *Pariahs*, untouchables. Lowest on the social scale, the untouchables are considered outcasts of society.

The system of jatis is complex and varied, depending greatly on region and history. Once a new jati is established, its members are again encouraged to marry within its ranks.

It is important to remember that rank in the caste system is linked to dharma. By performing familial and social duties honestly, a Hindu strives to be born into a higher caste in his or her next incarnation. But the opposite is also true. If a member of an upper class is without virtue, he or she may be born a Shudra or Pariah.

Presently, the constitution of India does not recognize the ancient caste system, prohibiting its social distinctions. Many Hindus believe the varna is unjust, separating the wealthy from the poor while providing no opportunity for betterment. Still, many of the system's jatis still exist, especially in India's countless villages.

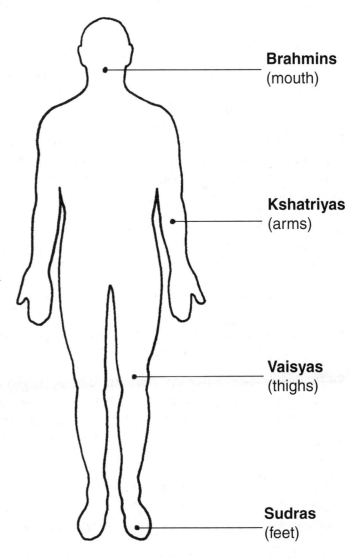

Brahmins (mouth)

Kshatriyas (arms)

Vaisyas (thighs)

Sudras (feet)

Hindu Rites of Passage

Birth

Even before a baby is born, Hindus perform rituals and recite prayers to protect the fetus from illness or harmful spirits. The mother eats only healthy foods to ensure the newborn's well-being.

In some families, the father performs a ceremony immediately after the birth. He dips a gold pen into a jar of honey and writes the sacred Sankrit symbol, Om, onto the infant's tongue. The symbol, which stands for truth, is written in hope that the child will be honest and speak only the truth, which is sweet as honey. The symbol looks like this:

After a little more than a week, the baby's name is formally given. Usually the name of a favorite god or goddess is chosen and whispered into the child's ear.

Within the first few years of her life, a Hindu girl has an ear-piercing ceremony. Both boys and girls have their hair cut, symbolic of renewal and the shedding of wrongdoing in past lives.

The Ceremony of the Sacred Thread

The Ceremony of the Sacred Thread is an ancient rite of passage into adolescence reserved for male members of the three upper castes, the Brahmins, Shatriyas, and Vaishyas. Like the Jewish bar mitz-vah, it represents a rebirth or initiation into the religious community.

Traditionally, this rite of passage served to introduce the devotee into religious life. In the presence of a guru, or holy teacher, the young man shaves his head and dons a saffron robe. Taking up a simple walking stick, he renounces all material possessions and then receives the sacred thread. The unadorned Thread is symbolic of the interconnectedness of all things. It consists of seven strands, each of which represents a different virtue or quality. They are as follows:

1. Power of speech

2. Memory

3. Intelligence

4. Forgiveness

5. Steadfastness

6. Prosperity

7. Good reputation

The boy promises to embody these qualities, and for the rest of his life he wears the sacred thread as a symbol of his coming-of-age.

The ceremony concludes with a fire sacrifice, the most common form of ritual in Hinduism. In early times, the initiate would follow his teacher into a faraway dwelling to study scriptures and to lead a life of spiritual practice and austerity. Afterwards, he would reenter society, marry, and raise a family. Nowadays, only young men seeking to become priests or ascetics live with a guru.

Name _____

Hindu Rites of Passage *(cont.)*

Marriage

Most Hindu marriages are arranged by the parents, although the children must also be happy with their chosen partner. Hindus almost always marry within the same caste, although in modern times there are increasing exceptions.

A wedding is one of the most colorful and important ceremonies in all of Hinduism. Although customs vary greatly in different regions, marriages are always joyous, momentous occasions, rich with decorations and food. In fact, some Hindu weddings last as long as three days!

The ceremony centers around a sacred fire, a manifestation of the god, Agni. Family and friends surround the couple as a priest chants Sanskrit verses. Next, he leads the bride and groom around the flames which burn in a brick firepit. Bells are sounded, and many offerings are made to the fire, including clarified butter, grains, and flowers. Each time the couple completes their circuit, the bride stands on one of the bricks. This act affirms her strength and loyalty.

Finally, the bride and groom take seven steps around the flames. These steps are the most significant action in a Hindu wedding. Now the couple is bonded for life, their union sanctified.

Death

Since ancient times, cremation, or the burning of corpses, has been a Hindu custom. Like the marriage ceremony, the rite of passage into death centers around the sacred fire.

The funeral begins when the body is wrapped in cloth and carried away on a stretcher. As family and friends leave their village for the cremation grounds, they recite prayers to the chosen deity of the deceased. Traditionally, the eldest son lights the wood of the funeral pyre with a flame lit in a nearby temple. Prayers and offerings are made in the belief that the deceased is going through a process of rebirth, cleansed by the fire into new life. The ritual also protects the relatives from evil spirits.

The ceremony concludes when the ashes are thrown into a river. Many Hindus want their remains to be left in the River Ganges, believing that its waters will help purify their souls.

Response:

Choose one of the previous four rites of passage. On the lines below, freewrite your response to the customs of the rite.

_____

_____

_____

_____

_____

Hindu Holidays

Divali

Divali, which means "a row of lights," celebrates the Hindu New Year. Because Hindus follow a lunar calendar, this holiday can fall in either October or November. Also known as the "Festival of Lights," people decorate their streets and doorways with small clay lamps called *divas* (or *idpas*). All this is done in anticipation of the coming of Lakshmi, the goddess of prosperity and good fortune. Colored lights and fireworks add to the festive atmosphere, for only if Lakshmi is greeted with light will she offer her blessings of wealth and abundance.

Divali lasts for five days. The faithful carefully clean their homes and businesses, while decorating their floors with colorful floor paintings made of rice flour. Everyone wears his or her finest clothes and jewelry and, in the spirit of generosity, offers sweets and gifts to friends and neighbors.

For some Hindus, Divali also commemorates the homecoming of Rama and Sita after their long years in exile. When the royal couple returned, their city was alight with lamps.

Extension:

Before a friend's birthday, or to welcome somebody home, make several small ceramic pots, leaving enough room in each for a candle. Surprise the person by lining his or her house with these handmade lights!

Holi

Holi is the Hindu spring festival, celebrating the equinox and the coming of Lord Krishna, who played with the colors of life. In northern India, Holi is also the time to gather the winter harvest.

A favorite among children, the holiday begins in the evening when bonfires are lit. These fires are meant to empower the sun as it moves into the warmer and longer hours of spring. All night the faithful sing and dance and pray around the bonfires. When dawn arrives, the fires are extinguished with water.

Now, instead of fire, water becomes the center of the festival. Colored with special dyes, people throw the water at each other in a playful spirit. These antics last for three days, during which people spend leisure time together, eating special holiday foods and sweets.

Extension:

With your teacher's permission, celebrate the spring equinox (March 20) with water games. Do some research to find out how you can safely color the water so that it does not stain.

Hindu Floor Paintings

If you were to visit India, you would notice colorful floor paintings decorating the entrance to many homes. These designs, which are not permanent, are made with chalk or rice flour. The patterns can be simple or complex: in either case, they keep alive a spirit of blessing and care for the home.

You can use colored chalk to design your own floor painting. Look through a book with Indian art and, with permission, copy a design for your school or home.

Here is one challenging design, the Sri Yantra. Hindus use this design as a focus for meditation.

Another way of emulating a floor design is by using colored beans, grains, and cardboard. After choosing a pattern you like, sketch it onto cardboard or construction paper. Now, plan your colors by writing them on the areas where they belong. Next, take turns filling the sections with glue and covering them with beans and grains. Let the painting dry thoroughly.

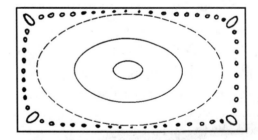

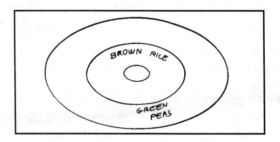

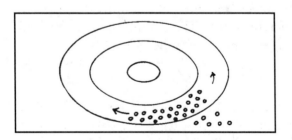

Mandir: The Hindu Temple

Like a church, synagogue, and mosque, the Hindu *mandir*, or temple, is a holy place of gathering and worship. Although mandirs vary in grandeur, they all share some specific features.

To begin with, each temple is dedicated to a particular god, although representations of other gods are allowed. In fact, *mandir* actually means "dwelling." At the heart of the temple rests a shrine to the chosen deity. These shrines contain an image—usually a statue or painting—of the god. Each morning the priest

adorns the shrine, surrounding the image with fresh flowers, fruit, incense, candles, lamps, and other decorations.

Hindus believe that although an image cannot contain God, deeper understanding can be achieved by meditating on a representation of Krishna, Vishnu, Brahma, or other deities. It is in this spirit that Hindus perform *puja*, daily worship. Temple pujas are performed at dawn, noon, dusk, and midnight. Participants take an active role in their worship, beginning with *darshan*, which simply means "to focus upon a deity." Next, the devotee makes a food offering. The priest blesses the *prasad*, or food, which is then consumed by the worshipper. It is also common for the priest to burn some of the gift and smear the consecrated ashes on the giver's forehead. Finally, some temples have room for followers to circle the shrine in a clockwise motion, another popular form of worship.

Traditionally, the outside walls of a mandir are decorated with sculptured representations of an array of mythic and worldly happenings. In fact, some older temples are literally carved out of rocks and caves. Some of these sculptures are magnificent, intricate works of art. Other temples are simple, unadorned buildings. Some rise into spires, or towers, symbolizing the meeting of the celestial and earthly. The entrance, usually facing east, welcomes the guest into a pillared hallway, an assembly hall, or both. These lead to the shrine room, the heart of the structure. Many temples also contain bathing tanks where devotees cleanse themselves.

Unlike the members of many other religions, Hindus may maintain their spiritual devotion without visiting their house of worship. As you will see, many worship their chosen deity at their family shrine. Still, the mandir serves an essential role in the spiritual life of a Hindu. It is a place where the world is left behind for awhile, a place of ritual, devotion, and cleansing.

Extension:

On the next page, study the sketch of the essential parts of a mandir. Follow up by finding some photos of a Hindu temple and locating these features.

Mandir: The Hindu Temple *(cont.)*

Mandir means "abiding place" or "dwelling." It is the home of the god worshipped there. The main services at a mandir are at sunrise and sunset.

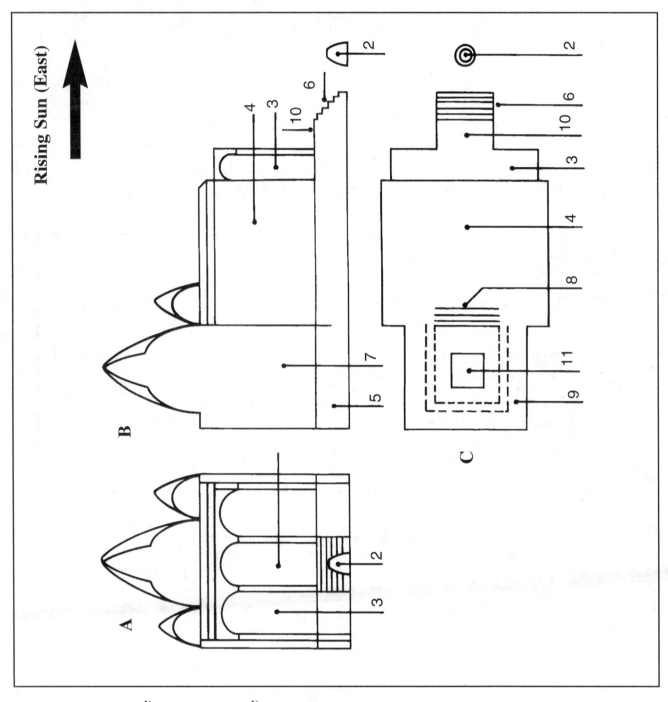

A   Temple entrance

B   Side view of temple

C   Plan of temple

1   Temple entrance

2   Stone Image

3   Pillared hallway

4   Hallway

5   Basement

6   Steps

7   Shrine room

8   Steps to the shrine

9   Processional passage

10   Porch

11   Images

A Hindu Family Shrine

Almost all Hindus keep a shrine in their home, regardless of their caste or economic status. These shrines, dedicated to a particular god, vary in size. Some families can afford to leave aside an entire room while others can devote only a corner of the bedroom. In either case, the sacred space, like the shrine of a temple, is tended to religiously. Here, family members worship collectively or individually.

On the following page, notice the common features of a family shrine. On a table or shelf rests a photograph of the chosen god. The fragrance of fresh flowers and fruit mixes with incense and perfumes in the air. A bell, which is rung for prayer, stands nearby. An oil lamp, lit during worship, sits beside the scripture from which prayers are read. Other symbols, gods, and gurus may also appear in the shrine.

Daily Duties

Beside daily worship, most Hindus attend to four other religious duties. Here is a list explaining all five daily duties:

1. **Worshipping God:** Hindus must devote part of their day to worship. This ensures spiritual contact.

2. **Reciting scripture:** By reciting from a sacred text, the faithful learn the lessons of worldly and religious life.

3. **Honoring to parents and elders:** Hindus are very loyal family members. Parents and elders are honored for their wisdom and self-sacrifice.

4. **Helping the poor:** Even the less fortunate try to obey this commandment. Guests, in particular, are given special attention in a Hindu home.

5. **Feeding animals:** Because Hindus consider all life a sacred part of one God, animals are respected and cared for.

Making Your Own Shrine

Set aside part of your room for a personal shrine. The shrine can focus on your religious tradition or it can just be a place to put special things. For example, you may want to decorate your area with a favorite souvenir or a letter from a dear friend. Take a picture of your shrine and bring it to class to share.

Be sure to look after the shrine area. Keep it decorated and clean.

A Hindu Family Shrine *(cont.)*

The Hindu Calendar

Like the Jewish and Islamic calendars, Hindus follow a lunar year. This means that each month begins with the appearance of the new moon, causing festivals and holidays to appear at a different date each year. The fortnight, or first two weeks, of the waxing moon is called *Shukla Paksha*. The fortnight of the waning moon is called *Krishna Paksha*.

Here are the months of the Hindu calendar along with their Gregorian equivalent. Below, you will also find a list of major festivals and the months on which they fall.

Magha (January/February)	**Phalguna** (February/March)	**Chaitra** (March/April)
Vaiskha (April/May)	**Jyestha** (May/June)	**Ashadha** (June/July)
Sravana (July/August)	**Bhadrapada** (August/September)	**Asvina** (September/October)
Karttika (October/November)	**Margasirsha** (November/December)	**Pausa** (December/January)

Some Significant Festivals and Holidays

Magha: *Maker Sankranti Lohri*, winter solstice festival

Phalguna: dedication to Saraswati, goddess of poetry and wisdom

Chaitra: *Holi*, spring festival

Vaisakha: *Ram Navami*, Rama's birthday celebration

Ashadha: *Ratha Yatra*, celebration of Krishna

Bhadrapada: *Raksha Bandhan*, holiday celebrating siblings; *Janamashtami*, celebration of Krishna's birth

Karttika: new year festival; *Divali*, festival of lights

Extension:

Research a holiday from this list and write a short essay on its history and festivities.

Hindu Symbols

Om or Aum

The symbol *Om*, or *Aum*, is the principal symbol of Hinduism. It is both a visual and an oral representation of Brahmin, or God. This mark has another name, *Pravana*, which means "that by which God is effectively praised," and "that which is ever new." Hindus repeat the word Om in order to transcend their individual thoughts and merge with God.

Actually, Om is comprised of three independent letters, "a," "u," and "m." The letter "a" represents beginning, "u" means progress and "m" stands for dissolution. Thus, Om reflects the power responsible for the creation, development, and destruction of the universe.

This symbol is the most widely used in all Indian religions, appearing in both Buddhism and Sikhism.

Sri Yantra

The geometrical pattern, *Sri Yantra*, is commonly used as a visual focal point for meditation. It originated with the Sakti cult, the votaries or worshippers of the Divine Mother. The design itself represents the form of the goddess. The Sri Yantra consists of nine triangles which intersect to form forty-three triangles in all. Three concentric circles surround the triangles. The shape is framed by a square.

This symbol represents spiritual evolution. The triangles stand for the many aspects of God, which, when focused upon, merge into one. When this occurs, consciousness of unity appears in the circles. Finally, the entire symbol is seen as a single unit mirroring the Absolute, or God.

Hindu Symbols *(cont.)*

The Swastika

The swastika is an ancient symbol of auspiciousness, good fortune, and protection. The root, "swasti," literally means "auspicious." Besides being used as a symbol for Vishnu, it also represents the eternal wheel of life which rotates upon an unchanging center, God. In India, it is not uncommon to find swastikas marked on buildings and animals. Some Hindus believe it protects them from evil spirits and natural disasters.

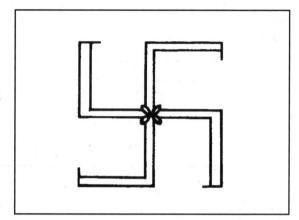

It is important to understand that the Hindu swastika pre-dates the swastika of Nazi Germany by centuries. In fact, the Nazi symbol is actually drawn in the reverse of the Hindu one.

The Lotus

The lotus bud, which is born in water and unfolds itself into a beautiful flower, symbolizes the birth of the universe, manifesting itself in all its glory. It is also a symbol of the sun, which rises in the navel of Vishnu. The lotus is the seat of Brahma as well. In fact, many deities are depicted sitting atop the sacred lotus flower.

The Cow

For ages, the cow has been held sacred by Hindus. The cow is the offspring of the celestial cow, which was created by Lord Krishna from his own body. Another Hindu myth says the cow was born of the churning of the ocean. Also, the Earth often approaches God in the form of a cow.

For many Hindus the cow is a sacred animal, providing milk and butter. Both these products are used in rituals of atonement.

Name _____

Hindu Crossword Puzzle

Across

1. Hinduism originated in the _____ Valley.
2. "What goes around comes around."
3. Considered the world's oldest writings
4. The most sacred river in India
5. An _____ lives a life of solitude and meditation.
6. Daughter of Brahma, she is the goddess of knowledge and art.
7. Hindu heaven
8. Pariahs, or _____ , are at the bottom of the social scale.
9. Krishna dances on these.
10. The goddess of destruction

Down

1. The sacred text which opened the doors of spirituality to all castes
2. The goddess of wealth and good fortune
3. The destroyer
4. Stands for the moral balance of all things
5. Cultures combined to form Hinduism when the _____ tribes invaded.
6. In the Western world, samsara means _____ .
7. Brahma is known as the _____ .
8. The priests, or elite of society
9. The _____ system divides people into different social levels.
10. The preserver, he has ten incarnations

Name _____

Quiz and Review

Part One: For questions one through ten, fill in the spaces with the correct answers.

1. When a child is born, Hindus use _____ to write the sacred symbol _____ on the newborn's tongue.

2. The rite of passage into adolescence for male Brahmins is called the ceremony of the _____ .

3. A Hindu wedding is complete when the bride and groom take _____ steps around the flames.

4. _____ is the customary rite of passage into death.

5. Many Hindu rituals center around _____ , the god of fire.

6. _____ , or the Festival of Lights, celebrates the New Year. This holiday is in honor of the goddess _____ .

7. Holi celebrates the _____ equinox and welcomes Lord _____ .

8. A Hindu temple is called a _____ .

9. An image of the chosen deity is kept in a _____ .

10. The geometric Sri Yantra is used for _____ . It originated with worshippers of the _____ .

Part Two: Answer the following prompts in the spaces below.

1. Hinduism was born from the meeting of the Indus and Aryan peoples. List and describe aspects of Hinduism particular to each.

_____

_____

_____

_____

_____

2. Describe briefly the qualities of an ascetic. How did these individuals affect Hinduism?

_____

_____

_____

Name_____

Quiz and Review *(cont.)*

Part Two *(cont.)*

3. Explain the three main principals of the Hindu belief system: dharma, karma, and samsara.

   _____

   _____

   _____

   _____

4. Discuss and describe the Hindu caste system. Why does it exist? Is there a caste system in your country?

   _____

   _____

   _____

   _____

5. Explain the role and meaning of fire in Hindu weddings and funerals.

   _____

   _____

   _____

   _____

6. How do Hindus worship? Describe what you might see if you were to visit a Hindu temple.

   _____

   _____

   _____

   _____

7. List and describe the five daily duties of Hinduism.

   _____

   _____

   _____

   _____

The Story of Buddha's Enlightenment

Buddhism began almost 2,500 years ago. The foundation of Buddhism rests on the life of one teacher, an Indian prince named Siddhartha Gotama. Prince Siddhartha grew up in small kingdom in northeast India, an area which now rests in Nepal. His father, King Sudhodana, ruled over the Shakya people. Although the King hoped his son would carry on his legacy, the prince had a very different calling, one which made him one of history's most famous and influential figures.

In order to understand the principals of Buddhism, one must begin with the life of its founder. The deeds and words of Lord Buddha are the source and inspiration behind this popular faith. As you read the story of Buddha's enlightenment given below and on the following pages, be sure to locate all place names on the map, page 173.

Prince Siddhartha was born around 563 BCE, son of King Sudhodana and Queen Maya. Even before the birth, the queen had premonitions of great happenings. Legend tells that in her dreams a radiant white elephant descended from the sky. As the elephant descended, its six large tusks pierced the queen's womb, and she was filled with light.

That morning, the king and queen sought the counsel of the wise, for this was no ordinary dream. The fortune tellers explained that the queen would give birth to a son, and he would be a great leader. The couple was overjoyed at hearing this. King Sudhodana was thrilled, for now he would have a successor.

About ten months later, on the full moon night, in the Indian month of *Vaisakha* (May/June), Queen Maya was on her way to her father's house in the town of Lumbini. Suddenly, she halted her escorts, descended from her carriage, and entered a lush, beautiful garden. There she gave birth to a son. Legends tell of the sacred silence which anointed the garden that night and of a peace which flowed throughout the land.

The royal couple decided to name the baby Siddhartha, which means "the one who brings all good." News of the prince's birth spread, and there was much celebration. Many visitors came to pay tribute to Siddhartha. One of these visitors was the holy sage, Asita. Asita told the parents that the prince would be either a great king or a great saint. Then something strange happened. When Asita's eyes met the infant's, the sage began to weep. This worried the king and queen, but Asita explained that these were bittersweet tears he shed for himself, for he saw that this indeed was a special child, one who could lead others to peace. Now the holy man wept because, after a lifetime of searching, he would not live to hear Siddhartha's teachings.

Both the king and queen were happy, but Sudhodana wanted to be certain that his son became a great emperor, not a saint. Therefore, he set out to give Siddhartha all he could desire.

But the couple's joy was quickly ended when Queen Maya shortly became seriously ill. Within seven days of giving birth, she lay on her bed dying. She asked her sister, Prajapati, to mother her son. Prajapati consented. Soon afterwards, the queen passed away.

Prajapati raised Siddhartha as though he were her own son, and the prince lived a carefree childhood within the palace walls. King Sudhodana made certain that the boy received the finest education, for Asita's prophecy remained with him. The prince learned quickly. In fact, legend has it that after only a few lessons he had no need of teachers—he had learned all they could teach him.

The Story of Buddha's Enlightenment *(cont.)*

As Siddhartha grew, his intelligence was matched with a compassionate gentleness. Unlike his peers, he spent a great deal of time alone, wandering the palace gardens. He did not participate in the common games of boys but sought the company of animals and nature.

It was on one of these garden days that the prince came upon a wounded white swan, an arrow still piercing its wing. He removed the arrow and comforted the bird, tending to its wounds. Shortly thereafter, Devadatta, Siddhartha's cousin, came running. Adorned with bow and arrow, Devadatta demanded the swan he had hunted. But the Prince refused. The boys argued until they agreed to settle their dispute in the palace's court.

When Devadatta came before the judges, he claimed that because he shot the bird, it should belong to him. When Siddhartha spoke, he said that he had saved the swan's life, and therefore it belonged to him. The judges sided with the prince, agreeing that the bird's savior has a greater right.

Years went by, and as the prince became a young man he continued in his gentle, quiet ways. This disturbed his father, who wanted his son more involved in worldly matters. But the King's worries were allayed when Siddhartha met Princess Yasodhara, daughter of King Suprabuddha. The young couple wanted to be married, but the neighboring king needed proof of Siddhartha's bravery and skills. Only then would he give his daughter in marriage. Although he had little experience in warrior games, the prince gladly agreed to take part in a contest against other suitors. Now even Siddhartha's father was worried. How could the prince compete against the other young men who had spent years in training?

But the prince surprised everyone with his abilities. He began by winning the archery match, defeating his cousin, Devadatta. Next, he won the swordsmanship contest when, in one lightning quick stroke, he slashed through a tree—a tree with two trunks! However, though the prince was powerful, it was his gentleness which won him the final contest.

Each of the suitors was given an opportunity to mount a wild horse. One by one they were thrown by the wild, kicking beast. In fact, the horse was so ferocious that the judges were about to stop. But when Siddhartha approached the horse, stroking it softly and speaking kind words, the horse mellowed. The prince mounted the horse, and the contest was over. Prince Siddhartha and Princess Yasodhara were wed.

Although King Sudhodana was happy, he remained worried that his son may yet become a saint. So, he built the newlyweds two enormous, heavenly palaces—one for winter and one for summer. These dwellings were surrounded by walls. Only beautiful servants, accomplished musicians, and the finest foods were allowed in the lush, natural settings. In this way, the king hoped Siddhartha would never be disturbed or seek to go outside the palace, and for years the prince and princess lived undisturbed within the palace walls. In time, they gave birth to a son, Rahula.

Now, although Siddhartha had all the luxuries in the world, he had yet to do one thing: venture outside the palace grounds. From servants he heard tales of other lands and wonders of different peoples, languages, and landscapes. A stirring began inside him. Shortly after, he asked his father's permission to visit the capital city of his kingdom. The king consented, but he ordered his subjects to hide away anyone who was ill or old and to decorate their houses in festive colors, for Sudhodana did not want any sights to trouble his son.

So, aboard his chariot the Prince entered the city of Kapilavastu. The streets, lined with onlookers, were filled with gaiety and celebration. The cheerful citizens, all of them healthy and young, showered the prince with praise. For a moment, Siddhartha was pleased, thinking that this city was like his

The Story of Buddha's Enlightenment *(cont.)*

Amidst the crowd stood an elderly man, saddened and bent with age. In all his years, the Prince had never seen such a sight. In fact, he did not even know that people grew old. This knowledge stunned him, and when he returned to the palace, he sat alone in deep contemplation.

In time, the Prince journeyed again into the city, and again the streets were lined with happy faces. However, among the citizens was a sick man, coughing and pale. In all his palace years, sickness was unknown to Siddhartha. Now, he learned of disease. He learned that anyone can fall ill at anytime. This news saddened him.

But the prince's third trip to the city affected him most deeply. Riding along in his chariot, he saw a group of mourners carrying a coffin. Inside the coffin, he saw a dead man wrapped in white. Now he learned of death and the rites of cremation. He was overwhelmed with the thought that even his beloved wife and son would someday die.

Siddhartha became very depressed and spent his time alone. His father tried to cheer him, but to no avail. The prince wondered how people could live happily knowing that old age, sickness, and death awaited them. His gloom deepened, until one day he rode out again on his chariot. This time, he traveled to the countryside. There he saw a saint meditating under a tree. He learned that this hermit had exchanged all worldly pleasures to seek for truth. This man had also seen the suffering in the world and sought to go beyond it to enlightenment. Prince Siddhartha was deeply moved by the sight. He returned to the palace, sure of his calling.

Siddhartha's mind was made up: he would leave his life of luxury and search for truth. Knowing he would not receive consent, that very night as everyone lay sleeping, he bid a silent farewell to his wife and son. He mounted his horse and set out for the forest in the far reaches of the land where the holy men gather. When he arrived, he cut his long hair and donned the robe of an ascetic, a man of solitude searching for wisdom. Now, at the age of twenty-nine, his journey had begun.

Prince Siddhartha spent the next six years in the forest. He studied with the most famous sages, but still he did not find an end to suffering. He joined a group of men who believed enlightenment could be found by denying the body nourishment and sleep, thereby mastering pain. For years the prince ate and slept very little. He grew as thin as a skeleton, and though the rain and sun beat down on him, he did not waver from his practices.

Finally, he realized that he was getting nowhere. Though he had neglected his bodily needs, he had not found an end to suffering. Thus, when a young woman came to him offering food, he accepted. Now that he was nourished he sat in meditation under a bodhi tree in the town of Bodhgaya. He sat down and vowed, come what may, he would not move until he found an end to sorrow. Although demons tempted him with images of his past and evil spirits brought nightmares upon him, the prince was centered on his goal.

Finally, under the Tree of Enlightenment, Siddhartha became Buddha, the Enlightened One. He went on to become a great world teacher, as Asita had prophesied, and from his teachings, Buddhism was born.

Places in the Life of Buddha

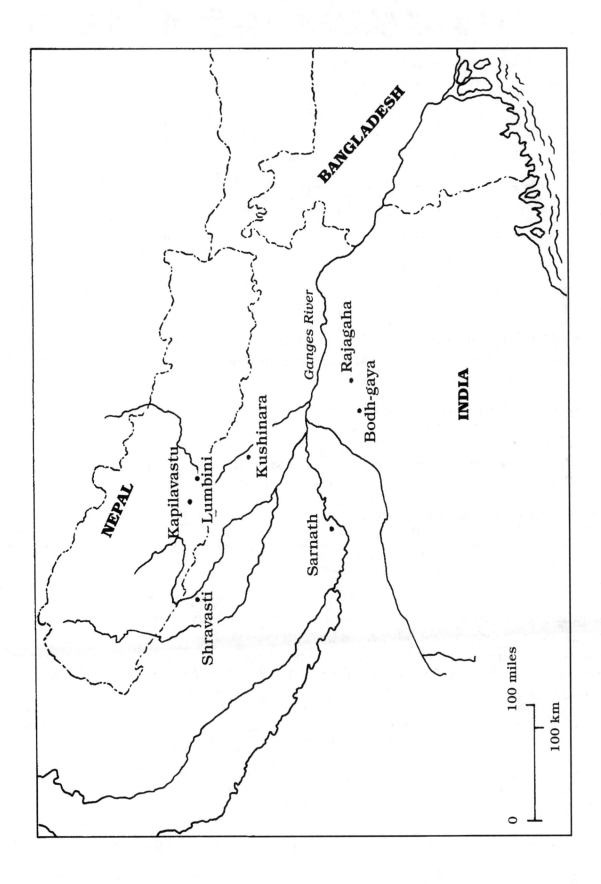

Name _____

Buddha's Enlightenment: Comprehension

Directions: Answer the following comprehension questions. (You may need to review the story.) Be sure to use full sentences. Continue on the back of the paper when necessary.

1. When was Prince Siddhartha born? What does his name mean?

   _____

2. Describe Queen Maya's dream. What does it mean?

   _____

3. Why does the sage Asita weep when he sees Siddhartha?

   _____

4. What is Asita's prophesy about the Prince?

   _____

5. What becomes of Queen Maya?

   _____

6. What does the King do to ensure Siddhartha's fulfillment?

   _____

7. As a child, how does the Prince spend most of his time?

   _____

8. What happens when the Prince finds a wounded swan?

   _____

9. Why must Siddhartha enter a contest to win Princess Yasodhara's hand in marriage?

   _____

10. The Prince triumphs in three contests. Describe them.

    _____

11. What does King Sudhodana give the prince and princess? Why?

    _____

12. List the three troubling sights Siddhartha witnesses during the visits to Kapilavastu.

    _____

13. What symbolic act does the prince perform when he arrives at the forest? How old is he when he arrives?

    _____

14. Why does Siddhartha starve himself?

    _____

15. In what city and under what kind of tree does Siddhartha become enlightened?

    _____

Name _____

Buddha's Enlightenment: Critical Thinking

Directions: Answer the following questions, using details to support your responses. Be sure to use full sentences. Continue on the back of the paper when necessary.

1. Why do the palace judges award the wounded swan to Siddhartha? Do you agree with their decision? Explain.

   _____

   _____

   _____

2. Discuss King Sudhodana'a actions throughout the story. What are his motivations for sheltering Siddhartha?

   _____

   _____

   _____

3. Describe Siddhartha's feelings when he sees old age, sickness, and death. How does his upbringing contribute to his reaction?

   _____

   _____

   _____

4. In his search for enlightenment, Prince Siddhartha leaves behind his wife and son. In so doing, he became one of the most influential figures in history. Do you feel he is justified in leaving his family behind? Explain.

   _____

   _____

   _____

5. Can you think of someone other than Siddhartha who left behind a life of luxury in order to pursue wisdom? Explain.

   _____

   _____

   _____

Buddha's Teachings

After his enlightenment under the bodhi tree at Bodh-gaya, Buddha (the "Awakened One") began teaching others. Once he truly understood the cause of sorrow, he could begin to free people. What, then, did he teach?

Buddha delivered his first sermon in a deer park in the city of Sarnath. He taught that all humans are caught in the *Wheel of Dharma*. They go through lifetimes in a cycle of birth and death, creating situations which create consequences. (To review *dharma*, see the chapter on Hinduism.) Until an individual can free him or herself from the wheel, he or she will be subject to the ups-and-downs of life. The only way to free oneself, preached Buddha, is to be free of desire. Thus, desire is the root of suffering. Then he taught his first disciples *The Four Noble Truths*. These truths form the bedrock of Buddhist belief.

The Four Noble Truths

I. **Dukkha: The Noble Truth of Suffering**

Life is full of suffering, full of sickness and unhappiness. Although there are passing pleasures, they vanish in time.

II. **Samudaya: The Noble Truth of the Cause of Suffering**

People suffer for one simple reason: they desire things. It is greed and self-centeredness which bring about suffering. Desire is never satisfied.

III. **Nirodha: The Noble Truth of the End of Suffering**

It is possible to end suffering if one is aware of his or her own desires and puts an end to them. This awareness will open the door to lasting peace.

IV. **Magga: The Noble Truth of the Path**

By changing one's thinking and behavior, a new awakening can be reached. This is called the *Middle Way* and can be followed in the *Eightfold Path.*

Buddha's Teachings *(cont.)*

The *Eightfold Path*, also called the *Wheel of Law*, contains eight steps for eliminating *dukkha* (suffering). By following this path, one can bring an end to his or her own *karma* and be released from continuous rebirth. (To review *karma*, see the chapter on Hinduism.) Buddha introduced these ideas during his first sermon at Sarnath. This teaching is often symbolized by a wheel with eight spokes. Later in this chapter, you will read more about this symbol.

The *Five Precepts* represent the third set of laws governing Buddhist thought. Although these are not "commandments" in the strict sense of the word, they are vows which ensure right behavior.

The Eightfold Path

- **Right Understanding**

  Strive to clearly understand the Four Noble Truths. Strive to understand the workings of your own mind.

- **Right Thought**

  Think kindly of others and avoid dwelling on the past or future.

- **Right Speech**

  Speak kindly and truthfully.

- **Right Action**

  Act kindly toward all living things. Do not be attached to the results of actions.

- **Right Work**

  Have a vocation that does not harm others.

- **Right Effort**

  Be determined to cleanse the mind.

- **Right Mindfulness**

  Be fully aware of what you are doing, always with concern for others.

- **Right Concentration**

  Intensely concentrate during meditation to focus on being one with any situation.

The Five Precepts

- **Do not harm any living thing.**
- **Do not steal. Take only what is given.**
- **Avoid over-stimulation.**
- **Do not say unkind things.**
- **Do not take alcohol or drugs.**

Buddha's Teachings *(cont.)*

The Wheel of Law

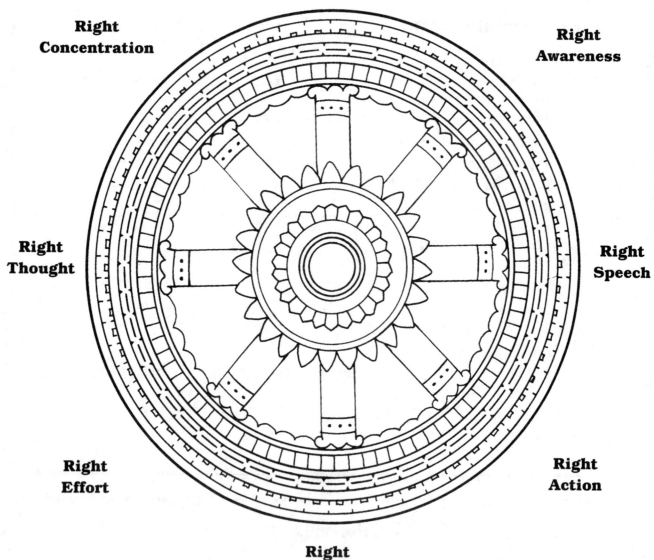

Right
Understanding

Right
Concentration

Right
Awareness

Right
Thought

Right
Speech

Right
Effort

Right
Action

Right
Livelihood

Name _____

The Eightfold Path: Personal Response

Directions: There are millions of Buddhists around the world trying to live in the spirit of the Eightfold Path. Opportunities to live in the spirit of the path manifest themselves in many different ways. Under each idea, write about how it might show up in your life. Think about school, home, sports, and hobbies.

1. Right Understanding

   _____

   _____

2. Right Thought

   _____

   _____

3. Right Speech

   _____

   _____

4. Right Action

   _____

   _____

5. Right Work

   _____

   _____

6. Right Effort

   _____

   _____

7. Right Mindfulness

   _____

   _____

8. Right Concentration

   _____

Branches of Buddhism

There are two main branches of Buddhism, **Mahayana** and **Theravada**. These schools of thought formed after Buddha's death in 486 BCE when disciples began disputing one another's interpretations of the Master's sayings. The Theravada branch, also called the "doctrine of the elders," is most popular in Southern Asia in countries like Burma, Thailand, Laos, Sri Lanka, and Cambodia. (See the map on page 181.) The underlying basis of the faith is that an individual is responsible for his or her own salvation. No god or image can bring enlightenment. Only by following the example of Buddha's life can an individual be free from the chain of rebirths. To a Theravada Buddhist, a person must be responsible for every act and thought. Salvation is an individual's duty. A devout Theravada Buddhist is called an *arhat*, a monk. Although there are no priests, these monks teach other Buddhists. They live in monasteries where they study the words and deeds of Buddha, striving to live pure lives and thereby achieve *nirvana*, enlightenment.

Mahayana Buddhism is most common in countries of Northern Asia: Tibet, Nepal, China, Korea, and Japan. This school differs in some fundamental ways from the Theravadas. First of all, Mahayana Buddhists believe that religious growth can be nurtured through the help of others. They do not idealize the lonesome ways of the monk. Rather, they maintain reverence and seek help from a *bodhisattva* (*bodhi* means "wise" and *sattva* means "being"). A bodhisattva is a saint who is so full of compassion that he will not enter into a state of nirvana until others can enter with him. Later in this chapter, you will learn more about some of these bodhisattvas.

Mahayana Buddhism has attracted more followers than the Theravada School and has been called the "greater vehicle." Priests, temples, and gods have been established as the faith spread worldwide. Again, the most fundamental doctrine here is that people are not isolated but part of a network of other souls. Some of these souls are more evolved, thereby able to guide others. Finally, it is believed that the spirit of Buddha is universal and timeless. It was discovered by Prince Siddhartha, but it is accessible to all. In fact, Mahayanas believe there have been others who have embodied that same spirit. They await the coming of *Maitreya*, the Buddha of the coming age. (You might recall that Buddha himself is considered by Hindus to be the ninth incarnation of Vishnu.)

Two other branches stem from the Mahayanas: **Tibetan** Buddhism and **Zen** Buddhism. These schools of thought are considered later in this chapter.

Mahayana and Theravada Buddhism in Asia

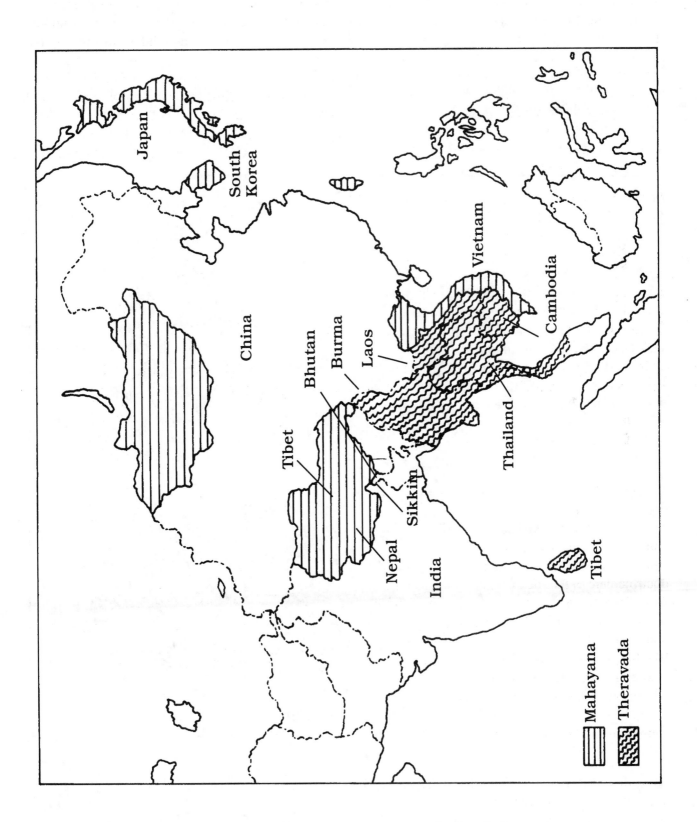

The Spread of Buddhism

Buddhism began to spread rapidly around 270 BCE during the reign of King Asoka, the ruler of the greater area of Northern India. After engaging his empire in a terrible, bloody war, he underwent a spiritual transformation that included embracing Buddhism. He sent missionaries throughout southern Asia. They met with great success, although they did not convert others through either excessive persuasion or violence.

Beginning in the first century CE, Buddhism spread slowly into China and Japan. The first Dalai Lama, the Grand Lama of Lhasa, was responsible for the extension of Buddhism into Mongolia during the 16th century CE.

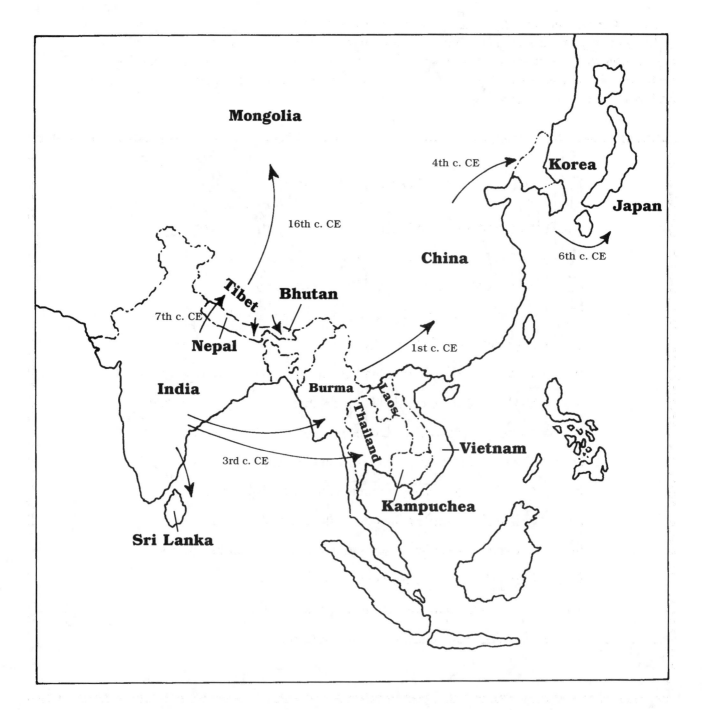

Buddhist Scriptures

From the two main branches of Buddhism—Mahayana and Theravada—come different sets of holy scriptures. Both texts evolved after Buddha's death, though they were not translated into written form for close to 500 years. Instead, like the Hindu Vedas, they were passed on by word of mouth.

The Theravada scriptures were compiled by Sri Lankans who wrote in the Indian language of *Pali*. They called these teachings the *Tipitaka*, which are divided into three "baskets of law." The first basket, the *Vinaya Pitaka*, contains the laws governing the life of a Buddhist monk or nun. The second basket, the *Sutta Pitaka*, contains dialogues and teachings delivered by Buddha himself. The third basket, the *Abhidamma Pitaka*, contains commentary on Buddha's teachings.

Sanskrit, the ancient language of India, was the means for transmitting the Mahayana scriptures. Although many of the earlier Mahayana scriptures were destroyed, their messages were kept alive in the writings of Tibetan and Chinese sages. There are now several of these scriptures recognized by Mahayana Buddhists. One of these sacred texts is a long poem written around 690 CE by Seng Ts'an, a Chinese sage. The poem is called "Trust in the Heart."

Trust in the Heart

The Perfect Way is only difficult for those who pick and choose;

Do not like, do not dislike; all will then be clear.

Make a hairbreadth difference, and Heaven and Earth are set apart.

If you want the truth to stand clear before you, never be for or against.

The struggle between "for" and "against" is the mind's worst disease;

While the deep meaning is misunderstood, it is useless to meditate on them.

It is as blank and featureless as space; it has no "too little" or "too much";

Only because we take and reject does it mean to us not to be so.

Do not chase after Enlightenment as though it were a real thing;

Do not try to drive pain away by pretending that it is not real;

Pain, if you seek serenity in Oneness, will vanish of its own accord.

Stop all movement in order to get rest, and rest will itself be restless;

Linger over either extreme and Oneness is forever lost.

Those who cannot attain Oneness in either case will fail.

To banish reality is to sink deeper into the Real . . .

Buddhist Scriptures *(cont.)*

The Sutta Pitaka records actual dialogues and sermons of Buddha himself. This is an excerpt from one of these teachings. You may need to use your dictionary!

Thought

As an arrow-maker makes straight his arrow, a wise man makes straight his trembling and unsteady thought, which is difficult to guard, difficult to hold back.

As a fish taken from his watery home and thrown on the dry ground, our thought trembles all over in order to escape the dominion of Mara, the tempter.

It is good to tame the mind, which is difficult to hold in and flighty, rushing wherever it lists; a tamed mind brings happiness.

Let the wise man guard his thoughts, for they are difficult to perceive, very subtle, and they rush wherever they list; thoughts well-guarded bring happiness.

Those who bridle their mind, which travels far, moves about alone, is incorporeal, and hides in the chamber of the heart, will be free from the bonds of Mara, the tempter.

If a man's faith is unsteady, if he does not know the true law, if his peace of mind is troubled, his knowledge will never be perfect.

If a man's thoughts are not scattered, if his mind is not perplexed, if he has ceased to think of good or evil, then there is no fear for him while he is watchful.

Knowing that his body is fragile like a jar, and making his thought firm like a fortress, one should attack Mara, the tempter, with the weapon of knowledge; one should watch him when conquered, and should never rest.

Name _____

Questions: The Branches and Spread of Buddhism

Directions: After reading the material on pages 180–184, answer the following questions.

1. Describe the fundamental beliefs of Theravada Buddhism.

_____

_____

_____

2. Describe the fundamental tenets of Mahayana Buddhism.

_____

_____

_____

3. What is a *Bodhisattva?*

_____

_____

_____

4. In both "Trust in the Heart" and "Thought," the mind and its restlessness is the central issue. According to these passages, why is thought problematic? Be sure to support your answers with details from each excerpt.

_____

_____

_____

5. If thought is the core problem according to these scriptures, what is the solution? Again, be sure to use details to support your response.

_____

_____

_____

6. What does Buddha mean when he talks about Mara?

_____

Tibetan Buddhism

If you look on the map entitled "The Spread of Buddhism," you will notice that Buddhism expanded into Tibet in the 7th century CE, more than 1,500 years ago. The people of Tibet are mostly nomadic, moving about the high Himalayan plateaus with their herds. For centuries, Mahayana Buddhism thrived in this rugged, undeveloped country.

Until China invaded Tibet in 1950, this vast natural setting was spotted with Buddhist monasteries. In fact, Buddhism defines both the religious and political climate of Tibet. The ruler of the country, the *Dalai Lama*, is chosen by spiritual merit. His compassion and wisdom are meant to inspire the people. Like the Catholic Pope, the Tibetan Dalai Lama is believed to be the closest link to the spiritual realm.

The foremost quality the Dalai Lama possesses is compassion. In fact, Tibetan Buddhists believe that the Dalai Lama is a manifestation of the *bodhisattva Avalokiteshvara.* (See page 187.) This god embodies the spirit of compassion, the same spirit alive in Buddha. The Dalai Lama is, therefore, a vehicle in which the bodhisattva's mercy can radiate to the people. Finding the Dalai Lama, however, is not always easy.

Tibetans believe that when the Dalai Lama dies, Avalokiteshvara is reborn as a baby. The Dalai Lama usually gives some indication of the baby's whereabouts, after which the search begins. *Lamas*, Tibetan monks, quest for the newborn, looking for proof of his heritage. They put the candidate through different tests. A true Dalai Lama, for instance, should recognize four of the previous ruler's possessions.

Besides the Dalai Lama, there exists up to 200 *tulkus*. These holy men and women are also revered as embodiments of Avalokiteshvara. These leaders are often responsible for spreading the message of Buddhism.

In 1950, Tibet was conquered by communist China. The Chinese government held that Tibet was part of their country. Although the Tibetans rebelled, the Chinese took over, destroying most of the monasteries and causing most of the monks and nuns to flee the country. In fact, while in 1930 there were about 738,000 monks and nuns in Tibet and China, by 1986 only 28,000 remained. Many Tibetans settled in India, while others exiled themselves to the West.

Extensions:

1. Write a report about the history of Tibet. Record the lineage of Dalai Lamas.

2. Find out about the present Dalai Lama. Report what you learn to the class.

Bodhisattvas

Here are a few famous bodhisattvas. In Mahayana Buddhism, these god-like beings are believed to help mankind by extending compassion and guidance. Followers try to embody the bodhisattva's qualities. These figures, which differ from country to country, are also used for meditation.

Avalokiteshvara

Avalokiteshvara is one of the foremost bodhisattvas. Tibetan Buddhists consider this saint to be the spirit of Buddha. They also believe the Dalai Lama is a reincarnation of Avalokiteshvara.

Tara

In Tibet, the goddess Tara is the consort of Avalokiteshvara. She is an embodiment of compassion.

Bodhisattvas *(cont.)*

Manjushri

Manjushri, the destroyer of ignorance, wields the Sword of Knowledge.

Amida

To northern Buddhists, Amida is next to Buddha himself in importance. Legend has it that Amida was a monk who devoted himself to saving others. Over the centuries, he has stored up a treasury of goodness which the faithful can access, thus freeing them from the Wheel of Life. As a bodhisattva, he is the source of infinite goodness.

Extensions:

1. Find an illustration of the bodhisattva Maitreya, the Buddha to come.

2. Find colored illustrations of the bodhisattvas above and on the previous page. Color the saints here accordingly.

Zen Buddhism

Transmission outside doctrine,
No dependencies on words.
Pointing directly at the mind,
Thus seeing oneself truly,
Attaining Buddhahood.

–Bodhidharma, 520 CE

This poem, written by the famous Indian monk, Bodhidharma, embodies the spirit of Zen Buddhism, a school of thought born in China around 520 CE. Zen arrived in China in 1191. Unlike other branches of Buddhism, Zen places no emphasis on either scriptures or bodhisattvas. Rather, practitioners of Zen believe that direct experience alone can lead one to truth. In other words, scriptures and teachers can serve only to point to enlightenment. It is the individual who must live and understand. In fact, mentors and theories must be destroyed before the mind is free, because their ideas and opinions about enlightenment prevent understanding. This point is illustrated in a story of a well known Zen master who shocked his students by tossing all the statues of Buddha into a fire in order to warm the room. Like these clay idols, images should be burned out of the mind: a person must be self-reliant, his or her own master.

Students of Zen practice meditation in order to increase their awareness and purify their minds. They hope to undo their opinions and preferences and reach a state of *satori*, or illumination. With this clarity, they can live calmly and compassionately in the world. A poem by the Chinese master, Tessho, describes this freedom of mind:

Finally out of reach—
No bondage, no dependency.
How calm the ocean,
Towering the void.

Although Zen does not emphasize scripture, it has a rich body of literature which points to understanding. Besides poetry, these books contain dialogues between pupils and teachers. These discussions are meant to illuminate the reader.

Zen Buddhism also finds expression in the martial arts, which arrived in Japan about 800 years ago. The schools of karate and judo, among others, are meant to enhance discipline and self-awareness. Gardening is also a popular expression of the Zen spirit. These gardens are simple but exact, mirroring the tranquility of Zen.

Japanese Haiku

You may already be familiar with the most popular form of Zen poetry, the *haiku*. The haiku originated in Japan during the 15th century CE. It began as a 17-syllable stanza but soon became a poem by itself. (The poems below are translations, so the syllable count is not exact.) Still popular among poets, the haiku is concise, combining images to produce emotion and meaning. Most often, the haiku is a celebration of nature and the wholeness and union of all living things.

Here are several haikus written by famous Japanese poets. Read them carefully and pay attention to the imagery. How does each one make you feel? After reading, write some of your own. Each three-line poem must have five syllables in the first and third lines and seven in the second.

To the willow—
all hatred, and desire
of your heart.
        —*Basho*

White lotus—
the monk
draws back his blade.
        —*Buson*

Under cherry trees
there are
no strangers.
        —*Issa*

Dew of the bramble,
thorns
sharp white.
        —*Buson*

Sacred night,
through masks
white breath of dancers.
        —*Kikaku*

Come, see
real flowers
of this painful world.
        —*Basho*

Buddha's Nirvana,
beyond flowers,
and money.
        —*Issa*

May he who brings
flowers tonight,
have moonlight.
        —*Kikaku*

Here is a 17-syllable haiku:

> The light rising fast (5)
> Over the far eastern plains (7)
> Brings daytime to all. (5)

Meditation

You have probably heard the word "meditation" many times in your life. You may have seen pictures of people sitting in meditation with crossed legs and eyes closed. You may even know someone who meditates. But what exactly is meditation? What is its purpose?

In Buddhism, followers meditate in order to still their minds, to let go of the running thoughts inside their brains. If you stop to notice, thoughts go on from the moment of waking until sleep. They even appear in dreams. For Buddhists, meditation is a means of finding what lies beyond these thoughts. Of course, this takes practice.

There are many forms of meditation. Usually, Buddhists sit still, spine straight and eyes closed. By focusing on their breath, they become more "present," more aware of themselves. Although the stream of thoughts continues, the student simply watches them go by like clouds in the sky. Thus, he or she begins to be free of the grip of thinking.

Zen Buddhist have some unusual meditation practices. One such practice is called a *koan*, or a riddle. The master asks a puzzling question which the student must answer correctly—although it may take days to comprehend! Thus, the koan provides the means for meditation.

One famous riddle tells the story of a high government official who approached a Zen master:

Officer: A man once kept a goose in a bottle. The goose grew larger until it could not escape. The man, not wishing to harm the goose, could not break the bottle. How would you remove the goose?

Master: O, Officer!

Officer: Yes!

Master: There, the goose is out!

Discuss the meaning of the koan with your fellow students.

Tibetan Buddhists like to focus on *mandalas* during meditation. Mandalas are elaborate designs rich with color and detail. They are often circular, containing either portraits of various gods or intricate patterns. After meditating on the mandala, the student will close his or her eyes and try to visualize the picture. Thus, the mind is disciplined while the heart merges with the spirit of the mandala.

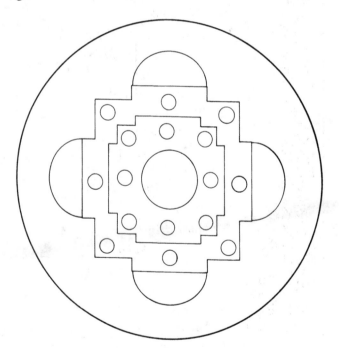

Extension

Try sitting quietly five minutes a day. Just sit and listen to the sounds around you, even the sound of your breathing. After a few days, try ten minutes. Keep a journal of your "quiet time" experiences.

Name _____

Mandalas

Directions: Below and on the following two pages you will find three different mandalas. Color them. If you feel adventurous, try designing your own!

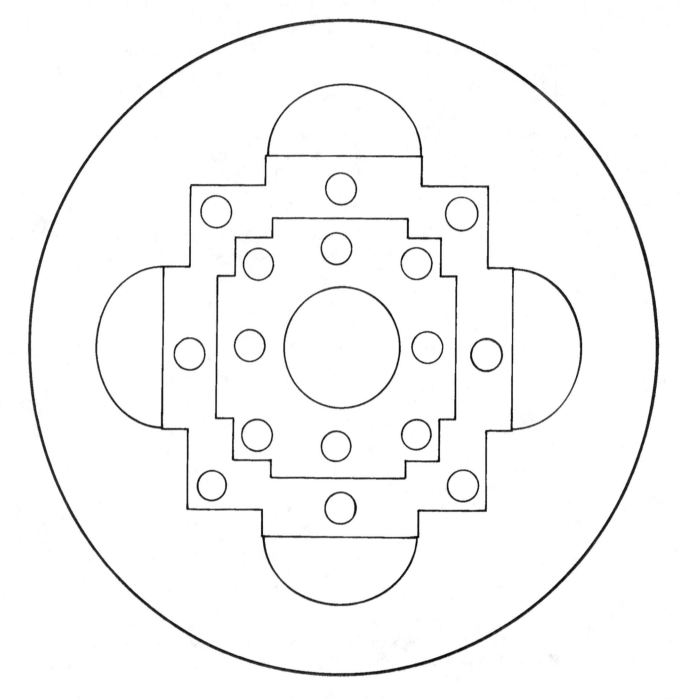

Typical Design

Name _____

Mandalas *(cont.)*

Tibetan

Name _____

Mandalas *(cont.)*

Sri Yantra

Rites of Passage

Unlike most other faiths, Buddhism does not require strict observance of custom. Because Buddhism is so focused on the internal life, some Buddhists practice privately without visiting temples or participating in rituals. Most, however, visit temples regularly, seek the counsel of monks, and partake in rites of passage ceremonies. These ceremonies differ greatly depending upon the country of origin.

Birth

When an infant is born, Theravadin Buddhists usually have the formal naming at a nearby temple. Afterward, monks bless and sprinkle holy water on the newborn. The closing ritual, the melting of candle wax into a bowl, symbolizes the union of the four basic elements: earth, air, fire, and water.

Marriage

In some Buddhist countries, monks never attend weddings because marriage ceremonies are believed to bring bad luck. In most countries, however, Buddhist monks do attend. Take, for instance, the example of a common Theravadin wedding. The ceremony takes place at the local temple. Here the bride and groom are surrounded by friends and relatives. First, the image of Buddha is wrapped with a long cotton thread, and then the thread circulates to all those in the congregation. The thread symbolizes the union of all present. All the while, the chanting of the monks fills the temple. After the principal monk blesses the couple, two pieces of the thread are cut. A monk ties one around the groom's wrist, and then the groom ties the other piece around the wrist of his bride.

Death

Theravadin Buddhists do not believe in the reincarnation of individual identities. Rather, it is the person's dharma, the balance of good and evil, which is cast into a new life. Because the body of Buddha was cremated, Theravadins cremate their dead. It is common for monks to visit the home of the dying person, comforting him or her with religious chants. These verses remind the person that although the body decays, goodness and mercy are timeless. This chanting continues even after death, in order to ensure purification of the soul.

According to Mahayana Buddhism, immediately after the moment of death, an individual experiences a state of trance which lasts four days. The deceased is not aware of his or her death. These days are called the *First Bardo*, during which monks can communicate with the dead by chanting certain verses. After these days, the person sees a very bright light. If the soul can embrace the light, it will be free of rebirth. Usually, however, the light's radiance frightens the deceased, in which case rebirth follows. The *Second Bardo* begins when a person sees the events and thoughts of his or her life. Now the knowledge of death is clear, and the *Third Bardo* starts. Now the deceased is free to choose new parents and a new identity.

Name _____

Rites of Passage *(cont.)*

Directions: There are numerous rituals, ceremonies, and even holidays dedicated to those who are born, marry, or die. Find out about your own family's traditions and beliefs concerning one of these stages of life. Do you have a ritual? How have things changed over time? Write your response below.

_____

_____

_____

_____

_____

_____

_____

_____

_____

_____

_____

_____

_____

_____

_____

_____

_____

_____

_____

_____

_____

_____

_____

_____

_____

Buddhist Temples and Shrines

The Stupa

The design of Buddhist temples originated with the *stupa*, which was used to cover Buddha's ashes and relics. Made out of mud bricks, this ancient Indian shrine was originally shaped like a simple bell—a mound with a small spire on top. Inside the stupas are Buddhist relics. The circularity of the dome resembles the wheel of life.

Gradually, the stupa became larger and more elaborate. Soon, reliefs of Prince Siddhartha's life began appearing on its outer walls.

The worlds's largest stupa rests on the island of Java, Indonesia. Toward the top, this elegant Mahayana shrine contains grand images of Buddha and statues of bodhisattvas. Below, there are sculptures of the mass of humanity caught in the Wheel of Life. At the peak there is a large, plain stupa which represents Nirvana, or enlightenment.

The Pagoda

In China, the stupa grew taller and thinner and adopted a new identity: the pagoda. Pagodas are eight-sided towers which contain an odd number of stories-between three and thirteen. Soon pagodas became popular; thousands were built throughout China, Japan, Vietnam and Burma. Although many of the older wooden pagodas have disappeared, the architecture still endures. In Japan, for example, small stone pagodas often appear in cemeteries. They have five levels, symbolizing the void and the four basic elements.

Buddhist Temples and Shrines *(cont.)*

The Monastery

The Buddhist monastery originated around the same time as the pagoda. As early as 200 BCE, these structures were providing shelter and study space for monks. Some were made of stone or wood while others, amazingly, were forged out of mountains of rock. Monks literally carved their sanctuary into cliff sides. Once this was done, they designed the interior with an assembly hall and living quarters, including a small stupa at the heart of the monastery. Detailed reliefs of Buddha and various bohisattvas often decorate the rock walls.

Theravadin Shrine

Theravadin shrine rooms are relatively unadorned places of meditation. An elevated statue of Buddha, surrounded by offerings of incense, candles, and flowers, rests at the center. A carpet decorates the floor. The meditation instructor sits in a chair at the foot of the rug.

Thai Temple

In Thailand, Buddhists temples, or *wats*, appear in almost every town. Attended to by monks, the wat is a place of worship and community gathering. Colorful and exotic, the temple contains a shrine room housing an image of Buddha. Followers usually bow to the statue. Then, they may light a candle, burn some incense, or offer flowers. The entrance to the temple, facing east, is decorated with curtains and serpent-like ornaments. The top of the wat is usually a towering pinnacle.

The following page contains an illustration of a typical Thai temple. As a challenge, color and label the features of the picture.

Buddhist Temples and Shrines *(cont.)*

Thai Temple *(cont.)*

Buddhist Symbols

Wheel of Law

You are already familiar with the principal symbol of Buddhism, the Dharma Wheel or the Wheel of Law. This sign is associated with Buddha's first sermon at a deer park in Sarnath. It is said that he used grains of rice to draw the symbol, which signifies the rounds of births and deaths a person experiences. The eight spokes of the wheel represent the eightfold path. Occasionally, the hub contains images of the three causes of pain: the serpent of ill will, the pig of ignorance, and the rooster of lust.

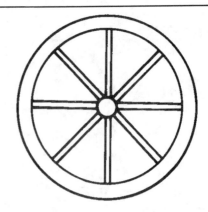

Lotus

Like many of the Hindu gods, Buddha is often shown sitting on a lotus throne. In Buddhism, the lotus flower is meaningful because its roots are mired in the mud; yet its flowers bloom above water. This mirrors the life of Buddha who journeyed through a troubled world yet remained holy.

White Elephant

The White Elephant symbolizes the birth of Prince Siddhartha. The Prince's mother, Queen Maya, dreamt that a bright elephant of light descended upon her—a sign that her son would be great among men.

The Bodhi Tree

The bodhi tree in Bodh-gaya is sacred to Buddhists for it is here where Prince Siddhartha attained nirvana. The bodhi tree has thus become a symbol associated with Buddha's enlightenment.

Buddhist Symbols *(cont.)*

Rupas: Images of Buddha

The images of Buddha, or *rupas*, are many, each with its own significance. In many representations Buddha has a halo around his head, a symbol of divinity. He is also shown with a topknot of hair which signifies his superior wisdom. In each figure, his position is related to his actions—teaching, blessing, or meditating. As you will see, even his hand gestures, or *mudras*, have become traditional gestures.

The Starving Prince Siddhartha

Lotus Pose, Hands in Teaching Position

Japanese Buddha Dressed as Monk

Full Lotus Position for Meditation

Mantras and Mudras

Many Buddhists use *mantras*, or chants, when they pray. These mantras consist of one or more sounds which, like the mandala, are meant to focus the mind and involve a state of grace. The most sacred sound, Om, has a Hindu origin. It is often part of a longer mantra which reads like this: Om Mani Padme Hum (pronounced "om manee padney home"). Translated, it means "the jewel in the lotus" or "the heart of the teaching."

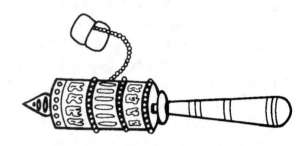

In Tibet, this prayer is often heard in the streets. It appears on flags above every temple and it is inscribed on prayer wheels. People spin these bronze cylinders in order to spread the message of the prayer.

Mudras are the hand positions of Buddha, many of which have become conventionalized. Each gesture has its own meaning. Try them yourself.

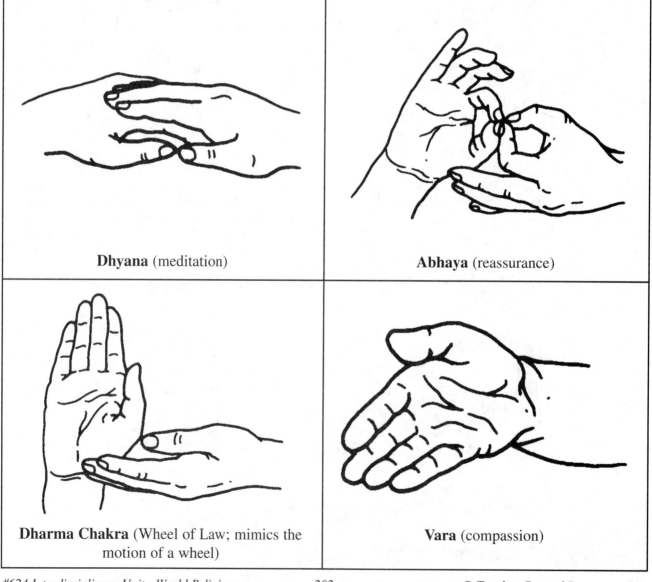

Dhyana (meditation)

Abhaya (reassurance)

Dharma Chakra (Wheel of Law; mimics the motion of a wheel)

Vara (compassion)

Buddhist Festivals and Holidays

The Month of Vesak

The month of *Vesak* (in May) contains holidays celebrating the birth, enlightenment, and death of Buddha. In some countries, all three events are celebrated on the full moon in May. Others observe these events as individual holidays in different months of the year.

One of the common features of Vesak is the lantern. In Thailand, people also decorate their homes with garlands of flowers and attend temple ceremonies. Followers polish the temple's statues of Buddha. After dark, the images are sprinkled with scented water as the followers take up their lanterns and walk in a circle surrounding Buddha with light.

Buddha's Birthday

In Japan, the birth of Buddha is celebrated on April 8 during a festival called *Hana Mastsuri*. Followers gather on the weekend nearest the holiday to ensure that they can attend. Outside the sanctuary, booths and games provide a festive atmosphere; however, at the heart of the shrine the mood is austere. The image of Buddha is strewn with flowers and surrounded with burning incense. People bow before the statue and pour a ladle of tea over it, thus commemorating the birth of Prince Siddhartha when the heavens rained sweet tea.

In the country of Laos, Buddha's birthday is combined with the New Year's celebration. During this lively festival, caged birds are set free and captured fish are returned to their native rivers. In temples and homes, holy water is poured on statues of Buddha. Then, the streets are busy with people drenching one another with buckets of water!

The Festival of the Tooth

The Festival of the Tooth takes place in the beautiful lakeside city of Kandy in Sri Lanka. On a hillock near the lake there is a temple which houses one of the most sacred Buddhist relics: Buddha's tooth. The tooth is kept hidden within seven jeweled caskets. But each year, on the full moon night in the month of Savana (August), a colorful procession transports Buddha's tooth through the city of Kandy. Pilgrims journey far distances to watch elephants, adorned with golden headdresses and silver jewels, parade the streets. Some of the elephants are painted while others wear multicolored clothing on their mammoth backs. Aboard the largest elephant is a pagoda inside of which rests the casket holding Buddha's tooth. Followers celebrate as the tooth passes by them, trailed by dancers and fire swallowers. The festival lasts into the evening when fireworks color the sky above Kandy.

Obon

Obon, or the Feast of Obon, is a popular Japanese holiday in which Buddhists pay homage to the dead. Tradition has it that on this day the souls of the deceased mix and mingle with the living. The making of paper boats is one of the many ceremonies of Obon. At daybreak, followers gather at a lake or stream and release the boats, transporting the souls of the dead.

The Feast of Obon is inspired by the legend of Maudgalyayana, a follower of Buddha. Maudgalyayana had a nightmare in which he saw his mother cast into the underworld. There, she joined other spirits who were tortured by having a banquet set before them, but when they tried to eat, the food turned to fire. The troubled man sought the counsel of Buddha, who advised him to practice kindness and to purify himself. The man became a generous monk, giving to all. After some years, he dreamed that his mother was free. Overjoyed, he set out a great feast for the villagers. In this spirit, Japanese Buddhists partake in a great feast.

The Buddhist Calendar

Like most religious calendars, the Buddhist calendar is based on the lunar year. That is, each month ends on a full moon, and most major festivals are celebrated on these days. Celebrations occur at different times depending on the country.

Here are the months of the Buddhist calendar along with their Gregorian equivalents. Below, you will also find a list of major festivals.

Citta (April)	**Vesak** (May)	**Jettha** (June)
Asalha (July)	**Savana** (August)	**Potthapada** (September)
Assayuja (October)	**Kattika** (November)	**Maggasira** (December)
Phussa (January)	**Magha** (February)	**Phagguna** (March)

Some Significant Festivals and Holidays

Citta: celebration of Buddha as peacemaker

Vesak: celebrations of the birth, enlightenment, and death of Buddha

Jettha: commemoration of the spread of Buddhism

Asalha: Buddha's journey from home and his first sermon

Savana: a special meditation retreat during the beginning of the rainy season when it is difficult for monks and nuns to travel

Kattika: end of the rainy season; Buddhist missionaries remembered

Maggasira: first community of Buddhist nuns founded in Sri Lanka

Phussa: celebration of Buddha's first visit to Sri Lanka

Phagguna: celebration of Buddha's return home

Places of Pilgrimage

India

The four primary places of Buddhist pilgrimage are located in India, Buddha's homeland. Pilgrims from all over the globe visit these holy places. Probably the most popular destination is the deer park in Sarnath where Buddha preached his first sermon. Sarnath is now a suburb of the sacred city of Varanasi. This location also features a gigantic stupa built by King Ashoka in honor of Lord Buddha.

King Ashoka also built a monument at Lumbini Grove in Nepal, where Prince Siddhartha was born. Pilgrims who travel here will see a stone pillar which was built in honor of the holy birth.

At Bodh-gaya, followers behold the place of Buddha's enlightenment. In fact, an actual descendent of the ancient bodhi tree still exists. Under this tree, which is often decorated with prayer flags, rests a stone inscribed with a footprint. There are many who believe this is literally Buddha's own print.

Another place of pilgrimage is in Kusinara where Buddha died. People gather here to pay tribute and to visit the famous stupa containing the relics and ashes of Buddha.

Sri Lanka

Towering high over the seaside, Adam's Peak is the principal place of pilgrimage in Sri Lanka. Pilgrims ascend countless flights of steps in order to reach the summit where there rests a rock bearing the footprint of Buddha. Although it remains unclear whether or not Buddha ever went to Sri Lanka, some people believe that this print marks the site where Buddha stepped ashore during his third visit to the island.

In addition, there are two famous monasteries in Sri Lanka: Anaradhapura and Polunnaruwa. These contain massive and inspiring rock depictions of Buddha.

Tibet

One of the most popular religious sites in Tibet is the palace of the Dalai, the Lake of Padmasambhava. Padmasambhava is the founder of Tibetan Buddhism. Legend has it that from this lake he was born in a lotus blossom. This popular leader is said to have spread Buddha's teachings in exchange for bags of gold dust. When he had gathered a great amount of gold, he loosened the bags and the precious dust flew away in the breeze. In doing so, he wanted to prove that only what is eternal is of value.

The Cat Who Went to Heaven

by Elizabeth Coatsworth
(Macmillan, 1990)
(Canada: Collier Macmillan; U.K. and AUS.: Maxwell Macmillan)

The Cat Who Went to Heaven is a wonderful story about a Japanese artist, his housekeeper, and a curious cat named Good Fortune. It is a beautifully written tale, rich with wisdom and compassion. Published in 1930, it won the Newbery Medal for distinguished contribution to children's literature and has remained a classic ever since.

Now that you have a good understanding of the principals and spirit behind Buddhism, your reading of *The Cat Who Went to Heaven* should be an inspiring one.

The purpose of this mini-unit is to encourage some deep thinking, especially about the four main characters: the artist, the housekeeper, Good Fortune, and Buddha. You will also be asked to respond to the reading on a personal and artistic level. Read the novel carefully. The following pages can be completed at its conclusion.

The Jataka Tales

The Cat Who Went to Heaven contains several stories of Buddha's former animal incarnations. The source of these stories is the charming *Jataka Tales* which are found in the Theravada scriptures. Legend has it that when Buddha attained enlightenment under the Bodhi tree, he remembered all 550 of his previous incarnations as a bodhisattva. The *Jataka Tales* are a collection of 557 such accounts, some of them repeated in a variety of ways. Each account is told by Buddha as instruction to his students, and each points out a moral or inspires virtue.

Finally, the heart of every story is a verse of poetry spoken by Buddha. In one tale called "The Cold Half of the Month," a lion and a tiger are arguing. The lion says it is cold in the light half of the month, while the tiger says it is cold in the dark half. Buddha, living as a hermit, responds with these words which unite the two animals in friendship:

> "In light or dark half, whensoe'er the wind
> Doth blow, 'tis cold. For cold is caused by wind.
> And, therefore, I decide you both are right."

Each of the animals in *The Cat Who Went To Heaven* appears in the *Jataka Tales*. Later, you will have a chance to write your own original tale of compassion.

Response:

Freewrite a response to the quote above. Do you think it shows wisdom?

_____

_____

_____

_____

Name _____

The Cat Who Went to Heaven *(cont.)*

Buddha

The great thread in this story, of course, is the life and the past lives of Buddha. You are familiar with the life of Prince Siddhartha, upon which the artist meditates for three days. Each day, the artist discovers a quality which must be alive in the face of the painted Buddha. Below are three quotes from the story. Explain how each one relates to the life of Buddha.

1. "Yet now he understood that the Buddha he painted must have the look of one who has been gently brought up and unquestioningly obeyed."

   _____

   _____

2. ". . . he must have the look of one who has suffered greatly and sacrificed himself."

   _____

   _____

3. ". . . he must have the look of one who has found peace and given it to others."

   _____

   _____

The Death of Buddha

The artist is commissioned to paint the death of Buddha. We learn of the assembly of animals, humans, and gods paying homage to their teacher. However, we learn little about the historical facts of Buddha's death.

At around the age of eighty, Buddha received a meal from a blacksmith. Afterwards, he fell ill. Knowing his time was near, Buddha walked to the village of Kushinagara. Legend has it that he lay down on his right side, under a grove of shala trees. He called forth his followers and spoke his last words:

> "Desire is the root of suffering. Everything is subject to change, to decay and death. Therefore, do not become attached to anything; instead, clear your mind and devote yourself to your own salvation."

> Then he rested his right hand under his head, closed his eyes, and passed away into eternal enlightenment. This image, called *parinirvana* (the final state of nirvava), is the subject of many statues of Buddha.

Name _____

The Cat Who Went to Heaven *(cont.)*

Buddha and the Animals

From the *Jataka Tales* comes the stories of Buddha manifesting as various animals. The first animal we learn about in *The Cat Who Went to Heaven* is the elephant. An animal of Indian royalty, the white elephant which appeared in Queen Maya's dream has come to symbolize Buddha's birth.

In our story, the elephant sacrifices himself for the good of a group of fugitives starving in the desert. After the elephant throws himself off a cliff, "the spirits of the trees had thrown their flowers upon his body." (Legend has it that the moment after Buddha's own death, the trees, though not in bloom, sprouted and showered blossoms upon him.) The artist thinks about the elephant's "sagacity and dignity and kindness" as he prepares to paint him.

Below is a list of the animals appearing in the book. For each one, tell briefly what act of kindness it showed. Then, find at least two direct quotes to describe its goodness. You can use the paragraph above as a model.

1. the king's horse _____

   _____

   _____

   _____

2. the buffalo _____

   _____

   _____

   _____

3. the banyon deer _____

   _____

   _____

   _____

4. the ape _____

   _____

   _____

   _____

Name _____

The Cat Who Went to Heaven *(cont.)*

The Housekeeper

The housekeeper is the quiet heart of *The Cat Who Went to Heaven*. After all, on the very first page she arrives with Good Fortune, an act which changes the artist's—and the town's—life. She also has eight "songs," or poems, which introduce each chapter and end the book. Yet, she is so gentle and quiet a character that we must look closely in order to discover her qualities, her own Buddha-nature.

Begin by taking a look at "The First Song of the Housekeeper," which, along with her next three poems, is centered on the artist.

What does this song tell you about the old woman? How does she feel toward the artist? How does she use the word "master"? What kind of living conditions does the poem relate?

_____

_____

_____

_____

_____

_____

_____

_____

_____

_____

_____

_____

_____

Extension:

Read all eight of the housekeeper's songs. On a separate sheet of paper, write about the content of each one and what each tells you about the artist's helper. Be sure to address the tone and feeling behind the poem. Finally, explain the prosody (poetic form) of each verse. For example, this first song has three stanzas, it rhymes A-B-C-B, and it contains between five and six syllables per line. (Your teacher will help you on this). Ask yourself how the form of the poem is related to the meaning of the poem.

As an additional challenge, copy and decorate the housekeeper's songs.

Name _____

The Cat Who Went to Heaven *(cont.)*

The Housekeeper *(cont.)*

The following questions will test both your comprehension and understanding of the housekeeper. Answer each one in full sentences and with supporting details. Use additional paper as needed.

1. When the housekeeper first arrives with Good Fortune, the artist is very upset. "Here we are starving and you must bring home a goblin," he says to her. First of all, why does she bring Good Fortune to the house? Secondly, describe the story she tells in response to the artist's complaints.

    _____

    _____

2. Early in the story, the housekeeper says, "There is not a kinder heart in the whole town than my master's." Indeed, she shows great loyalty and love toward the hungry painter. First, write about the different ways she expresses her loyalty. Secondly, discuss what qualities she sees in the artist. Why is she so loyal to him?

    _____

    _____

3. What does the housekeeper do each morning in preparation for and in honor of the artist's work?

    _____

    _____

4. What present does the artist bestow upon the housekeeper?

    _____

    _____

5. When the artist cannot recall a story about a dog, the housekeeper helps. What story does she tell?

    _____

    _____

6. In "The Fourth Song of the Housekeeper," she writes about how concentrated the artist has become—so much so that he "does not know/That I am I./He does not see/Our cat pass by." However, in her wisdom she knows that the three of them are connected: "And yet our love/Has its share, too,/In all things/His two hands do."

    _____

    _____

For this final question, discuss the spirit of the housekeeper. Use examples like the one above to show her part in the miracle at the end of the book. Finally, how is she like Buddha?

Name _____

The Cat Who Went to Heaven *(cont.)*

The Artist

Although the artist in *The Cat Who Went to Heaven* is not a monk, he is an embodiment of the Buddhist spirit. Indeed, the way he approaches his painting teaches us a great deal about Buddhism, just as his final act of compassion and self-sacrifice mirrors Buddha's own.

Again, you should answer the questions below in full sentences, using details from the book. Also, get together with a classmate and discuss them. As you respond, keep in mind how the artist changes from the beginning to the end of the book.

1. Although it is not clear whether the Japanese artist is a Zen Buddhist, his lifestyle reflects simplicity and aesthetic beauty, qualities inherent in Zen. Find some details which illustrate these qualities.

    _____

    _____

2. How does the artist first feel about Good Fortune? What names does he call him? Why is he so upset that the housekeeper brings home a cat?

    _____

    _____

3. What are the artist's living conditions? How does he feel inside in the beginning of the book?

    _____

    _____

4. The artist begins to look differently upon Good Fortune when the cat performs a surprising act of mercy. What act is this? How does it make the artist feel?

    _____

    _____

5. How is it that priests come to choose the artist to paint the death of Buddha? What happens right after the artist hears the news?

    _____

    _____

6. The artist is puzzled as to why Buddha blessed the tiger, a fierce and sometimes cruel creature, and will not paint the "killers among the reeds." What answer helps him come to terms with this dilemma?

    _____

    _____

Name _____

The Cat Who Went to Heaven *(cont.)*

The Artist *(cont.)*

Buddhism is sometimes called a religion without a God. In fact, some people do not consider it a religion at all, but a philosophy or school of thought. This is partly because Buddhists do not pray in the common sense of the word.

Most people consider prayer an act of petition or repentance to a higher force. Some people pray to God for guidance, forgiveness, or even a new car! Buddhists, however, do not believe in a God "up there" who will answer personal prayers. Rather, they seek self-understanding. Their model, of course, is Lord Buddha, whose qualities and state of enlightenment they try to emulate. Thus, when Buddhists pray, they are praying inwardly, to their own Buddha nature. As a perfect being, Buddha provided guidance. It is up to the individual, however, to come to perfect understanding.

This spirit of prayer is evident in the artist, even though before Good Fortune arrived "he was a little ashamed to remember how seldom he prayed." Rather than beginning his painting, he spends three days meditating upon the life of Prince Siddhartha:

> "There were no rolls of silk near him, no cakes of ink with raised patterns of flowers on their tops, no beautiful brushes, nor jar of fresh spring water. He must strive to understand the Buddha before he could paint him."

Extension:

Use your understanding of Buddhism and the life of Buddha to help answer each of the following essay questions. Give detailed examples from the book.

1. Why must the artist understand what he is painting? Why not simply draw the picture and collect the fortune?

   _____

2. Describe the artist's direct experiences with the lives of Buddha. What qualities does he touch upon?

   _____

3. When the artist completes the paintings, he is purified. Find some excerpts which describe this purity. How do these descriptions relate to Buddhism?

   _____

4. Although the artist experiences Buddha's compassionate nature, it is not until the end of the book that he actually performs his own act of self-sacrifice. Explain what he does, what he gives up, and why he does it.

   _____

   _____

Name _____

The Cat Who Went to Heaven *(cont.)*

Good Fortune

Both the Hindu and Buddhist faiths have great reverence for all living things. Animals, therefore, are considered to come from the same source of life as humans. Tibetan Buddhists, for instance, believe that all creatures experience rebirth, but most are reborn as animals. To be born a human is considered an honor. And, of course, Buddha himself had many animal incarnations. Because of these beliefs, many Buddhists practice vegetarianism.

In *The Cat Who Went To Heaven*, Good Fortune has the "distinction" of being an animal apart, a creature who did not receive Buddha's blessings. But we learn that she is a special cat, a cat who resurrects a lifeless household. By paying attention to Good Fortune's actions, then, we can understand a great deal about devotion and steadfastness—qualities Buddhists strive to embody.

Begin by answering the comprehension questions. You may need to review the book. Then, respond to the critical thinking questions in full sentences, using details to support your writing. Use additional paper as needed.

Comprehension:

1. Describe Good Fortune's physical appearance. Use at least two of the artist's similes in your description. (A simile is a comparative description which uses "like" or "as.")

   _____

2. From where did the housekeeper get Good Fortune? Explain Good Fortune's family lineage.

   _____

3. Why does the housekeeper choose the name "Good Fortune"?

   _____

4. Describe Good Fortune's eating habits when she first arrives.

   _____

5. When the housekeeper leaves the house, why does she put Good Fortune in a bamboo basket?

   _____

6. After the housekeeper tells the story of Shippeitaro, the dog, something occurs which saddens Good Fortune. Explain what happens and how the cat responds.

   _____

7. Does Good Fortune eat meat? Use a direct quote to support your answer.

   _____

8. Use direct quotes from the story to explain why cats were not given Buddha's blessing.

   _____

Name _____

The Cat Who Went to Heaven *(cont.)*

Good Fortune *(cont.)*

Critical Thinking:

"Good Fortune, having found that she was unable to help either of them, sat quietly in the sun, ate as little as she could, and often spent hours with lowered head before the image of Buddha on its low shelf."

'She is praying to the Enlightened One,' said the housekeeper in admiration." (chapter 2)

1. The above quote introduces us to Good Fortune's virtue and religious character. Write down other times when the cat is a spiritual support and inspiration to the artist and housekeeper. How does Good Fortune embody Buddhism?

   _____

   _____

   _____

   _____

   _____

2. After the artist paints each animal, Good Fortune arrives to look at the painting. List at least three of these instances. Describe her feelings after each one. Does she become more emotional each time?

   _____

   _____

   _____

   _____

   _____

3. Why is Good Fortune finally accepted by Buddha? How is her relationship to the artist instrumental in this acceptance?

   _____

   _____

   _____

   _____

   _____

Name _____

The Cat Who Went to Heaven *(cont.)*

Creative Writing:

The story of Good Fortune is a story of compassion and self-sacrifice. Like Buddha's animal incarnations, the cat brings out the artist's true spirit of selflessness. Below, write a story about an animal—a story which could fit into *The Cat Who Went to Heaven* or even the *Jataka Tales*. The story can be fiction or non-fiction.

_____

_____

_____

_____

_____

_____

_____

_____

_____

_____

_____

_____

_____

_____

_____

_____

_____

_____

_____

_____

Name _____

Vocabulary

Match the letter of the appropriate definition to each vocabulary word.

_____ 1. stupa   A. principal Buddhist symbol

_____ 2. bodhi tree   B. a compassionate deity

_____ 3. Vesak   C. helped spread Buddhism

_____ 4. Mahayana   D. a design used for meditation

_____ 5. King Ashoka   E. Southern branch of Buddhism

_____ 6. Siddhartha   F. Siddhartha's father

_____ 7. haiku   G. mound-like building

_____ 8. Obon   H. where Buddha was enlightened

_____ 9. *Jataka Tales*   I. leader of Tibetan Buddhism

_____ 10. monastery   J. month of three celebrations

_____ 11. Theravada   K. a position of the Buddha image

_____ 12. Queen Maya   L. Northern branch of Buddhism

_____ 13. bodhisattva   M. tall, thin tower

_____ 14. Dalai Lama   N. Siddhartha's mother

_____ 15. rupa   O. "one who brings all good"

_____ 16. mandala   P. short Japanese poem

_____ 17. pagoda   Q. abodes for monks

_____ 18. King Sudhodana   R. animal stories

_____ 19. mudras   S. conventionalized hand positions

_____ 20. Wheel of Law   T. Japanese holiday for the dead

Name _____

Quiz and Review

Part One: For statements 1-10, fill in the spaces with the correct answers.

1. Prince Siddhartha was born around _____ , in the town of _____ .

2. The Four Noble Truths state that _____ is the root of suffering.

3. Three of the steps on the Eightfold path include right _____ , right _____ , and right _____ .

4. Three countries in which Theravada Buddhism is popular include _____ , _____ , and _____ .

5. Three countries in which Mahayana Buddhism is popular include _____ , _____ , and _____ .

6. The three Theravadin scriptures are contained in the _____ .

7. Buddhists practice _____ in order to quiet their minds.

8. Some Zen Buddhists use riddles, or _____ , in their practice.

9. Buddhist architecture originated with the _____ .

10. When Buddha died, he lay down on his _____ side.

Part Two: Respond to the following prompts in the spaces below.

1. Why did King Sudhodana want his son to witness no suffering?

   _____

   _____

   _____

   _____

   _____

2. List and explain briefly the Four Noble Truths.

   _____

   _____

   _____

   _____

   _____

Name _____

Quiz and Review *(cont.)*

3. What is the purpose of meditation? Describe at least two different types.

    _____

    _____

    _____

4. Explain the role of the Dalai Lama in Tibetan Buddhism. How is a new Dalai Lama chosen?

    _____

    _____

    _____

5. Describe the fundamental principals of Zen Buddhism.

    _____

    _____

    _____

6. Describe the features of a stupa, pagoda, and monastery.

    _____

    _____

    _____

7. List and describe three places of pilgrimage for Buddhists.

    _____

    _____

    _____

8. What are some of the qualities most Buddhists strive to embody? Why?

    _____

    _____

    _____

Origins of Sikhism: The Life of Guru Nanak

Of all the major world religions, Sikhism is the youngest, beginning around the year 1500 C.E. The majority of its eighteen million followers still live in the Punjab, the northwest region of India, although Sikh communities now exist in every continent.

Most Westerners know very little, if anything, about the Sikh religion. A faith rich in history, tradition, and hardship, Sikhism combines traces of both Hinduism and Islam. From Hinduism it adopts the doctrine of reincarnation and karma, and from Islam stems its monotheism and rejection of the caste system. Although Sikhs comprise only two percent of India's population, they are among the country's most influential groups, cherishing religion, education, work, and family.

Like so many other religions, Sikhism began with the teachings of one man. He was Guru Nanak. (The word *guru*, borrowed from the Hindus, means "a teacher or holy man.") But unlike many other faiths, Nanak was followed by another guru, Angad. In all there were ten Gurus, each one responsible for carrying on the teachings and leadership of the Sikh people. All ten leaders will be attended to later in the chapter.

Guru Nanak is considered the spiritual founder of Sikhism. Understanding his life and spirit will help one to understand the principal beliefs and customs of Sikhism.

Most of what we know about Guru Nanak's life comes from a series of stories called *Janamsakhi*. The first book ever composed in the Punjabi language, these accounts were written shortly after Nanak passed away. As can be seen, Nanak's life contains similarities to the lives of other prophets.

For example, Nanak was born on April 15, 1469, in an Indian village which is now part of Pakistan. As at the birth of Prince Siddhartha, a priest envisioned the newborn as a prophet, speaking especially of Nanak's love for all people, regardless of caste or religion. Born a Hindu, Nanak belonged to one of the higher castes. (See page 155.)

However, during his childhood, Muslims ruled India. Although the young Nanak grew up in a world of political disharmony, he already inspired togetherness. In fact, he was taught and admired by both Hindu and Muslim priests. And like Siddhartha, Nanak soon outgrew his teachers.

A telling moment in his life came at eleven years of age when he refused to participate in the ceremony of the sacred thread. (See page 156.) This distaste for external rituals, along with the rejection of the caste system, was already a keynote to Nanak's teachings. So, when the priest, or Brahmin, questioned the boy Nanak, he answered with words which have become a popular Sikh hymn:

> "Make compassion the cotton, contentment the yarn;
> Give it chastity's twist and knot;
> Such is the true thread of the self.
> Put such on me, thou Brahmin, should thou have it."

To young Nanak, an individual's behavior and internal life mattered more than any external adornment. In fact, he felt that the life of the spirit was often eclipsed by ceremony or ritual. Education, too, he found uninspiring, and soon dropped out to work in the fields and to contemplate God.

Several stories tell of Nanak's mystical experiences in the fields, including one hot summer day when he slept under a tree. Legend has it that a deadly cobra slid before him, opened its hood, and shaded his face from the burning sun. Another account tells of the miracle of the wheat. Nanak's cows had wandered off and consumed a neighbor's crops. But when the angry man returned with the village chief, they witnessed an untouched field where only moments before no crop stood.

Origins of Sikhism: The Life of Guru Nanak *(cont.)*

Like many prophets before him, Nanak experienced a divine revelation, an experience of enlightenment which launched his teachings. By the age of twenty-eight, Nanak was wed and had fathered two sons. The family lived in the city of Sultanpur. Each morning, Nanak bathed at a nearby river, But one day, he did not return. Relatives found his clothes beside the river, and after two days passed, they assumed the young man had drowned. To their surprise, three days later Nanak returned and boldly proclaimed, "There is neither Hindu nor Muslim." He said that he had been in communication with the Almighty and had been instructed to become a leader. His first message, he explained, did not renounce religion, but forced the truth at the heart of all creeds: faith and devotion to one, unchangeable, universal reality. This reality, he declared, is beyond description, yet attainable in the heart. Here is Nanak's revelation as recorded in the *Janamsakhi*:

> "As the Almighty willed, Nanak the devotee was ushered into the Divine Presence. Then a cup filled with nectar was given him with the command, 'Nanak, this is the cup of Name Adoration. Drink it . . . I am with you and I do bless and exalt you. Whoever remembers you will have my favor. Go, rejoice in My Name, and teach others to do so…I have bestowed upon you the gift of My Name. Let this be your calling."

For the next two and one-half decades, Nanak traveled as far as the holy city of Mecca, preaching his message of divine Oneness. He dialogued with Buddhists, Hindus, and Muslims while making known his own philosophies. Although he counseled people to reject rituals, he advised against renouncing religion altogether. Rather, they should seek within their faith and within themselves for the universality of God, which transcends boundaries.

Journeying with Nanak was a Muslim servant, Mardana, who played a three-stringed instrument called the *rebec*. Nanak composed and sang hymns to the music of the rebec, songs which still remain popular among Sikhs. Some of these poems also appear in the *Guru Granth*, the sacred Sikh scripture. Here is the first of the thirty-eight psalms of Nanak, which focuses on the nature of God:

> "Thinking comprehendeth him not, although there be thoughts by the thousands,
> Silence discovers him not, though it be continuous silence,
> Man is persistently hungry, though he eats of tasty abundance;
> Not one of a hundred thousand artful devices avail him!
> How may the truth be attained, the bonds of falsehood be broken?
> By obeying the will of God as surely recorded, saith Nanak."

In many artistic depictions, Mardana appears with Guru Nanak. As you will see, music is a crucial part of Sikh daily life.

Origins of Sikhism: The Life of Guru Nanak *(cont.)*

Of course, from the travels of Nanak many stories were born. One account tells of the leader being invited to dinner by a rich officer and by a poor man. When the guru chose to eat with the poor man, the rich man was angered. Nanak then changed his mind, and together with the poor man sat down to dine at the rich man's house. Legend tells that the guru took a piece of bread from both houses, lifted them up, and squeezed them. Blood poured form the rich man's bread while milk came from the other. Nanak explained that the wealthy man exploited people while the poor man was honest. Each way of life, he instructed, has its own consequences.

Wherever he traveled, the holy teacher gathered followers. His message of universal brotherhood appealed to people from a variety of religions and social classes. These disciples came to be called Sikhs. But when Guru Nanak was about 50 years old, he halted his travels and built a town on the banks of the Ravi River in the Punjab. He called this settlement Kartarpur. Here, many of his devotees lived in a community. This group considered men and women equal. While studying the guru's teachings, followers continued with daily life, including working and raising children. Never were they asked to renounce the world and live a monastic life, actions common to devout Hindus and Buddhists.

This emphasis on everyday living and equality is one of the principal characteristics of Sikhism. Nanak himself ate meals with his visitors, an uncommon gesture in a land defined by social classes. In the sight of God, he explained, all people are equal. It was also at Kartarpur that Nanak founded the three most important ingredients of Sikh social behavior: voluntary labor, partaking in community meals, and social gatherings. Later in the chapter, you will take a closer look at each of these institutions.

Around the time Nanak arrived in Kartarpur, a man called Lehna came to visit. Lehna soon became the guru's closest devotee. In 1539, to the surprise of Nanak's two sons, their father pronounced Lehna the next Sikh guru. Nanak gave Lehna a new name, Angad, which means "part of me," and then laid a coconut and five copper coins in front of his disciple. Finally, Nanak bowed before Lehna's feet, proclaiming him Guru Angad.

Nanak's two sons, Sri Chand and Lakhmi Chand, were not pleased with their father's decision, feeling that a natural heir should be guru. However, Nanak said he had chosen the most capable, sincere, and humble of his followers—a precedent upon which all ten Gurus were named. In fact, several times Guru Nanak had asked his sons to perform tasks normally carried out by lower castes, but they refused. For example, one stormy night, part of Nanak's house collapsed. He asked his sons to rebuild it, but they refused, complaining of the cold and baseness of the task. Lehna, however, humbly completed the menial labor, reconstructing the damaged section many times over until Nanak was satisfied.

Guru Nanak died on September 7, 1539. The story goes that after his death, both Hindus and Muslims wanted to perform the last rites. The Hindu custom of cremation was thus pitted against the Muslim practice of burial. But when they removed the white sheet covering Nanak's body, only flowers remained! Fittingly, the sheet and flowers were evenly divided between the two religions, reminding them of Guru Nanak's message of peace and brotherhood.

The Punjab and Surrounding Countries

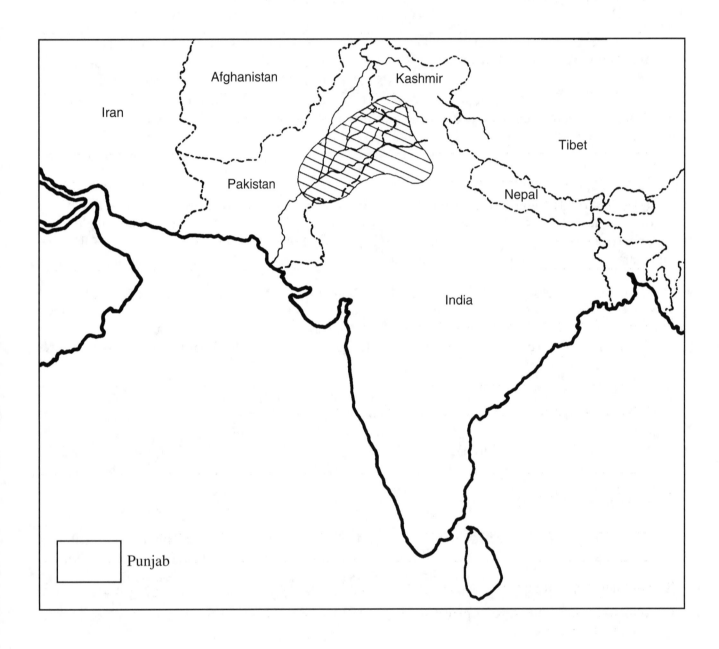

Name _____

Origins of Sikhism: Comprehension

Respond to the following comprehension questions and prompts. Be sure to use full sentences. Use additional paper if necessary.

1. Around what year did Sikhism begin? When was Guru Nanak born?

    _____

2. Where do the majority of the Sikhs live?

    _____

3. What significant event took place when Nanak was eleven years old?

    _____

    _____

4. Describe one of Nanak's mystical experiences when he worked the fields.

    _____

    _____

    _____

5. What did Nanak say after returning from his days of revelation?

    _____

    _____

6. Who accompanied Nanak in his travels? What did this person do?

    _____

    _____

7. Briefly retell the story of the rich man and the poor man.

    _____

    _____

8. On your map, find the Ravi River and the town of Kartarpur.

9. Who did Nanak choose to follow him as guru? What new name did Nanak bestow on him, and what is its meaning?

    _____

10. What happened to Guru Nanak's body after his death?

    _____

    _____

Name _____

Origins of Sikhism: Critical Thinking

Respond to the following questions and prompts in complete sentences. Be sure to use details to support your answers. Use additional paper if necessary.

1. Guru Nanak has been likened to other prophets of God, such as Christ, Buddha, Moses, and Muhammad. Describe at least two events in Nanak's life which are similar to happenings in the life of another prophet.

   _____

   _____

2. Why did Nanak refuse to participate in the ceremony of the sacred thread?

   _____

   _____

3. Describe Nanak's vision or revelation. What happened to him? What was the essence of the divine message? In what ways is this message unique?

   _____

   _____

4. Explain Guru Nanak's ideas about religion and religious practice. How does this relate to his feelings about the caste system?

   _____

   _____

5. Why did Nanak favor Lehna when choosing a successor? How is this consistent with the spirit of Sikhism?

   _____

   _____

6. What dispute took place after Nanak's death? How does the miracle of flowers epitomize the life and message of Guru Nanak?

   _____

   _____

The Sikh Gurus

Here is a list of the ten Sikh gurus, including their birthplaces, life spans, the year they became guru, and one achievement for which each was known. You will want to use this chart as reference for the chapter ahead.

Name and Life Span	Birthplace	Became Guru	Achievement
Nanak (1469-1539)	Nankana Sahib	1469	founded Sikhism
Angad (1504-1552)	Mukatsar	1539	Gurmukhi alphabet
Amar Das (1479-15720	Amritsar	1552	social reform; began langar
Ram Das (1534-1581)	Lahore	1574	founded "Pool of Nectar"
Arjan (1563-1606)	Amritsar	1581	founded Golden Temple
Har Gobind (1595-1644)	Amritsa	1606	two swords of earthly and spiritual power
Har Rai (1630-1661)	Kiratpur	1644	spread the religion
Har Krishna (1656-1664)	Kiratpur	1661	the child guru
Tegh Bahadur (1621-1675)	Amritsar	1665	martyred for religious freedom
Gobind Singh (1666-1708)	Bihar	1675	created the Khalsa

Extension:

As you read about Sikhism, choose one of the ten gurus who interests you and write a short essay about his life.

The Guru Granth: Sikh Holy Book

Before passing away in 1708, Guru Gobind Singh, tenth in the line of gurus, instructed that there would be no more human gurus. Instead, followers would be guided by the *Guru Granth*, the Sikh holy book. As you will see, the *Guru Granth* (*granth* means "book") is revered in the same manner as a living, breathing guru.

The *Guru Granth* is actually a massive compilation of poems and hymns from various contributors beginning with Guru Nanak. Containing 5,894 verses, it the largest single compilation of rhymed poetry. The text began when followers of Nanak copied his spontaneous hymns which they accepted as the words of God. In all, 974 of Guru Nanak's hymns appear in the scripture.

Guru Angad also contributed 62 couplets (two-lined rhymes) to the holy book. In doing so, he created the written form of the Punjabi language, Gurmukhi. In an act of fealty to his predecessor, Angad signed each of his poems "Nanak." This tradition continued with succeeding Gurus, including Amar Dar who composed 907 hymns and Arjan's 2,218 hymns.

The *Guru Granth* also included works by Hindu saints as well as *Sufis*, members of a mystical branch of Islam revered poets. One of these contributors is the famous poet Kabir who greatly influenced Guru Nanak. On page 228, you will read one of his verses.

As mentioned above, the *Guru Granth* receives the reverence of a human guru. It is the central focus of the gurdwara. During worship, it rests on a quilt and three cushions beneath the protection of a beautiful canopy. Because the Ten Gurus were comforted by the waving of fans, the *Guru Granth* is given the same respect. If a family owns a copy, they are expected to provide for it a room of its own. In fact, Sikhs remove their shoes and cover their heads in an act of reverence to the holy scripture.

Some gurdwaras have a designated reader of the *Guru Granth* who may also act as a teacher. Otherwise, it may be read by any Sikh man or woman. There are several special occasions when the entire text is read—a task which takes two days!

Reading from the Guru Granth

Four Hymns by Guru Nanak

I have no friend like God
Who gave me soul and body, and infused into me understanding.
He cherishes and watches over all creatures; He is wise and knows the secrets of hearts.
The Guru is like a lake; we are his beloved swans;
In the water are many jewels and rubies.
God's praises are pearls, gems, and diamonds; singing them makes soul and body happy.

My soul is in fear; to whom shall I complain?
I have served Him who causes us to forget our sorrows; He is ever and ever the Giver.
My Lord is ever young; He is ever and ever the Giver.
Night and day serve the Lord, and in the end He will deliver thee.
Hark, hark my friend, thus shall you cross over.
O Merciful One, by Thy name shall I cross over; I am ever a sacrifice unto Thee.

He who knows the two paths to be one, will alone find fulfillment;
The evil slanderer must burn in hell-fire;
The whole universe is Divine in essence—
Merge yourself into Truth.

Know the Lord to be One, even though the paths be twain.
Through God's Word learn His commandment:
Give equal place in thy heart to all human forms and castes!
Saith Nanak, only the One is worthy of worship.

Reading from the Guru Granth *(cont.)*

A Poem by Kabir

Why so impatient, my heart?
He who watches over birds and beasts and insects,
He who cared for you while you were yet in your mother's womb,
Shall He not care for you now that you are come forth?
O my heart, how could you turn from
The smile of your Lord and wander so far from Him?
You have left your beloved and are thinking of others and this is
    Why all your work is in vain.

A Song by Guru Angad

They who possess the greatness of Thy name, O god,
    are happy at heart.
Nanak, there is only one nectar; there is none other;
Nanak, that nectar is in the heart, but it is only
    obtained by the favor of the Guru;
Those who were so destined from the beginning
    drink it with delight.

A Song by Guru Ram Das

They who leave the Guru, who is present with them, shall find no entrance into God's court.
Let any one go and meet those slanderers, and he will see their faces pale and spat upon.
They who are accursed of the Guru are accursed of the whole world, and shall ever be vagrants.
They who deny their Guru shall wander about groaning.
Their hunger shall never depart; they shall ever shriek from its pangs.
No one heareth what they say; they are ever dying of fear.

A Song by Guru Arjan

Though art, O God, an ocean of water; I am thy fish . . .
In thee is my hope, for Thee I thirst, my heart is
    absorbed in Thee
As a child is satisfied by drinking milk,
As a poor man is happy on finding wealth,
As a thirsty man is refreshed by drinking water, so
    is my soul happy with God . . .
God is mine; I am his slave.

Name _____

Questions: Reading from the Guru Granth

Respond to the following questions with complete sentences. Use additional paper if necessary.

1. Use details from these poems to explain the role and function of the Sikh guru.

   _____

   _____

   _____

2. Knowing what you do about the life of Guru Nanak, explain what he means by "two paths" in the third hymn. Where else does he address these paths? What is his message?

   _____

   _____

   _____

3. What is the cause of Kabir's unhappiness?

   _____

   _____

   _____

4. What is the meaning of Guru Angad's poem? What is the nectar? (Review Guru Nanak's life.) What is the role of predestination?

   _____

   _____

   _____

5. What message is shared among the poem of Kabir, the song of Guru Arjan, and the second hymn of Nanak? Offer details in your response.

   _____

   _____

   _____

   _____

   _____

The Khalsa

The *Khalsa* group, one of the most unique features of Sikhism, was founded by Guru Gobind Singh on April 13, 1699, the day of the Indian New Year. Members of the Khalsa are called the "Pure Ones" because they have sworn their lives to defend the Sikh faith. But why was this militant group started in the first place? What does it entail to become a member?

By the early 17th century, Sikhism was an established religion growing in numbers. This popularity was threatening to the Muslim leaders who wanted India to become an Islamic nation. In 1606, the Sikh leader, Guru Arjan, was imprisoned and tortured to death by Muslim rulers. Instantly, Arjan became a martyr, inspiring the Sikhs towards a spirit of self-defense which lives to this day.

Hargobind, Arjan's son, championed this martial spirit. For his initiation as guru, he dressed as a warrior clad with two swords. One weapon represented the guru's spiritual power while the other symbolized earthly powers. Like the Christian cross, they embrace as one the material and the divine. Soon, Guru Hargobind had organized a small army and erected a fortress in Amritsar. Suddenly, the identity of the gentle Sikh community was transformed.

The martyrdom of the ninth guru, Tegh Bahadur, added fuel to Sikh militarism. In 1675, Tegh Bahadur led a resistance against the forced conversion of Hindus. The guru led some followers into the Muslim center in the city of Delhi. Soon, they were imprisoned and threatened: either they become Muslims or were put to death. Without exception, they chose to die. Guru Tegh Bahadur was beheaded, leaving behind a nine-year-old son. Twenty-four years later it was this son, Gobind Singh, who established the Khalsa. The moment of its inception is one of the most dramatic events in Sikh history.

Decades after Tegh Bahadur's death, Sikhs were still being persecuted. So, on New Year's Day, 1699, Guru Gobind Singh called the Sikh community together. Dressed for battle and wielding a sword, he called for unity and courageousness. Lifting his sword, he asked who among the crowd would be willing to die for Sikhism. A man volunteered. The guru led him to a nearby tent and returned to the crowd with a bloody sword. Again he asked for volunteers. In all, five men were led into the tent. Finally, Gobind Singh returned with all five men, each dressed and armed like the guru. These men, willing to die for their faith, were the first members of the Khalsa.

The Khalsa ceremony which followed remains the model for today's initiation. Along with the Guru Granth, five members of the Khalsa must be present. An iron bowl is filled with *amrit*, the nectar used in Sikh rituals, and the liquid is stirred with a sword. After the initiates drink from the bowl, amrit is sprinkled on their faces and hair. Finally, each swears allegiance to the Khalsa, shedding his or her family name. Men adopt the surname Singh which means "lion," while women are given the name Kaur which means "princess." The candidates are then considered part of the family of Gobind Singh and his wife, Mata Sahib Kaur. Their vow is summed up in this statement, made by Gobind Singh at the original Khalsa Ceremony:

> "I wish you all to embrace one creed and follow one path, rising above all differences of religion as now practiced. Let the four Hindu castes, who have different duties laid down for them in their scriptures, abandon them altogether, and adopt the way of mutual help and cooperation . . . Do not follow the old scriptures . . . but all should cherish faith in the teachings of Guru Nanak and his successors. Let each of the four castes receive my Baptism of the double-edged sword, eat out of the same vessel, and feel no aloofness from . . . one another."

Name _____

Essay Response

Throughout history, there have been many groups like the Khalsa, people willing to defend their religion or nationality at all costs. In the space provided below, compare one of these groups to the Khalsa. How are they similar? How are they different?

_____

_____

_____

_____

_____

_____

_____

_____

_____

_____

_____

_____

_____

_____

_____

_____

_____

_____

_____

_____

_____

_____

_____

_____

The Five K's and the Sikh Turban

Along with their spiritual baptism, members of the Khalsa agree to adorn themselves with the Five K's, making visible their allegiance to Sikhism. These were implemented by Guru Gobind Singh who instructed the first members to appear with the Five K's. As you will see below, each sign relates to a spiritual quality of Sikhism.

Kesh: Uncut Hair and Beard

Honoring the ways of nature,
many of India's spiritual people
do not cut their hair or their beard.
This is the spirit of *kesh*.

Kangha: Comb Holding Hair in Place

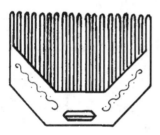

Unlike many of the Indian saints, however, Sikhs do not allow their long hair to become matted or dirty. Thus, the *kangha* functions as a comb (hair must be combed twice daily) while keeping the kesh in place.

Kara: Steel Bracelet

The *kara*, usually worn on the right arm, is made of steel, symbolizing strength. The bracelet also represents the unity of God and of the Khalsa.

The Five K's and the Sikh Turban *(cont.)*

Kirpan: The Double-Edged Dagger or Sword

The *kirpan* is not meant for attack. Rather, it reminds Khalsa members of their duty to defend Sikhism.

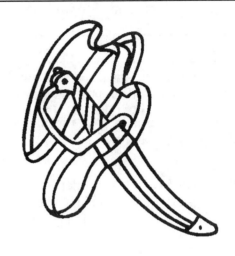

Kaccha: Trousers Worn by Warriors

When the Khalsa began, Sikh soldiers wore the *kaccha*, which has become a symbol of modesty and moral restraint.

The Sikh Turban

Guru Gobind Singh, who wore a turban as a sign of power, instructed his followers that they embody his qualities as much as possible. Thus, most male—and some female—Sikhs wear turbans. Although they are not included in the Five K's, turbans are the most visible Sikh adornments.

Sikh Social Customs

At Kartarpur, Guru Nanak established three important elements of Sikh behavior: *sewa* (voluntary labor), *langar* (community meal), and *sangat* (social gathering). Each of these practices strengthens the bonds of the Sikh community while bringing into application the principals Guru Nanak upheld.

Sewa

Service to others, or sewa, is a vital part of Sikh ethics and behavior. It is an action of selflessness which manifests itself in three ways: *tan* (physical), *dhan* (material), and *man* (mental).

Physical service usually means manual labor. Sikhs perform sewa by cleaning the local gurdwara (Sikh temple), or they may help feed those less fortunate, sweep the temple steps, or offer water to weary pilgrims.

Giving money is another manner of Sikh service. Although it is not required, Guru Gobind Singh, the tenth guru, said Sikhs should try to donate to charity ten percent of their incomes. Donating a tenth, called *tithing*, is common to many religions. Those who cannot afford to give money often offer food to the gurdwara.

But sewa is not limited to manual labor or money. Guru Nanak also instructed followers to speak with others about the nature of God. However, Sikhs do not try to convert people to their religion. Rather, they hope to spark in others the love of God.

Importantly, in line with the spirit of Sikhism, sewa extends to all peoples, regardless of religious or racial background. One famous story tells of a Sikh soldier, Ghanaya, who, in the midst of battle, carried water to the wounded enemy. He was reported to Guru Gobind Singh who questioned the soldier. Ghanaya said that as he moved through the battlefield, he saw only the face of the guru in both enemy and comrade. The guru praised Ghayana and sent him back with a fresh supply of ointments and bandages.

Langar

The langar, or open kitchen, was established by the third guru, Guru Amar Das. Inspired by Guru Nanak, Amar Das wanted to continue the tradition of community dining. These meals continue as an expression of equality between men and women as well as people of different origins. Originally, anyone who sought counsel with the guru was required first to eat at the langar. Many Sikhs believe langar is helpful in purifying their souls, cleansing them in preparation for rebirth.

The langar is still very active today, alive in every Sikh community. Men and women help to prepare and serve the vegetarian meals, and afterwards, they clean up together. After the worship service, participants sit in long rows and share the meal in the spirit of togetherness.

Sangat

"One disciple is a single Sikh, two form a holy association, but where there are five present, there is the Ultimate Reality itself."

This popular saying captures the spirit of sangat, a Sikh gathering and sense of community. Guru Nanak considered religious interaction critical to the preservation and health of the Sikh faith. Spiritual togetherness, he felt, hastened illumination. Thus, the sangat was established at Kartarpur and remains active today.

Typically, hymns are sung and verses are recited during sangat. Like the langar, anyone can join in sangat, irrespective of race, religion, or gender.

Name _____

Sikh Social Customs *(cont.)*

Respond to the following questions and prompts in complete sentences. Use additional paper if necessary.

1. In many religions, selfless service is an esteemed action. Give examples of religions or religious figures extending service as part of their ministry.

    _____

    _____

    _____

    _____

    _____

    _____

2. The langar is one of many examples of a shared meal. Describe other holiday or religious meals which honor this spirit of togetherness.

    _____

    _____

    _____

    _____

    _____

    _____

3. Besides these Sikh institutions, give examples of others which provide for people regardless of background.

    _____

    _____

    _____

    _____

    _____

    _____

Name _____

Community Service

Sikhs uphold community service as one of the most virtuous actions. In fact, most religions consider self-giving an honorable and cleansing act. Of course, the spirit of selflessness is not relegated only to the religious minded.

In the space below, write about a time when you helped someone or when you volunteered your services. How did you feel? Next, on a separate sheet of paper, brainstorm for some concrete projects you could undertake to help others in your community. What kind of preparation and commitment would they take? (Of course, this is not an assignment, but if you feel inspired, try giving some of your time to service.)

_____

_____

_____

_____

_____

_____

_____

_____

_____

_____

_____

_____

_____

_____

_____

_____

_____

_____

_____

_____

The Gurdwara

The *gurdwara*, "door to the guru," is the Sikh place of worship. Like the synagogue, church, mosque, and temple, the gurdwara offers a religious sanctuary where worshippers can gather. And also like these buildings, gurdwaras everywhere share some special features.

One distinguishing mark of a gurdwara is a yellow flag which holds the principal Sikh symbol. (See page 248.) The emblem also appears within the walls and doors of the temple. All gurdwaras must have a separate room to house the *Guru Granth* and a room for worship. The faithful remove their shoes before entering the worship area, and after leaving offerings of food and money before the *Guru Granth*, they bow and are seated for prayer.

You have already learned about another feature common to the gurdwara: the langar room. Here Sikhs and non-Sikhs gather for a shared meal following worship.

Gurdwaras vary in structure and grandeur. In India, their white domes and minarets are unmistakable. Like Hindu temples, many have a pool of water where Sikhs can bathe or walk nearby in contemplation. These Asian gurdwaras are commonly modeled after the Golden Temple, the most important Sikh shrine. (See page 239.) Outside India, gurdwaras are sometimes converted houses or other simple buildings. Others are vast structures which act as community and educational centers, as well as places of worship.

There are also some common rules governing gurdwaras. For example, tobacco, alcohol, and drugs are strictly forbidden. Following tradition, men and women sit separately on carpeted prayer areas or mats. People listen to hymns of the *Guru Granth*, joining in toward the end of the service. The reader then recites from a random section of the scripture which the seeker accepts as the day's guidance. Finally, the congregation enjoys a traditional offering of *prasad* (sweets).

Extensions:

1. The following page contains a diagram of a typical gurdwara. Familiarize yourself with its features and then find a photograph of a real gurdwara. Are the same features present? Try to find gurdwaras of different shapes.

2. Locate and visit the nearest gurdwara. Although they are not common, you may be surprised to find one near your town.

The Gurdwara *(cont.)*

1. room for *Guru Granth*
2. palki (canopy over *Guru Granth*)
3. takht (raised platform)
4. ragis (musicians)
5. donations of food and money
6. carpeted prayer area for women
7. carpeted prayer area for men

8. cloak/shoe room
9. nisan sahib (flag)
10. washing area
11. pictures of gurus
12. langar dining room/kitchen
13. steel bowls of kara prasad, a sweet made of flour, butter, sugar, and water, and given to all Sikhs at the end of a service

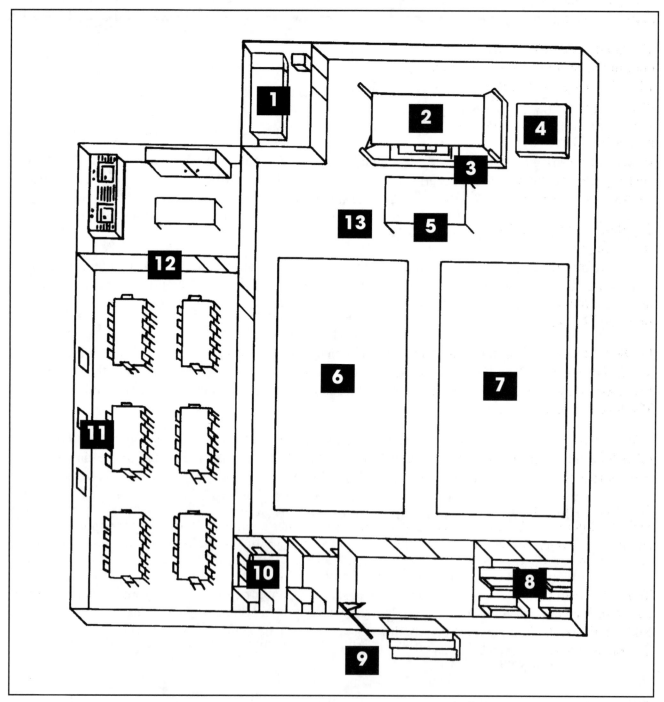

The Golden Temple

Constructed by Guru Arjan in 1581, the Golden Temple in Amritsar is the physical heart of the Sikh religion, the holiest of Sikh places. Like the Ka'bah for Muslims and the Western Wall for Jews, the Golden Temple is a place of pilgrimage, a reminder of the faith's history and spiritual foundation. Sometimes called the "Throne of the Almighty," the Temple also houses the Sikh administration.

The Golden Temple stands in a sacred pool of water built by Guru Ram Das in 1577. He named it Amritsar, which means "pool of nectar." Because the water is believed to have healing properties, Guru Arjan wanted the shrine in the heart of the pool. Before entering the Temple, pilgrims purify themselves by bathing in the pool.

The design of the Golden Temple has some unique features which set it apart from Hindu shrines. For example, the Temple has four doors—one for each direction—in which pilgrims from all castes, religions, and races are welcome. Rather than ascending to the shrine, the visitor descends a set of stairs in an act of humility. Finally, despite a history of bloodshed and animosity between Sikhs and Muslims, it is believed that a Muslim laid the first stone of the Temple's foundation.

In 1802, Maharajah Ranjit Singh had the Temple rebuilt out of marble and its upper walls inlaid with jewels and layered with gold leaf, giving the shrine its name. Verses from the Guru Granth are inscribed on these walls, while sections of the original scripture itself rest in the heart of the shrine. The text is read aloud continuously, sanctifying the atmosphere.

Like so many holy places, the Golden Temple has been destroyed and rebuilt. Sheltering swords and other Sikh relics, the Temple is the seat of political as well as religious power. Sadly, the shrine has been unable to escape the consequences of political conflict.

This was seen perhaps most dramatically in 1984 when a small band of Sikhs made the Golden Temple their headquarters. Accused of separatism and terrorism, the group was attacked by the Indian army. In the battle which followed, at least 500 Sikhs and 83 Indian soldiers were killed. Meanwhile, the Temple suffered great damage. Assaulted by tanks and bullets, the marble walls were shattered.

Today, the restoration of the Temple in Amritsar is nearly complete. Interestingly, before returning the shrine to Sikh authorities in 1986, the Indian government repaired much of the damage. However, Sikhs believed the Temple must be rebuilt as an act of sewa, community service. They demolished the Temple and began reconstruction again.

The Punjab

The Punjab, which means "five rivers," is the fertile area of land where Sikhism began. Although the Punjab is not a separate country, for centuries Sikhs have considered this region of northern India to be their homeland. And like many religions which have suffered persecution, the Sikhs have had to battle for their territory.

The political turbulence began after the death of Guru Gobind Singh, who established the Khalsa. The earlier execution of their two gurus by Muslim leaders inspired the Sikhs to establish their own nation where they would enjoy religious freedom. So, in 1710, they captured the town of Sirhind gaining control of the Punjab. However, this action backfired in 1716 when the Sikhs were defeated and their religion outlawed. For decades, the Khalsa groups wandered the hills of the Punjab, in danger of persecution.

The political climate changed in the middle of the 18th century when Afghanistan gained control of northern India. Sikhs then gathered together into twelve Khalsa groups and took control of the Punjab. In 1799, a nineteen-year-old warrior named Ranjit Singh gained control of the city of Lahore. He went on to become the *Maharajah*, or ruler, joining the separate Khalsa groups into an independent Sikh state.

The reign of Maharajah Ranjit Singhs lasted forty years, during which the Punjab and Sikh nation enjoyed independence, prosperity, and international respect and acceptance. Although the British were taking hold of India, the boundaries of the Punjab continued to extend, encompassing all five of the region's rivers.

In 1839, Maharajah Ranjit Singh died. Afterwards, the Sikhs' leadership was in disarray and their armies left unorganized. The British took advantage of this weakened state and defeated the Sikh army in 1846. By 1849, the British gained complete control of the Punjab, and the kingdom was annexed by the British Empire.

When India gained its independence in 1947, part of the Punjab became the Muslim nation of Pakistan. This forced most Sikhs into India, where again they hoped to establish their homeland. Although they were not granted secession from India, from 1966-1980 they had their own Punjabi government. However, in 1983, their state government was eliminated altogether. Since then, the Sikh nation has suffered major setbacks from within and without its ranks. Nevertheless, millions of Sikhs remain in the fertile region of the Punjab, cultivating the land just as their ancestors did.

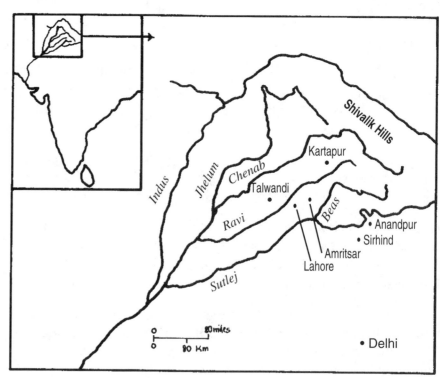

Rites of Passage

Because rites of passage establish religious commitment and understanding, they are especially important to Sikhs. The gurdwara, of course, is where many of the rituals take place. Most ceremonies are hallowed by the reading of the *Guru Granth*, although it may not be read from cover to cover each time.

Birth and Childhood

As soon as possible after the birth of a child, he or she is brought to the gurdwara for the naming ceremony. Relatives gather and celebrate as musicians sing hymns of gratitude for the heavenly gift of the newborn.

The naming of the infant is considered an act of providence. The reader opens the *Guru Granth* randomly and announces the teaching. The child's name must begin with the same letter with which the reading begins. As you recall, male Sikhs adopt the surname Singh, which means "lion", while female Sikhs are called Kaur, meaning "princess."

Some parents also request the amrit ceremony which originated with the Khalsa. After the sugar water is stirred with a sword, a few drops are fed to the infant, and the mother drinks the rest. In addition to a name, the baby receives its first *kara*, or steel bracelet.

Traditionally, Sikh birthdays are not highly festive events. Sometimes, the parents, in honor of their child's birth, provide for the langar, or community meal, in the gurdwara. Normally, a family celebrates quietly. Although presents are not usually given, money may be accepted on the child's behalf.

As they grow, Sikh children will be exposed to the teachings and lives of the ten gurus. One of the most challenging aspects of their education is learning Gurmurkhi, the language of the *Guru Granth*. Although it may take years to master Gurmurkhi—especially for Sikhs outside India—it is considered an essential part of the Sikh religion.

Finally, children will wear the Five K's. (See pages 232-233.)

Marriage

Marriage is a sacred event in Sikh life. Believing matrimony to be an expression of divine service to God and the Sikh community, all but one of the ten gurus married. Most marriages are arranged by the couple's families, as is customary in India. Sikhs believe that marriage includes the wedding of two families, not only two individuals.

Most Sikh couples enjoy an engagement ceremony, although it is not required. Interestingly, the bride and groom celebrate their engagement separately. First, in the presence of the *Guru Granth*, men from both families gather at the groom's house, bestowing gifts of money and food. Likewise, women gather at the bride's house where she accepts presents, including the red head scarf—sent by male relatives—which she will wear at the wedding ceremony. Although not required, the bride's hands and feet are often decorated with beautiful designs drawn in henna, a red dye.

Rites of Passage *(cont.)*

Marriage *(cont.)*

Most weddings happen at the gurdwara. The only requirement, of course, is that *Guru Granth* be present. The bride dresses in a traditional Indian *sari* while the groom wears a turban. Amidst the singing of hymns, the congregation gathers and is seated. The groom bows to the *Guru Granth* and then is joined by the bride. Next, a Sikh leader delivers a speech expounding on the significance of Sikh marriage, which is seen as the union of two souls. The father of the bride then ties together the newlyweds' scarves, placing his daughter into her husband's care and symbolizing their devotion to God.

The heart of the marriage occurs with the reading of the sacred marriage hymn written by Guru Ram Das. After each of the four verses, the couple circles the *Guru Granth* in an act of reverence, symbolizing the spirals of spiritual fulfillment marriage offers. During the fourth circuit, the couple is joyously showered with flower petals.

Death

Like Hindus, Sikhs believe in reincarnation—that human life is a passage in a great spiritual evolution. Therefore, Sikhs do not mourn after a person's death. Rather, they look upon death as a transition toward God, the ultimate reality. Sikhs cremate their dead, returning the body to the natural elements.

After the body is cleansed and dressed, it is blanketed with a white sheet and carried on a platform to the cremation grounds. Verses from the *Guru Granth* are recited, hymns which offer strength to the soul of the deceased and those who remain behind. The body is laid on the funeral pyre which is lit by a family member. Afterward, *prasad*, traditional Indian sweets, are distributed, signifying the continuance of life.

Shortly thereafter, relatives of the deceased read the *Guru Granth*. The family receives visitors who wear white, black, or brown. Ten days after the funeral, the *bhog* ceremony is performed. This time is spent reciting hymns and praying in silence. In the years to come, the anniversary of the departed is commemorated with bhog ceremonies and annual offerings to charities.

Name _____

Women and Sikhism

Sikhism was born in India, a religious country where women were, and continue to be, treated subordinately. Although Sikhism synthesizes fundamental beliefs from Hinduism and Islam, it assumes its own stance toward the dignity and equality of the sexes. Guru Nanak and his successors did not accept women and men as separate aspects of humanity. Rather, they are seen as part of a whole, born with the same divine potential. This equality is manifest in the gurdwara, where a man or a woman may lead the congregation in prayer or read from the *Guru Granth*. Women are also ensured a political voice in their communities.

Some of the religious customs which the Sikh gurus had to dispel are quite disturbing. Take, for example, the Hindu practice of *sati* whereby a widow is expected to commit suicide at her husband's cremation, or the Islamic custom which requires women to veil themselves. Perhaps most shocking is the practice of destroying female infants, considered less worthy than males. Finally, there is the Hindu belief, *sutak*, which considers the house of a newborn impure for forty days following the birth. To this belief, Guru Nanak responded thus:

> "All belief in sutak is superstition, born of illusion.
> Birth and death come by decree; man comes and goes by His will.
> Food and drink are all pure, coming as apportioned by God.
> Nanak, those who have acquired awareness of God,
> By his grace are not deluded by thought of sutak."

Guru Nanak liberated his followers from the belief in sutak by placing the source of purity and impurity in the individual's mind, rather than in some preordained time or place.

Although the Ten Gurus are Sikhism's most famous figures, several women have taken their places in Sikh history. In Hazus Sahib, a town in South India, a monument commemorates the heroism of one such woman, Mai Bago. In the early 18th century, she rallied disheartened Sikh soldiers back into besieged Anandpur. In 1705, she participated in the battle of Mukstar.

Mata Sahib Kaur, wife of Guru Gobind Singh, sweetened the amrit at the original Khalsa ceremony. In a manner of speaking, she is the mother of the Khalsa. She assumed the surname Kaur, now used by all Khalsa women. In fact, Khalsa members considered themselves to be blessed as sons and daughters of Guru Gobind Sing and Mata Sahib Kaur.

Extension:
Freewrite your response to the role of women in Sikhism.

_____

_____

_____

_____

_____

Sikh Holy Places

You have already read in detail about the most holy of Sikh places, the Golden Temple in Amritsar. Besides this sacred shrine, there are five other significant places of Sikh pilgrimage. They are called *takhts*, or places of authority. These are the locations where most of the Sikh religious and political policies are made. Of course, there are many other holy Sikh sites throughout India.

Akal Takht

Akal Takht, or the "Throne of the Formless," actually faces the Golden Temple. Constructed by Guru Hargobind in 1609, the Throne is a five-story, golden-domed building which houses the Sikh administration. Visitors witness daily ceremonies commemorating Sikh leaders. Gurus' weapons are displayed, including the actual swords of Hargobind and Gobind Singh. While honoring the past, the Akal Takht remains the center of Sikh authority and political decision making.

Patna Sahib

Patna Sahib, the birthplace of Guru Gobind Singh, is another place of Sikh pilgrimage. Five hundred miles east of Delhi, this city rests on the Ganges River. Sikhs who travel there visit a shrine to Gobind Singh, who lived his childhood in Patna. Here, the guru's relics are displayed, including his weapons, a pair of sandals, and some writings. There are also many tales about Gobind Singh's early years. One tells about the childless queen, Mania. When Gobind Singh was only four years old, he told Mania that he would be her son. The Queen often fed corn to her "honorary" son. In remembrance of their bond, langars at Patna Sahib serve corn.

Anandpur

Anandpur is the site where Guru Gobind Singh formed the Khalsa. A monument honoring this event is a popular destination for Sikhs. Many visitors come here to watch the annual reenactment of the founding of the Khalsa.

After Guru Tegh Bahadur was martyred in 1675, a disciple carried the guru's head to Anandpur for cremation. In commemoration of the guru, a gurdwara was built on the spot where his ashes were buried.

Takht Sri Hazur

The temple of Hazur Sahib stands at the place where Guru Gobind Singh died in Nander, South India. Built by Maharajah Ranjit Singh between 1832 and 1837, it is an elaborate two-story gurdwara modeled after the Golden Temple. The *Guru Granth* is read aloud constantly.

The temple's treasury contains a variety of the guru's relics, including five golden swords and royal clothing. Interestingly, the stable at the gurdwara has a horse believed to be a descendent of one of Gobind Singh's horses. This animal is decorated during holiday processions.

Damdama Sahib

South of Amritsar rests the gurdwara Damdama Sahib, another shrine to Guru Gobind Singh. This place, where Gobind Singh did much of his writing, is known as the seat of Sikh learning. In fact, it was here that the final version of the *Guru Granth* was completed under Gobind Singh's supervision. Among other relics on display are the guru's sword, gun, and mirror. Finally, a pillar at the gurdwara contains the following words of Gobind Singh:

> "To the Khalsa belongs all
> My home, my body, and all that I possess."

Sikh Holidays and Festivals

Guru Nanak felt that all days are holy since they are all expressions of the ultimate reality. In his time, he asked Sikhs to cast aside astrology, a popular Hindu custom. However, Sikhs do celebrate two kinds of holidays.

First, being part of India, Sikhs inherited the Hindu calendar and several Indian holidays which they imbue with special meaning. Secondly, several days in the Sikh calendar commemorate events in Sikh history. These days are called *gurbpurbs*, or "holidays of the gurus."

Baisakhi: New Year Festival

Baisakhi, falling on April 13 or 14, is the New Year's Day for both Indians and Sikhs. Commemorating religious, political, and social events, this holiday is among the most meaningful in Sikhism.

Like Hindus, Sikhs give thanks for the harvest, gathering to listen to the teachings of the gurus. Livestock are sold and the corn harvest begun.

The festival became more profound in 1699, when, on New Year's Day, Guru Gobind Singh created the Khalsa. Many Sikhs, therefore, choose to be initiated into the Khalsa during the festival of Baisakhi. Others regard it as a time to renew their religious commitment. As at most meaningful Sikh happenings, the *Guru Granth* is read aloud.

After the Baisakhi festival of 1919, the holiday was never the same. The Indian government, fearing a Sikh uprising, had forbidden Sikhs to gather during Baisakhi. But a group defied the government, assembling near the Golden Temple in Amritsar. The Indian army reacted, shooting into the Sikh crowd and killing hundreds. To this day, Sikhs commemorate the 1919 massacre with a rally at the site of the massacre.

Most Sikhs try to gather at the Golden Temple during Baisakhi. Pilgrims from all over the world pay homage to the spiritual and worldly significance of this holiday. Finally, in the spirit of renewal, gurdwaras replace their Sikh flags with new ones.

Divali

Another adopted Hindu festival is Divali, the "festival of light." Sikhs share some of the Indian customs, using the time to whitewash their houses and then decorating them with clay lanterns. But to Sikhs, Divali reminds them primarily of the imprisonment and valor of their sixth guru, Guru Hargobind.

In the early 17th century, Guru Hargobind, along with fifty-two Hindu princes, was imprisoned by Mogul rulers. On the day of Divali, the Emperor decided to release the guru. However, Hargobind refused to leave unless his companions were also liberated. Legend has it that the Emperor agreed upon one condition: that all fifty princes must leave together through a narrow passage while holding onto the Guru's clothing! How did Hargobind succeed? He had a cloak made with long tassels on its ends, tassels long enough for all fifty of the Hindu princes to grasp and walk the narrow passageway to liberation.

The festival of Divali lasts for three days. Crowded with music and celebration, the Golden Temple is alight with glory, while lanterns float on the surrounding sacred pool.

Name _____

Sikh Holidays and Festivals *(cont.)*

Basant

The spring festival of Basant, which means "spring," is a happy Punjabi celebration. In honor of the blooming mustard plants, Sikhs eat yellow rice and wear yellow clothes. Traditionally, children fly kites and take part in kite-flying competitions.

Gurpurbs

As you recall, gurpurbs commemorate events in Sikh history. The martyrdom of Guru Arjan, for example, is remembered in the Sikh month of Jaith (May or June). Guru Arjan was tortured to death with hot oils. Thus, on the anniversary of his death, Sikhs make offerings of cold milk. The martyrdom of the sons of Guru Gobind Singh is remembered when Punjabi farmers prepare a festive langar, or community meal. This is in contrast to the tragedy of Gobind Singh's sons who were kept captive by Muslim rulers. Rather than convert to Islam and be released, the boys died, heroes to their faith.

The birthdays of Guru Nanak and Guru Gobind Singh are internationally celebrated, while the birthdays of the other eight gurus are more locally observed. During most gurpurbs, a colorful procession carries the *Guru Granth* through the streets. Tradition is observed when the scripture is read from cover to cover.

Gurpurbs are most often celebrated in the gurdwara. They represent a chance for Sikhs to congregate and deepen their bonds. Often, leaders will lecture while others will perform Sikh plays and music. This is especially important outside of India where Sikh communities must work hard to martial their spirit.

Extension:

On the lines below, compare any one of these Sikh holidays and festivals to another holiday or festival with which you are familiar.

_____

_____

_____

_____

_____

_____

_____

_____

_____

The Sikh Calendar

The Sikhs use the Hindu lunar calendar, each month beginning with a new moon. Sikhs also share several celebrations with their cousin religion. Besides these holidays, they celebrate *gurpurbs* which commemorate an important event in the life of a guru.

Here are the months of the Sikh calendar, along with their Gregorian equivalents. Below, you will also find a list of major festivals.

Magh (January/February)	**Phagan** (February/March)	**Chait** (March/April)
Vasakh (April/May)	**Jaith** (May/June)	**Har** (June/July)
Sawan (July/August)	**Bhadro** (August/September)	**Asun** (September/October)
Katik (October/November)	**Magar** (November/December)	**Poh** (December/January)

Some Significant Festivals and Holidays

Magh: *Maghi*

Phagan: *Hola Mohala* (military festival)

Vasakh: *Baisakhi* (New Year festival, festival celebrating founding of Khalsa)

Jaith: martyrdom of Guru Arjan

Har: birthday of Guru Har Krishna

Asun: birthday of Guru Ram

Katik: birthday of Guru Nanak; Divali celebration

Magar: martyrdom of Guru Tegh Bahardur

Poh: birthday of Guru Gobind Singh

Sikh Symbols

Sword, Dagger, and Shield

The principal Sikh symbol is the sword, dagger, and shield. This emblem, which originated with the Khalsa, appears on a flag above every gurdwara. The curved swords represent both the ultimate truth as well as the willingness to defend it. The circle, also a shield, reminds followers that there is one source, yet again it must be defended. Finally, the martial spirit of the community is represented by the double-edged sword used to stir the amrit during Khalsa ceremonies.

Ik Oankar

Ik oankar is the symbol representing the first words of the most famous Sikh hymn, the "*Mool Mantra.*" This mantra, the first composed by Guru Nanak, states the basic beliefs of Sikhism and appears before each chapter of the *Guru Granth*. The first words, Ik oankar, mean "there is one God." This symbol appears on the canopy above the sacred text. Here is the symbol written in the Gurmukhi script.

The following page contains the "Mool Mantra" in its entirety.

The Mool Mantra

Ik Oankar
THERE IS ONE GOD

sat naam
TRUTH IS ITS NAME

karta purkh
CREATOR OF ALL

nir bhau
WITHOUT FEAR

nir vair
WITHOUT HATE

akal murat
TIMELESS AND FORMLESS

ajooni sabhang
UNBORN AND ENLIGHTENED

guru prasad
KNOWN BY THE GRACE OF THE GURU

Name _____

Vocabulary Wordsearch

Use the clues to discover which Sikh terms you should search for.

```
G J S F D H W O I R F W R T K A C C H A C L I D Q O R E P D J L A W E E S B
U F A S A T U R B A N S D R Y K U I R V K K P U Y W A A D U B N M G W E T Y
R D F H J K M U T A U R C Z A T E C H J A K F D W M E S R D N Q R D K E S H
U N V S F J W R R S D T T N Y G Z X D R R I Y G R A E Q I T T J U G X A S S
G H G U R U G A S L E T A U Y T U Y F D A F S I G V N B V V Z A A B N M L E
R C M L A I R U R A F N A F G H L R F D G H T X A Q W Y E N J C E B R F F R
A J F J A D J I W H F K S G S F F D D S A D J U Y U T V R C Z S E R A B G V
N M C V A A E W R K T Y S I N G H D A W H J K M F S A A S L P I H O G J K I
T S D G F G H J J N A P R I K L G H X S A F R H N B H K C G Z D H N N Y U C
H O N B L D A K F J T I P O T W J G D G N R E K A U R F F G N K M H A B D E
D A F E T G O L D E N T E M P L E G I I C N A Z P R A S A D R T W Q L V D W
A S D F N K S D G J L S K G J K S D R H T F N K A H G N A K A I W I O W A F
```

1. Most Sikhs wear these on their heads. _____

2. comb holding hair in place _____

3. Sewa is the act of _____ .

4. principal Sikh holy place _____

5. Sikh group started by Guru Gobind Singh _____

6. Most Sikhs live in this northern region of India. _____

7. the second Guru _____

8. uncut hair _____

9. the community kitchen _____

10. a Sikh holy leader _____

11. steel bracelet _____

12. Sikh temple _____

13. Sikh holy book _____

14. last name meaning "lion" _____

15. He founded Sikhism. _____

16. trousers worn by warriors _____

17. last name meaning "princess" _____

18. sweetened water used for ceremonies _____

19. There are five of these in the Punjab. _____

20. double-edged dagger or sword _____

Name _____

Quiz and Review

Part One: For questions one through fifteen, fill in the spaces with the correct answers.

1. Sikhism began around the year _____ .

2. When Nanak was born, _____ ruled India.

3. Two of the five rivers running through the Punjab are _____ and _____ .

4. Guru _____ founded the "Pool of Nectar."

5. Guru _____ founded the Golden Temple.

6. Guru _____ was martyred for religious freedom.

7. Guru _____ created the Khalsa.

8. The Punjabi alphabet is called _____ .

9. The Guru Granth contains 5,894 _____ .

10. Two countries bordering the Punjab are _____ and _____ .

11. Khalsa members wear the _____ as visible signs.

12. A Sikh temple is called a _____ .

13. In 1984, the Golden Temple was _____ .

14. Holidays commemorating Sikh history are called _____ .

15. The wife of Guru Gobind Singh, _____ , is considered the mother of the Khalsa.

Part Two: Respond to the following questions and prompts in the spaces below.

1. What happened when young Nanak was brought forth for the Hindu ceremony of the sacred thread? How does this relate to Sikhism?

_____

_____

_____

2. Community is very important to Sikhs. Describe at least two social customs or institutions capturing this spirit of togetherness.

_____

_____

_____

Name _____

Quiz and Review *(cont.)*

Part Two *(cont.)*

3. What is contained in the *Guru Granth*? Who are its authors? Briefly describe how it is treated. Why is it treated this way?

   _____

   _____

   _____

   _____

4. From what you have read about the Punjab and the Golden Temple, write a brief account of the political history of the Sikh people.

   _____

   _____

   _____

   _____

5. How do Sikhs look upon death? What are their funerals like?

   _____

   _____

   _____

   _____

6. What status do women hold in Sikhism? How is this different from other religions?

   _____

   _____

   _____

   _____

7. Explain in your own words the meaning of the "Mool Mantra."

   _____

   _____

   _____

   _____

Confucius: China's Great Teacher

In order to appreciate Taoism, we must first learn about the great Chinese teacher and sage, Confucius. Born in 551 BCE, many of the ideas Confucius taught still remain central to Chinese life.

Like the birth of so many sages, Confucius' birth also was preceded by a divine vision. Legend has it that his mother saw five elderly men leading a unicorn toward her. The magical animal knelt and spit out a piece of jade which was inscribed with the promise that her baby would be a "king without a crown." When his mother retreated to a cave to give birth, the dwelling was protected by dragons. The nature spirits rejoiced, and a heavenly stream appeared.

But Confucius was born in a difficult time. China, once unified, was now in disarray, divided by warring provinces. The Emperor, who once held the country together, was powerless within the separate provinces.

When Confucius was only three years old, his father died. His mother raised him, seeing him through school, where he excelled. Soon he went to work as a tax collector, but in time he was disillusioned by the ways of government and the condition of China. So, at the age of 22, the young man set out to become a teacher, feeling deeply that he had something useful to share.

In many ways, Confucius was a revolutionary teacher. Besides learning skills—such as writing, music, and mathematics—he felt that students should learn to be virtuous, to achieve moral character, and to live a life of harmony. He was also equally concerned with *how* to learn as much as *what* to learn. Education, he felt, is more than memorizing facts and learning skills. It is the flowering of intelligence and sensitivity. In this spirit, Confucius accepted all as his students, regardless of their social positions, as long as they were serious about learning. The only students he turned away were lazy ones! Soon he had thousands of followers.

In a time of political uncertainty and civil violence, Confucius looked to China's past for guidance. He felt that some rulers of the past maintained harmony because their own lives were in order. Thus, he taught that a peaceful society begins in the family. If there is goodness and respect in relationships, then the community will benefit.

Confucius focused on five basic relationships. These include (1) parent and child, (2) husband and wife, (3) siblings, (4) emperor and subject, and (5) friends. The most important of these is the relationship between parent and child. It is the child's duty to have reverence for the parent and for the parent to love the child. If this central connection is harmonious, then the other four basic relationships will follow.

Confucius believed most of all in moral conduct and good education. These would lead to wisdom. Therefore, he proclaimed that China's rulers should be the highly educated, those who have acquired wisdom from studying the Chinese classics. These texts of poetry and history contain rules of behavior from which Confucius gained many of his ideas. In fact, in the latter part of his life he studied and edited the classics. However, his ambition to advise China's rulers never came to pass. Sadly, at the time of his death in 479 BCE, Confucius considered himself a failure. He died at the age of seventy-two.

China in the Time of Confucius and Lao-Tzu

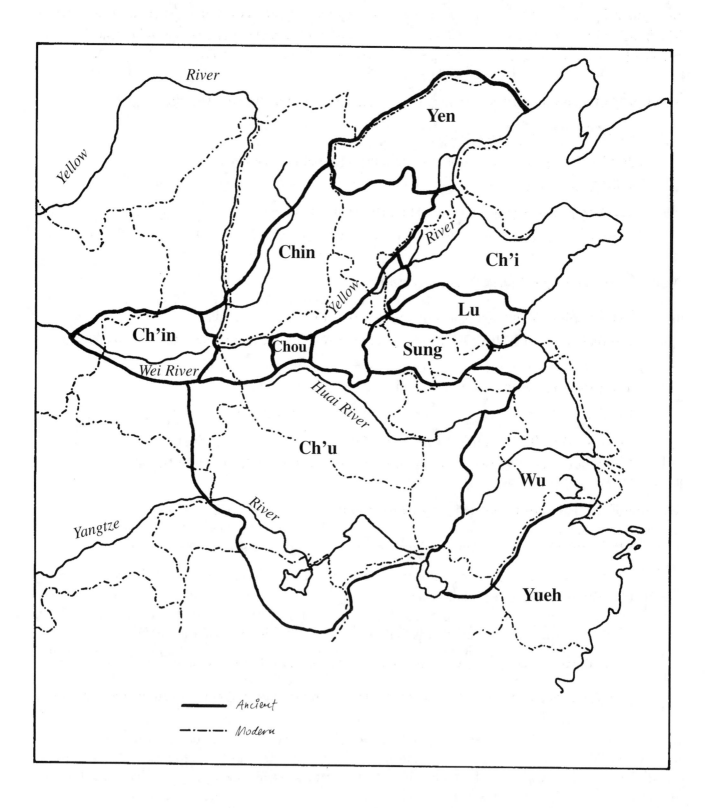

The Analects: Teachings of Confucius

Although Confucius felt himself a failure, his teachings were preserved by his students and spread throughout China. As his ideas gained popularity, they were written down in a text called *The Analects*. The book contains accounts of his life and conversations with students. The whole of his teaching became known as Confucianism. Here are a few passages from *The Analects*.

The first dialogue takes place as Confucius is traveling with a student, Jan Yu.

Confucius: What a dense population!

Jan Yu: The people have grown so numerous. What is to be done?

Confucius: Enrich them.

Jan Yu: And when they are enriched, then what is to be done?

Confucius: Educate them.

Next, Confucius is questioned by several students:

Tzu Lu: How should one worship ghosts and spirits?

Confucius: We still don't know how to serve people; how can we learn about ghosts and spirits?

Tzu Lu: What about death?

Confucius: We don't yet know about life; how can we know about death?

Tzu Kung: Is there one rule for moral conduct?

Confucius: Do not unto others as you would not want others to do unto you.

One day Confucius saw a woman weeping by a tomb.

"You weep as though so sad," he said.

"It is so," she replied. "Here where I stand my husband and son and father-in-law were killed by a fierce tiger."

"Then why don't you leave this awful place?" asked Confucius.

"Here there are tigers," the woman answered, "but at least the government is not bad."

"My students!" announced Confucius, "listen and remember: bad government is worse than a fierce tiger!"

Taoism

Name _____

Questions: The Life and Teachings of Confucius

Respond to the following questions in full sentences. Be sure to use details to support your answers.

1. In her vision, the mother of Confucius was told that her son would be a "king without a crown." In what ways did this prophecy hold true? In what ways did it not come to pass?

   _____

   _____

   _____

2. Describe the condition of China at the time of Confucius' birth. How did this state of affairs contribute to the content and effectiveness of his teaching?

   _____

   _____

   _____

3. According to Confucius, what constitutes a good education? What things are important for the student to learn? Do you feel like these things are valued in your own educational experience?

   _____

   _____

   _____

4. Deeply concerned about government, Confucius had strong feeling about who should govern the people. According to him, what are the qualities of a great ruler? Who should rule the country?

   _____

   _____

   _____

5. List the five relationships that Confucius considered most important. Of these, which was most critical and why?

   _____

   _____

   _____

Name _____

Relationships

Most religions and schools of thought emphasize the importance of right relationships. In fact, it is impossible to go through life without being related to people and to nature. Confucius, of course, emphasized the importance of relationships within the family.

In the space below, write about an important relationship in your own life. Why is it important to you? Does it achieve the sense of respect that Confucius preached?

_____

_____

_____

_____

_____

_____

_____

_____

_____

_____

_____

_____

_____

_____

_____

_____

_____

_____

_____

_____

_____

Lao-Tzu and the Origin of Taoism

Throughout Chinese history, Taoism has paralleled Confucianism, influencing all areas of Chinese culture, including literature, art, and government. Like Confucianism, the origin of Taosim can be traced back to one man. He is Lao-Tzu.

Lao-Tzu was a distinguished scholar and keeper of royal archives in the province of Luoyang. Interestingly, tradition has it that as a young man, Confucius met Lao-Tzu. But when he spoke to the scholar about his attempts to improve China's social order, Lao-Tzu answered thus: "This talk of duty to others drives me crazy! Leave the world in its original simplicity. As the wind blows where it will, let virtue establish itself." Finally, Lao-Tzu told Confucius that his teachings were "of no use."

Lao-Tzu's response captures the essential difference between Taoism and Confucianism: one is concerned with social order and regulating behavior, while the other focuses on individual life and spirituality. However, they are not mutually exclusive. In China, a person might be both a Taoist and a Confucian.

But how did Taoism begin? What are its doctrines? The essence of Taoism lies in a collection of meditations called the *Tao Te Ching*. These sayings set forth the virtue of *Tao*, the eternal "way." Although the origin of the book is disputed, legend tells us that when Lao-Tzu was preparing to leave his city for the remote West, the gatekeeper demanded that he leave the people some words of wisdom. He consented and created one of the most influential scriptures of all time.

Unlike Confucius' doctrines of moral conduct, the Way of the Tao is the way of "no action." This means allowing the universe to take its natural course, to be one with the flow of nature, and thus to penetrate the mystery and unfathomable source of all life. To be concerned with artificialities and personal ambitions could only interfere with the Tao. Lao-Tzu taught that human beings are inherently good, but blinded by their opinions and their need to do things. This creates internal disharmony, which contaminates social order and nature.

Lao-Tzu felt that people should not concern themselves with the "spirit world" or the formalities and superstitions of religion. Those were merely distractions. Rather, by being quiet and following the ways of nature, one would spontaneously discover what is true and eternal. However, as Taoism evolved, magical practices continued among the people.

Like Confucius, Lao-Tzu believed that those in power should be wise. If the leaders have no personal ambition, then the country will have harmony. But Lao-Tzu's emphasis on non-action included the government. Thus, he deplored taxation and warfare and social "improvement." In fact, the whole notion of morality, he believed, was deceptive. The *Tao Te Ching* stresses that both good and bad are only ideas. Ultimately, the answer lies in a life of simplicity, holding close to one's heart the "three treasures." They are love, frugality, and non-ambition.

Although Lao-Tzu never intended to begin a new religion, about 700 years after his death, a group adopted him as their leader and formed Taosim. As you will see, it is questionable whether Lao-Tzu would want to be associated with the pursuit of supernatural powers and mythic islands that are now found in popular Taoism.

Reading from the Tao Te Ching

One

The Tao that can be told is not the eternal Tao.

The name that can be named is not the eternal name.

The nameless is the beginning of heaven and earth.

The named is the mother of ten thousand things.

Ever desireless, one can see the mystery.

Ever desiring, one can see the manifestations.

These two spring from the same source but differ in name;
    this appears as darkness.

Darkness within darkness.

The gate to all mystery.

Six

The valley spirit never dies;

It is the woman, primal mother.

Her gateway is the root of heaven and earth.

It is like a veil barely seen.

Use it; it will never fail.

Thirteen

Accept disgrace willingly.

Accept misfortune as the human condition.

What do you mean by "accept disgrace willingly"?

Accept being unimportant.

Do not be concerned with loss or gain.

This is called "accepting disgrace willingly."

What do you mean by "accept misfortune as the human condition"?

Misfortune comes from having a body.

Without a body, how could there be misfortune?

Thirty-Seven

Tao abides in non-action.

Yet nothing is left undone.

If kings and lords observe this,

The ten thousand things would develop naturally.

It they still desired to act,

They would return to the simplicity of formless substance.

Without form there is no desire.

Without desire there is tranquility.

And in this way all things would be at peace.

Reading from the Tao Te Ching *(cont.)*

Forty

Returning is the motion of the Tao.
Yielding is the way of the Tao.
The ten thousand things are born of being.
Being is born of not being.

Forty-Three

The softest things in the universe
Overcomes the hardest things in the universe.
That without substance can enter where there is no room.
Hence I know the value of non-action.
Teaching without words and work without doing
Are understood by few.

Seventy

My words are easy to understand and easy to perform,
Yet no man under heaven knows them or practices them.
My words have ancient beginnings.
My actions are disciplined.
Because men do not understand, they have no knowledge of me.
Those that know me are few;
Those that abuse me are honored.
Therefore the sage wears rough clothing and holds the jewel in his heart.

Seventy-Eight

Under heaven nothing is more soft and yielding than water.
Yet for attacking the solid and strong, nothing is better;
It has no equal.
The weak can overcome the strong;
The supple can overcome the stiff.
Under heaven everyone knows this,
Yet no one puts it into practice.
Therefore the sage says:
    He who takes upon himself the humiliation of the people
        is fit to rule them.
    He who takes upon himself the country's disasters deserves
        to be king of the universe.
The truth often sounds paradoxical.

Name _____

Questions: Lao-Tzu and The Tao Te Ching

Respond to the following questions and prompts in full sentences. Be sure to use details to support your answers.

1. Explain briefly the essential difference between the teachings of Lao-Tzu and the teachings of Confucius. Why did Lao-Tzu discourage Confucius? What beliefs did they share?

   _____

   _____

2. How did the *Tao Te Ching* come to be written?

   _____

   _____

3. How is water like the Tao?

   _____

   _____

4. Explain what Lao-Tzu means by "non action." Why is it best?

   _____

   _____

5. What did Lao-Tzu feel about religious ritual and superstition?

   _____

   _____

6. According to the *Tao Te Ching*, what are the qualities of a great leader?

   _____

   _____

7. Describe the tone of the *Tao Te Ching*.

   _____

   _____

Taoist Magic: Chang Tao-Ling and the Elixir of Immortality

So far we have learned about a school of Taoism concerned solely with the natural order of life. Its followers try to harmonize with timeless rhythms of nature, thereby achieving wisdom. Another school, "popular Taoism," is quite different. This ancient sect is filled with gods and goddesses, with guardian spirits and magic elixirs. Rather than simply harmonize with nature, Taoist masters achieve power over the universe. Popular Taoism is therefore rich with tales of the supernatural, with sages disappearing into thin air, commanding the elements, and achieving immortality. While many of its deities came from Chinese cults, others were adopted from Buddhism and transformed into the colorful and instructive world of Chinese mythology.

Perhaps the greatest contributor to popular Taoism is Chang Tao-Ling, revered as the Heavenly Teacher. In the second century CE, he had a great following, for legend has it that he succeeded in discovering an elixir, or potion, for immortality. However, the mixture required very expensive ingredients which he could not afford. So Tao-Ling moved to the high mountains where he believed he could communicate with the immortals. The story tells that hundreds of immortals, including Lao-Tzu himself, descended and taught him secrets of healing. Soon Tao-Ling's magic powers of healing attracted a large community and great wealth. Now he was able to afford his elixir of immortality. However, he drank only half of the potion, for he wanted to remain with the living and lead them in the way. Apparently, he had all manner of terrific abilities. He could take on different forms, read minds, and divide himself into many parts!

Like most great teachers, Tao-Ling demanded great austerity and faith from his disciples. Only the truly dedicated could achieve mastery, and that only after they were severely tested. One such student was Chao Tzeng. He passed seven tests of devotion to Taoism. When he first arrived, he was scoffed at and humiliated, but his commitment remained fixed. He was also tempted by a beautiful woman, but he did not touch her. Then, as he was walking down a mountain path, caskets of gold appeared. But he took none of them, for he knew his treasure lay elsewhere.

Chao's final test of faith was the most dramatic. His teacher led several disciples to a towering cliff, where halfway down grew a peach tree. "Whoever retrieves a peach," announced the heavenly teacher, "will achieve immortality." Of all the disciples, only Chang was unafraid, leaping off the cliff and landing safely on the peach tree. After throwing the peaches up to his teacher, Chao had great difficulty climbing up the wall. And when he reached an impassable ledge, hanging on for his life, Tao-Ling helped him. The master reached over the cliffside, and his arm suddenly grew longer and longer until his hand met his student's and lifted him to safety.

But the test was not over. Now that all the peaches had been eaten, Tao-Ling leapt off the cliff to get some more. To his disciples' surprise, he fell all the way to the earth! Only Chao and one other student were not affected. Without a thought, they jumped off the cliff, landing safely in their teacher's company. Legend has it that at that moment Chang Tao-Ling and his two disciples ascended to Heaven forever.

The Eight Immortals

Popular Taoism is polytheistic. It contains many gods for specific aspects of life. There is a god of wealth, literature, medicine, and even a god of the kitchen! Some of these deities began as mortals, achieving immortality through time.

One famous group of deities is the Eight Immortals. Beloved by the people, they are depicted in paintings and statues, appearing in temples and in homes. By the 13th century CE, this eclectic group had a place in Chinese mythology and was featured prominently in Taoist tales. Their variety of personalities and positions mirror the differences of people in the world. However, each of these deities have one thing in common: they have rejected the world's values and sought for something deeper. Here, very briefly, is a description of each of the Eight Immortals.

Li Tieguai

Li Tieguai, whose name means "Li the iron crutch," began as a Taoist master who was able to leave his body and let his spirit wander. Legend has it that before one such journey he instructed a student to watch over his body for seven days. If he should fail to return after a week, the disciple should go ahead and cremate the body. However, on the sixth day the faithful student was summoned to his own mother's deathbed. In a moment of crisis, the student had his teacher's body cremated. Li Tieguai returned the next day to a pile of ashes.

Sadly, Li's spirit wandered. But soon he came upon the fresh corpse of a one-legged beggar. The master chose to inhabit his body, and the gods gifted him with a gold band to keep his hair neat and an iron crutch to help him walk. Now Li sought the disciple who cremated his body a day early.

When Li found the student, he did not reprimand him. Instead, in his compassion he brought the man's dead mother back to life!

Han Chongli

Some believe that Han Chongli was a Taoist priest trained in the art of alchemy. He could change base metals into gold and silver. Legend has it that he used his treasure house of wealth to feed the multitudes during a famine.

Others claim that Han was a hermit who achieved immortality. He is depicted as an elderly man with a fan made of feathers.

Lu Dongbin

A disciple of Han Chongli, Lu Dongbin was known for his miracles and acts of service. He is said to have turned an old woman's well water into wine. He is also known for stocking a lake with fish for a town suffering from hunger.

Lu is shown carrying a sword, which keeps away demons, and a fly whisk shaped like the tail of a horse.

Chang Guolao

The elderly Chang Guolao is based on an 8th century Taoist sage. As an immortal, he is always shown riding a white donkey. Fortunately, when he tires of riding, he can fold the donkey up and place it in his bag!

The Eight Immortals *(cont.)*

Tsao Guojiu

While all the immortals are virtuous, not all of them began so. Tsao Guojiu lived in the 11th century, the uncle of an empress. (His name actually means "uncle of the Emperor.") He is commonly illustrated wearing court robes and carrying a wooden tablet used when one stood before the emperor.

Tsao had a wicked younger brother who murdered a man and then seduced the man's wife. Legend has it that the man's ghost appeared in court, and the judge had the criminal arrested. Tsao, trying to protect his brother, attempted to murder the widow. She escaped, and now both brothers were locked in prison. Fortunately for them, the empress, their niece, took pity. She soon convinced her husband, the emperor, to declare general amnesty throughout the kingdom, and her uncles were set free. Rather than return to his worldly ways, Tsao devoted himself to Taoism.

Han Chiangzi

The nephew of a famous 9th century poet, Han Chiangzi's is a story of resurrection. The tale goes that this young man died when he fell from a peach tree, but soon afterwards came back to life. (The peach tree, you may recall, is associated with immortality.) This is why Han carries either peaches or flowers.

Lan Tsaiho

Lan Tsaiho is also depicted as a young man. Legend has it that he was a performer who renounced worldly ways. He sang and danced in the streets, convincing his countrymen to become Taoists.

Ho Chiangu

Ho Chiangu achieved immortality with a gift of grace from Lu Dongbin. When she was a little girl, she got hopelessly lost wandering the mountains. Lu Dongbin appeared and, with the gift of a peach, showed her the way home. After Ho arrived safely, she ate the heavenly fruit and instantly achieved the power of prophecy and the blessing of immortality. She is shown carrying a lotus.

264

Religious Customs

Even before the advent of Communism in China in the 1950s, Taoism began gradually to fade as a popular religion. According to United Nations figures, in 1985 there were an estimated 20 million Taoists, mostly in Taiwan and Hong Kong. Although many of the popular religious customs have faded, Taosim still influences Chinese thought. Here are a few ceremonies, some of which still remain alive in East Asian households. Like all Taoist actions, they are concerned with harmony, with the balance of *yin* and *yang*, the feminine and masculine energies.

Birth

When parents are expecting a child, they conduct ceremonies meant to drive away evil spirits. After the birth, the parents send announcements written on red paper. Red is the color of luck and the color of yang. When the baby is a month old, parents send eggs, dyed red, to friends and relatives—an even number for a boy and odd for a girl. (Even is yin and odd is yang.)

The father usually names the child, although he will probably consult an astrologer. Offerings of gratitude are made on the child's birthday until he or she turns sixteen. Taoists often take their child to the temple to receive a priest's blessing and to buy a charm. This charm is usually a piece of paper containing words of blessing and protection.

Marriage

Marriages are usually arranged, although consent on all sides is expected. On the wedding day, the groom, along with some friends, honors the bride by escorting her to his house on a "marriage chair." The chair is a hand-held, beautifully decorated carriage.

The marriage ceremony takes place at the groom's household. The newlyweds drink from wine glasses tied together with a red cord. This echoes an ancient fable of the Man in the Moon, who tied together a husband and wife with a red cord. The couple then bows before ancestral tablets, declaring their loyalty to one another.

Death

Traditionally, the Chinese believe that Yellow Springs, an area just beneath the ground, is the dwelling place of the dead. Therefore, until the birth of Communism, Taoists buried their dead. Food offerings were very important. Often, the corpse's mouth was actually filled with rice and meat. It was also believed that the body and animal soul go downwards, while the spirit is elevated.

Communist rulers, intolerant of religion and superstition, discouraged burial and encouraged cremation. Although cremation is now standard in the cities, villagers still commonly bury their dead.

The Chinese Calendar and Zodiac

The Chinese Calendar is lunisolar. The lunar year is divided into 12 months of 29-30 days. Every few years an extra month is added. A solar year of 24 months (15 days each) complements the lunar year. Most holidays are calculated on the lunar cycles.

The Chinese lunar calendar is also the basis for the Chinese zodiac. The calendar extends into 12–year cycles, with an animal for each year. Thus, each Chinese New Year celebrates a different animal until the cycle repeats itself. Like the Western zodiac, personalities and events are believed to be influenced by the signs. For example, you were born in the Year of the Rooster if you were born in 1981. This means that you are supposed to be organized and attractive!

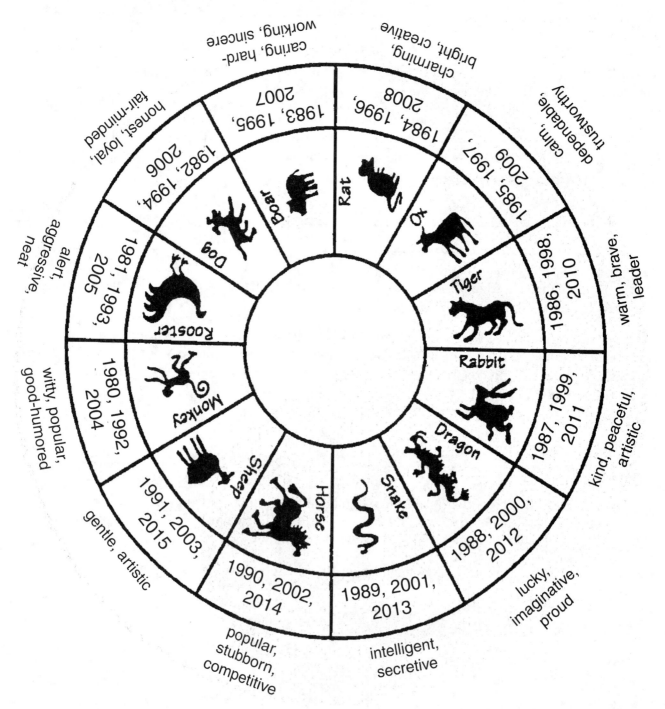

Taoist Symbols: The T'ai Chi

The T'ai Chi is the principal symbol of Taoism. As a circle, it represents the ultimate reality or the unchanging absolute. But within the eternal rests the temporal world, the world of happenings. This world is kept in harmony by the balance of opposites, known as yin and yang. Yin is represented in darkness and considered to be the feminine aspect; yin is the negative and destructive. Yang is the white area, the masculine, constructive principal. Importantly, both sides contain a small circle of the opposite. Thus, they exist in harmony with equality.

The T'ai Chi is one of the most popular religious symbols in the world. It has even been adopted by non-religious groups and popular cultures throughout the world. Brainstorm with the class for places you may have seen the T'ai Chi.

Name _____

Quiz and Review

Part One: For questions one through ten, fill in the spaces with the correct answers.

1. Lao-Tzu and Confucius were born in the _____ century BCE.

2. The teachings of Confucius are called the _____ .

3. The teachings of Lao-Tzu are called the _____ .

4. _____ Taoism was created about 700 years after Lao-Tzu.

5. Chang Tao-Ling was known as the _____ Teacher.

6. Some Taoist masters tried to achieve _____ .

7. One popular group of Chinese deities is called the Eight _____ .

8. Some believe that the dead live just below the ground, in the _____ .

9. In the T'ai Chi, the feminine aspect, or _____ , is dark. The masculine aspect, _____, is light.

10. To protect a newborn, parents often visit the temple and buy a _____ .

Part Two: Respond to the following questions and prompts in the spaces provided below.

1. Explain the differences between the two basic threads of Taoism—traditional Taoism and popular Taoism.

    _____

    _____

    _____

2. In your own words, try to define the Tao or the Way.

    _____

    _____

    _____

3. Choose one of the stories from popular Taoism—either the story of Chang Tao-Ling or the story of one of the Eight Immortals—and explain how the tale is instructive or moralistic. What lesson does it teach you?

    _____

    _____

    _____

Atheism and Agnosticism

In studying this book, you have learned a great deal about the most influential religions in the history of the world. But what about those people who do not belong to a religion at all? How do we refer to people who do not believe in God or a "higher" consciousness? For our purposes, we will use two defining words: *atheism* and *agnosticism*.

The dictionary defines atheism as the "disbelief in the existence of God." The key word here is "disbelief." In other words, atheism is the opposite of theism, which affirms spiritual reality and seeks to prove its existence. An atheist, however, does not necessarily abhor or disrespect religion or spirituality, which is a common misrepresentation. Rather, the atheist simply does not believe in a "higher power." Interestingly, the term "atheist" is commonly used to refute another's religious beliefs. This is known as theoretical atheism. For example, the Romans accused Jews and early Christians of being atheists because they refused to worship Roman gods.

The other form of atheism is practical atheism, which simply means a person who denies the existence of God. But again, this does not mean that life is meaningless. In fact, if there is no ordained order, argue some atheists, the humans are left to manage as dignified an existence as possible.

Agnosticism is defined as "the belief that there can be no proof of the existence of God without denying the possibility that God exists." The basic creed of the agnostic, is "I do not know."

In the case of both atheism and agnosticism, the impact of science cannot be underestimated. When Copernicus proved that the Earth was not the center of the universe, he was excommunicated. Charles Darwin shook the international religious community when he developed his theory of natural history, which challenged the validity of the Garden of Eden by suggesting that humans evolved from apes. Increasingly, scientific explanations for spiritual matters turned many people toward a materialistic view of the universe.

Of course, both these definitions oversimplify the non-religious. It would be silly to think that an atheist or agnostic lives without meaning, ethic, or beauty. In fact, there are many people who feel that religion has gone astray, that its followers have been deceived by the outer rituals and beliefs. Some even contend that religion has actually interfered with humanity's psychological evolution.

Extension:

Choose one of the following people and research to explain how he influenced atheism or agnosticism. Share what you learn with your class.

1. Charles Darwin

2. Ludwig Feuerback

3. Karl Marx

4. Immanuel Kant

5. Sigmund Freud

6. Thomas Huxley

Name _____

Religious Freedom and the First Amendment

Historically, religious freedom has not always come easily. There are countless examples of religious suppression and persecution. In World War II, as you recall, there was an effort to eradicate the Jews. Until 313 CE, Christians faced Roman persecution, forced to meet in secret and suffer the slaying of countless martyrs. Sadly, the list goes on. Even within a religion, certain denominations may be outcast. This was the case with the Quakers, a Christian sect which rejects formal ritual, sacraments, and priesthood. This non-violent group suffered great persecution during the United State's colonial period.

This is ironic, of course, because one of the central reasons the colonists came to the New World was for religious freedom. This liberty was so important that it was named in the First Amendment of the Bill of Rights. These amendments to the Constitution were put in place to secure the rights of individuals and to limit the power of the government. The First Amendment consists of three articles. The first article begins as follows:

> "Congress shall make no law respecting an establishment of religion, or prohibiting the free exercise thereof . . ."

In other words, the United States was not to have an "official" faith. The government was separate from religion. This is commonly known as the separation of church and state. People were free to practice their faith, whether they were Jews, Quakers, or Muslims. Unfortunately, this tolerance is difficult to achieve.

Another interesting development in the relationship between religion and government has to do with education. In the early 1960s, the Supreme Court said that public schools could not sponsor religious activities. In other words, religion—including prayer—was to be kept out of the schools. In school districts across the United States, this issue continues to be controversial. For instance, should a teacher be allowed to begin class with a prayer? Can a high school basketball team be allowed to say a prayer before its game?

Unfortunately, some schools have interpreted this Supreme Court decision to mean that they cannot teach about religion, while others have shied away from the subject because of its controversial nature. Nowadays, more and more educators and students are realizing it is essential to learn about religion—both for the sake of knowledge and for the sake of tolerance.

Extensions:

1. Make some notes here about your thoughts concerning religion and education. Then, as a class, discuss the issue.

   _____

   _____

2. Read the rest of the First Amendment of the Bill of Rights. How do the other articles support the first?

   _____

   _____

Religious Conflict and Religious Tolerance

> "God has made different religions to suit different aspirations, times, and countries. All doctrines are only so many paths; but a path is by no means God Himself. Indeed, one can reach God if one follows any of the paths with whole-hearted devotion. One may eat a cake with icing either straight or sidewise. It will taste sweet either way. As one can ascend to the top of a house by means of a ladder or a bamboo or a staircase or a rope, so diverse are the ways and means to approach God, and every religion in the world shows one of these ways."
> – Ramakrishna (1839-1886)

The sentiment behind the words of Ramakrishna, the 19th century Indian saint, echo in the hearts of many people throughout the world. Unfortunately, they have not been realized. Religious and racial conflicts are as old as the history of religion itself. Of course, what poses as religious conflict is often political or economic conflict. One group invades or destroys another for land or power. Still, there are those who believe that only their religion has validity, that all others are inaccurate. This has led to forced conversions and some of the most atrocious injustices in the history of mankind.

The dictionary defines tolerance as "The capacity for or practice of recognizing and respecting the opinions, practices, or behavior of others." What can bring about this tolerance? With our world getting so much smaller every day, how can we work to increase tolerance and erase prejudice?

Extensions:

1. The first—and perhaps most important—step in undoing prejudice and stereotype is to recognize it in ourselves. Although we may not think so, we probably all carry judgments and conclusions about people different from ourselves.

   Get together with a partner and discuss your own assumptions and opinions about a religious or racial group. Write down your findings.

   Please remember, the point of doing this is to increase tolerance and understanding, not to condemn ourselves or another. If you find this assignment too personal, feel free to do it on your own.

2. Research the history of a specific religious conflict. How did it come about? How might the groups have found another solution?

Interview

Another way to dispel prejudice and increase understanding is actually to make contact with people from other religions. Use the following questions to interview someone from a faith different from your own. Maybe you can find someone in your own classroom! At the end of this list, add three questions of your own.

1. What religion do you follow?

2. What branch of the religion do you belong to? What distinguishes it from other branches?

3. How long has your family belonged to this religion? From where did your religious traditions originate?

4. How do you worship? Do you attend a special place?

5. What kind of special clothing, if any, is required in your religion?

6. Describe some of the special holidays or festivals in your religion. Can you give a personal account of the happenings?

7. What are some of the rites of passage in your religion? Which did you go through and what was it like?

8. Are there special foods related to your religion?

9. Why is your religion important to you?

10. What are the basic beliefs of your religion?

11. Have you ever gone on a pilgrimage?

12. Please describe some of the special arts related to your religion, such as dance, music, literature, and drama.

13. Can you share a myth or legend involving your religion?

14. How does your faith look upon other religions?

15. What would you say is the message at the heart of your religion?

16.

17.

18.

Name _____

A Moral Universe?

If we review the religions we have studied, we notice that each faith suggests a moral universe. Although the nature of this universe varies, each contains an ethic which, if not followed, is met with punishment. Again, the nature of the punishment varies. The Jews, for example, feel that God has a distinct interest in human affairs, in history, and in the fabric of everyday life. If a nation is sinful, then sooner or later there will be judgment. In Taoism, a person suffers simply because he or she is not in harmony with the universe, while in Hinduism, past lives may be the cause of suffering.

Peace and happiness are likewise merited by living a moral life. The ultimate reward in Christianity and Islam is heaven, while a Buddhist attains enlightenment.

In the spaces below, write a brief summary of each religion's sense of morality. What are the rules of conduct? What, if anything, merits punishment? Who punishes? What kind of punishment is there? What are the rewards of living a virtuous life? How does one earn these rewards? Finally, ask yourself whether or not you live in a moral universe. Discuss this issue with your classmates.

1. **Judaism** _____

   _____

2. **Christianity** _____

   _____

3. **Islam** _____

   _____

4. **Hinduism** _____

   _____

5. **Buddhism** _____

   _____

6. **Sikhism** _____

   _____

7. **Taoism** _____

   _____

Name _____

My Own Symbol

Now that you are familiar with seven of the world's principal religious symbols, it is time for you to make up your own. In the space below, draw an original design which reflects your personal values and aspirations. The symbol does not need to be spiritual or religious in flavor.

Name _____

Comparison: Rites of Passage

All religions and cultures have rites of passage, or initiations, into different stages of life. Usually this begins with birth and ends with death, which many consider to be the passage into another life. In between, there are a variety of possibilities: adolescence, marriage, religious initiation, and so forth.

Each of the religions that you have studied approach these rites differently, yet all of them address these important moments of life. In the space below, discuss, first of all, the importance of each of these passages. Why are they given so much universal importance? Next, describe what some of the religions have in common in their rites of passage. What do they share? Lastly, describe some differences in the rituals and philosophies among a few religions.

_____

_____

_____

_____

_____

_____

_____

_____

_____

_____

_____

_____

_____

_____

_____

_____

_____

_____

Name _____

Biographies

Use an encyclopedia or other reference book to find information for a brief biographical sketch of each of the following famous figures. Each is connected to one of the religions we have studied. Afterward, feel free to add some of your own names to the list.

1. **Golda Meir** (Judaism)_____

   _____

   _____

   _____

   _____

2. **Mother Theresa** (Christianity)

   _____

   _____

   _____

   _____

3. **Malcolm X** (Islam)

   _____

   _____

   _____

   _____

4. **Mohandas Gandhi** (Hinduism)

   _____

   _____

   _____

   _____

276

Name _____

Biographies *(cont.)*

5. **The Dalai Lama** (Buddhism) _____

_____

_____

_____

_____

6. **Guru Gobind Singh** (Sikhism)

_____

_____

_____

_____

_____

7. **Chuang Tzu** (Taoism)

_____

_____

_____

_____

_____

Extension:

Here are five more modern figures. Report on their biographies and religious backgrounds.

1. Muhammad Ali

2. Catharine Burroughs

3. Martin Luther King, Jr.

4. Anne Frank

5. Vivekenanda

World Religions Final Exam

Name _____

Part One: Circle the correct answer for each.

1. If an event occurred in the 1700s, it happened in what century?
   A. 17th   B. 7th   C. 18th   D. 20th

2. The Jewish holiday which celebrates the Exodus out of Egypt
   A. Passover   B. Chanukah   C. Easter   D. Purim

3. The place of worship for Muslims
   A. temple   B. mosque   C. ashram   D. church

4. The branch of Buddhism inspired by bodhisattvas
   A. Mahayana   B. Zen   C. Theravada   D. Tibetan

5. Lao-Tzu and Confucius lived in this country.
   A. Japan   B. Taiwan   C. India   D. China

6. The founder of Sikhism
   A. Muhammad   B. Dalai Lama   C. Guru Angad   D. Guru Nanak

7. The "destroyer" god of the Hindu Trinity
   A. Vishnu   B. Shiva   C. Kali   D. Brahma

8. He baptized Jesus.
   A. Joseph   B. Paul   C. John the Baptist   D. Matthew

9. The first Jewish patriarch
   A. Moses   B. Abraham   C. Joseph   D. Adam

10. The most sacred river in India
    A. Ganges   B. Indus   C. Narmada   D. Jumma

11. This Empire ruled Palestine during the time of Jesus.
    A. Roman   B. Greek   C. Ottoman   D. French

12. Where Muhammad was born
    A. Medina   B. Cairo   C. Jerusalem   D. Mecca

13. Buddha was born in this country.
    A. China   B. Tibet   C. India   D. Japan

14. The Sikh holy book
    A. Bible   B. Guru Granth   C. Guru Gobind   D. Koran

15. The principal symbol of Taoism
    A. crescent and star   B. the Wheel of Law   C. the T'ai Chi   D. dove

16. If someone was born in a year B.C., he or she was born . . .
    A. before Christ   B. after Christ

17. The Semitic religions originated in this area.
    A. India   B. South America   C. Middle East   D. China

18. The youngest major world religion
    A. Taoism   B. Christianity   C. Islam   D. Sikhism

19. The world religion with the most followers
    A. Judaism   B. Christianity   C. Hinduism   D. Buddhism

20. A scripture sacred to both Jews and Christians
    A. Greek Scripture   B. Koran   C. Hebrew Scripture   D. Gospels

World Religions Final Exam *(cont.)*

Name _____

Part Two: Circle either T for *true* or F for *false*.

T F 21. Hinduism is a polytheistic religion.
T F 22. Jews celebrate Easter.
T F 23. Confucius was a hermit.
T F 24. The Sikh capital is the Punjab.
T F 25. Jesus raised Lazarus from the dead.
T F 26. Buddha was born a beggar.
T F 27. Mecca and Medina are located in Saudi Arabia.
T F 28. All religions try to convert others.
T F 29. Most Taoists can be found in Europe.
T F 30. Buddha had a son.

Part Three: Fill in the blanks with the appropriate words.

31. Jesus' mother and father were named _____ and _____ .

32. Moses received the _____ on Mount Sanai.

33. The _____ is the leader of Tibetan Buddhism.

34. The pilgrimage to Mecca is called the _____ .

35. _____ is the Hindu deity with the head of an elephant.

36. Sikhs formed the _____ group to defend their religion.

37. Lao-Tzu is believed to have authored the _____ .

38. Buddhists _____ in order to quiet the mind.

39. Most Sikh men wear _____ on their heads.

40. Communion is inspired by the events at the _____ .

41. The _____ is the leader of the Jewish synagogue.

42. The _____ and the _____ are two principal Hindu scriptures.

43. The _____ , or House of God, is sacred to Muslims.

44. Buddha taught that _____ was the root of suffering.

45. Indian authorities partially destroyed the _____ .

46. The most important holy site for Jews to visit in Jerusalem is the _____ , where King Solomon's Temple was destroyed.

47. In 1054, Christianity branched off into two groups, the _____ and the _____ .

48. Confucius put great emphasis on _____ in hope of restoring social order in China.

49. The Ramayana tells the story of the royal couple, _____ and _____ .

50. _____ is the oldest Indian religion, while _____ is the oldest Semitic religion.

World Religions Final Exam *(cont.)*

Name _____

Part Four: Respond in detail to the following questions and prompts.

51. Explain how Sikhism fuses Hinduism and Islam. How did this come to be?

_____
_____

52. Explain how the Indus and Aryan civilizations combined to form Hinduism.

_____
_____

53. Why was Moses so upset when his followers built the Golden Calf?

_____
_____

54. Explain the significance of the crucifixion and the resurrection.

_____
_____

55. What events lead to Prince Siddhartha's decision to leave the palace?

_____
_____

56. Explain why Muhammad, after capturing Mecca, went straight to the Ka'bah and destroyed the idols. Discuss the structure's historical significance as well.

_____
_____

57. Explain the difference between Tibetan Buddhism and Zen Buddhism.

_____
_____
_____
_____

World Religions Final Exam *(cont.)*

Name _____

Part Four *(cont.)*:

58. What are the principal differences between the Greek Orthodox and Roman Catholic churches?

_____

_____

59. What is Popular Taoism? Why would traditional Taoists look down upon it?

_____

_____

60. Explain the significance, the role, and the history of the guru in Sikhism.

_____

_____

61. Explain the aspects of the Hindu Trinity. How do they balance one another?

_____

_____

62. What are some of the stereotypes surrounding the religion of Islam?

_____

_____

63. What ties does Judaism have with Islam and Christianity? Why do all three of these religions consider Jerusalem a sacred city?

_____

_____

64. What is the difference between a fact and a belief? What is a belief system?

_____

_____

World Religions Final Exam (cont.)

Name _____

Part Five: This section can be completed with the use of notes and reference books. Each item has three answers. First, name the religion from which the passage is taken. Next, name the scripture from which it comes. Finally, if appropriate, name the author of the passage. (You may need to do some research.)

65. "In the name of Allah, the Compassionate, the Merciful. Praise be to Allah, Lord of the Universe, the Compassionate, the Merciful, Sovereign of the Day of Judgement! You alone we worship, and to You alone we turn for help. Guide us to the straight path, the path of those whom You have favored, not of those who have incurred Your wrath, nor of those who have gone astray."

_____ _____ _____

66. "Within thy home is the treasure,
     there is not without;
By the Guru's grace to it thou
     attainest and the door
         opens unto thee."

_____ _____ _____

67. "Every good tree bringeth forth good fruit; but a corrupt tree bringeth forth evil fruit. A good tree cannot bring forth evil fruit, neither can a corrupt tree bring forth good fruit. Every tree that bringeth not forth good fruit is hewn down, and cast into the fire. Therefore, by their fruits ye shall know them."

_____ _____ _____

68. "Let me now sing the heroic deeds of Vishnu, who has measured apart the realms of earth, who propped up the upper dwelling-place, striding far as he stepped forth three times."

_____ _____ _____

69. "And when, monks, in these four noble truths my due knowledge and insight . . . was well purified . . . I had attained the highest complete enlightenment. This I recognized. Knowledge arose in me, insight arose that the release of my mind is unshakeable: this is my last existence; now there is no rebirth."

_____ _____ _____

70. "Now, if you obey the Lord your God, to observe faithfully all His commandments which I enjoin upon you this day, the Lord your God will set you high above all the nations of the earth. All these blessings shall come upon you and take effect . . . ."

_____ _____ _____

71. "Empty yourself of everything.
Let the mind rest at peace.
The ten thousand things rise and fall while the Self watches their return.
They grow and flourish and then return to the source.
Returning to the source is stillness, which is the way of nature.
The way of nature is unchanging."

_____ _____ _____

Bibliography

General

Comparing Religions Series: a series of young reader's books which focus on various aspects of religion, including birth, death, food and fasting, initiation, marriage and pilgrimage. Thomas Learning, 1992.

Houston, Smith. *The Illustrated World's Religions.* HarperCollins, 1994.

Kollek, Teddy and Pealman, Moshe. *Jerusalem.* Steimatzsky, Jerusalem, 1985.

O'Brien, Joanne and Palmer, Martin. *The State of Religion Atlas.* Touchstone, 1993.

Ross, Floyd H., and Hills, Tynette. *The Great Religions by Which Men Live.* Fawcett, 1956.

Sever, Merle (editor). *Great Religions of the World.* National Geographic Society, 1971.

Swami Harshananda. *Principal Symbols of World Religions.* Sri Ramakrishna Math.

Thompson, Jan and Mel. *The Re Atlas: World Religions in Maps and Notes.* Hodder & Stoughton, 1986.

Ward, Hiley H. *My Friends' Beliefs.* Walker and Company, 1988.

Judaism

Burstein, Chaya M. *The Jewish Kids Catalog.* Jewish Publication Society, 1993.

Fackenheim, Emil L. *What Is Judaism?* Summit Books, 1987.

Singer, Isaac Bashevis. *The King of the Fields.* Farrar, Srauss, Giroux, 1988.

Tanakh: The Holy Scriptures. Jewish Publication Society, 1985.

Telushkin, Joseph. *Jewish Literacy.* William Morrow and Company, Inc., 1991.

Christianity

The Holy Bible. King James Version. Thomas Nelson, Publishers, 1972.

Jesus of Nazareth: A Life of Christ Through Pictures. Simon & Simon, 1994.

Brown, Stephen F. *Christianity.* Facts on File, 1991.

Haughton, Rosemary. *Paul and the World's Most Famous Letters.* Abingdon Press, 1970.

Petry, Anne. *Legends of the Saints.* Thomas Y. Crowell Co., 1970.

Islam

The Koran. Translation by N.J. Dawood. Penguin Books, 1990.

Denny, Frederick Mathewson. *An Introduction to Islam.* Macmillan, 1985.

Farah, Caesar E. *Islam: Beliefs and Observations.* Barron, 1983.

Gordon, Matthew. *Islam.* Facts on File, 1991.

Ingrams, Doreen. *The Arab World: Mosques and Minarets.* EMC Corp. 1974.

Hinduism

The Rig-Veda. Translation by Wendy Doniger O'Flaherty. Penguin, 1981.

The Upanishads. Translation by Swami Prabhavananda and Frederick Manchester. Vedanta Society, 1957.

Choudhry, Bano Roy. *The Ramayana.* Hemkunt Press, New Delhi, 1970.

Hirst, Jacqueline. *The Story of the Hindus.* Cambridge U. Press, 1989.

Nivedita, Sister. *Cradle Tales of Hinduism.* Vedanta Press, 1988.

Wangu, Madhu Bazaz. *Hinduism.* Facts on File, 1991.

Buddhism

The Teachings of the Compassionate Buddha, edited by E.A. Burtt, Mentor, 1955.

Bancroft, Anne. *The Buddhist World.* Silver Burdett Company, 1984.

Coatsworth, Elizabeth. *The Cat Who Went to Heaven.* Alladin, 1990.

DeRoin, Nancy. *Jataka Tales: Fables from the Buddha.* Houghton Mifflin, 1975.

Hodges, Margaret. *The Golden Deer.* Charles Scribner's Sons, 1992.

Landaw, Jonathan and Brooke, Janet. *Prince Siddhartha.* Wisdon, 1994.

Wangu, Madhu Bazaz. *Buddhism.* Facts on File, 1993.

Sikhism

Arora, Ranjit. *Religions of the World: Sikhism.* Bookwrights Press, 1987.

Singh, Daljeet. *The Sikh World.* Silver Burdett Company, N.J., 1985.

Singh, Gurbachan. *Guru Nanak.* Sahitya Akademi, 1990.

Singh, Harbans. *Mahindi and Other Stories.* Delhi: Navyug Publishers, 1984.

Singh, Nikky-Guninder Kaur. *Sikhsim.* Facts on File, 1993.

Taoism

Hoobler, Dorothy and Thomas. *Images Across the Ages: Chinese Portraits.* Raintree SteckVaughn Publishers, 1993.

Overmyer, Daniel L. *Religions of China.* Harper & Row, 1986.

Tsu, Lao. *Tao Te Ching,* Translation by Gia-Fu Feng and Jane English. Vintage Books, 1972.

Sanders, Tao Tao Liu. *Dragons, Gods & Spirits from Chinese Mythology.* Schoken Books, 1980.

Answer Key

Page 7: Reading a Time Line
1. 1760 BCE.
2. 15th century
3. 500 years
4. 2960 years
5. Answers will vary. One possibility is 1450-1550.
6. Through the year 2000, it is the 20th century. Beginning in 2001, it is the 21st century.

Page 10: Distribution of World Religions
1. Answers will vary.
2. the countries of northern Africa
3. North America, South America, Europe, and Australia
4. Africa, Middle East, or Israel
5. Answers will vary.
6. Answers will vary.
7. Christianity
8. Christianity has the most. Taoism, Sikhism, and Judaism have the least.

Page 11: Belief, Fact, and Opinion
1. B
2. F
3. F
4. O
5. B
6. O
7. F
8. F
9. O
10. B

Page 12: The Semitic Religions
1. people from the Middle East and their languages
2. Judaism, Islam, and Christianity
3. monotheistic

Page 14: The Bible
1. the first five books of the Bible; Genesis, Exodus, Leviticus, Numbers, and Deuteronomy
2. The Greek Scripture tells the story of Jesus and the spread of Christianity, and is holy only to Christians, not Jews.
3. The Sermon on the Mount or The Beatitudes

Page 17: Reading from the Bible
1. Do not eat of the tree of knowledge of good and evil.
2. to name the creatures
3. from the rib of Adam
4. Answers will vary.
5. sly, clever, or crafty
6. it tempted Eve
7. to be like God
8. They loose their innocence and they feel ashamed.
9. The snake will be lowly, crawl on its stomach, and be an enemy to people. The woman will suffer in child-birth but still be desirous to mate, and she will also be subject to the man. The man will be forced to work the fields, and he will one day die.
10. Answers will vary.
11. to keep them from the tree of life
12. Answers will vary.
13. Answers will vary.

Page 24: Exodus
1. a large group of people departed; about 1250 BCE
2. because he was drawn from the river
3. Answers will vary.
4. a. river of blood
   b. frogs
   c. lice
   d. flies
   e. death of Egyptian cattle
   f. sores
   g. hail
   h. locusts
   i. three days of darkness
   j. death of first-born children and cattle
5. They were worried about being alone. They did not trust their leader. It breaks the second commandement.
6. Ark of the Covenant; Tabernacle

Page 36: The Synagogue
1. H
2. B
3. G
4. D
5. C
6. E
7. J
8. I
9. F
10. A

Page 46: Vocabulary
1. N
2. J
3. D
4. X
5. M
6. U
7. T
8. W
9. P
10. H
11. A
12. R
13. L
14. S
15. E
16. V
17. I
18. K
19. G
20. F
21. O
22. B
23. Q
24. C

Page 47: Quiz and Review

Part One
1. covenant
2. Friday, Saturday
3. 1250 BCE
4. Sinai
5. plagues
6. King Solomon
7. (any two) matzah, beitzah (roasted egg), charoseth (an apple, nut, cinnamon and wine mixture), green vegetable, salt water, maror (bitter herb) or horseradish.
8. Syrian Greeks
9. concentration camps
10. "a son of the Commandment"
11. 17 million
12. Jordan, Egypt, Lebanon, Syria.
13. Babylonians
14. the United States
15. circumcision

Part Two
Answers will vary.

Answer Key *(Cont.)*

Page 53: Reading from the New Testament

1. Answers will vary.
2. to turn stones to bread, to jump from the temple, and to worship him
3. Answers will vary.

Pages 59–60: The Last Supper and Crucifixion

1. three
2. They felt threatened by him. Examples will vary.
3. The Temple was for the worship of God, not business transactions.
4. Bread and wine are blessed and offerred to the congregation. The exact method and meanings vary depending on the denomination. The service is modelled after the Last Supper.
5. blasphemy and organizing a revolt against Rome
6. Answers will vary.
7. Answers will vary.
8. the place were Jesus was crucified
9. the putting to death by nailing or tying to a cross
10. Answers will vary.
11. the series of events and route taken by Jesus on the way to and including his crucifixion and death

Page 61: The Resurrection

1. It means the raising of Jesus from the dead.
2. Answers will vary.

Page 75: Rites of Passage

1. marriage ceremony whereby the man and the woman devote themselves to one another for life in much the same fashion as Jesus and the church
2. induction into Christian society and Christian faith, mirroring the baptism performed by John the Baptist
3. last rites given to a gravely ill individual in the hope that he or she will be cleansed of his or her sins
4. sponsors for a baptized child who promise to provide the child's religious training if the parents are unable
5. period of mourning and prayer preceding a funeral
6. the naming of a child—usually for a saint—during or in place of a baptism

Page 87: Vocabulary Crossword Pzzle

Across

1. cross
2. Paul
3. Lent
4. Bethlehem
5. miracles
6. Catholic
7. purgatory
8. Spirit
9. protestant
10. apostles
11. Roman
12. Mary
13. Supper
14. rite
15. John
16. Easter
17. Trinity
18. Palestine
19. Christmas

Down

1. Jerusalem
2. Beatitudes
3. crucifixion
4. communion
5. baptism
6. Joseph
8. resurrection
9. Pope
10. priest
18. Prayer

Pages 88–90: Quiz and Review

Part One:

1. Herod the Great
2. Mediterranean
3. Star of Bethlehem
4. Messiah
5. Satan, or the devil
6. inherit
7. Sabbath
8. Supper, treason
9. rich
10. Reformation
11. missionary
12. Ash Wednesday
13. Easter
14. Francis
15. New

Part Two: Answers will vary.

Pages 95–96: The Life of Muhammad in Review

1. Abraham is considered the forefather of Islam. He was the father of Ishmael, from whose heels the sacred well, Zamzam, first sprung. Muhammad is also considered a prophet from Abraham's lineage.
2. Muhammad traveled to spread Islam and to protect himself from his enemies. The rest of the answer will vary.
3. Muhammad's first revelation was the appearance of the angel Gabriel. The rest of the answer will vary.
4. Muhammad urged Meccans to reject their idols. They disliked him for this.
5. Hijrah is the journey from Mecca to Medina made by Muhammad and his friend, Abu Bakr. He was followed by his enemies during the first portion of his journey, but they passed him by at a cave, the entrance of which was miraculously covered by a spider's web.
6. Muhammad had to deal with the violence of two warring tribes as well as assasination attempts on his own life. Muhammad attempted to bring the groups together through united prayer.
7. In 629 CE, Muhammad returned to Mecca. He immediately circled the Ka'bah seven times and then smashed the idols there. He did so because his message involved a belief in the oneness of God.
8. Mecca and Medina are in Arabia.
9. A. the religion founded by Muhammad,
   B. a follower of Islam
   C. a holy sanctuary built by Abraham; also called the "House of God"
   D. God in Arabic
   E. the sacred well that sprang up at Ishmael's heels

Answer Key *(Cont.)*

Page 99: Reading from the Koran
1. "In the name of Allah, the Compassionate, the Merciful"
2. God is almighty and all powerful. God is merciful and just.
3. Satan
4. Answers will vary.
5. Answers will vary.

Page 109: The Shi'ah and Sunni Sects
1. a Moslem leader of the Shi'ah sect; leads the community; guides community to salvation; people judged by the Twelfth Imam
2. the role of the imam and the issue of salvation
3. Answers will vary.

Page 113: Identifying Features of a Mosque
1. D   4. B
2. C   5. E
3. A

Page 121: Islam in the World Today
1. Africa and Asia
2. highest: Africa; lowest: Australia
3. warm climates; because they are near the equator
4. about 22-25
5. Saudi Arabia
6. Answers will vary.
7. centralized
8. Indonesia
9. Answers will vary.

Page 124: Wordsearch

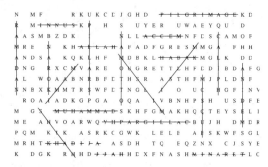

Page 125-126: Quiz and Review
Part One:
1. Ka'bah, Mecca
2. Semitic
3. Hirjrah
4. Koran, surah
5. Saudi Arabia
6. Shahada, "There is no God but Allah, and Muhammad is the messenger of Allah."
7. 5 times, Mecca
8. almsgiving
9. Ramadan, Eid-al-fitr
10. Pilgrimage

Part Two:
1. A caliph is a succesor to Muhammad. His role is to lead the Muslim community and to spread the message of Islam.
2. North Africa, Middle East, Eastern Europe (specific answers may vary.).
3. Shi'ah Muslims believe that descendants of Caliph Ali should lead Islam; Sunnis do not believe leader must be a descendant of Muhammad. (answers may vary.)
4. A. *birth–shahadah* read and head shaved

   B. *marriage*–men and women celebrate separately

   C. *death*–recitations from *Koran,* head towards Mecca

Part Three:
1. false   6. false
2. true   7. true
3. false   8. true
4. true   9. true
5. true   10. false

Part Four:
Answers will vary.

Page 127: The Indian Religions
1. because they originated in India
2. oldest: Hinduism; youngest: Sikhism
3. belief in more than one god
4. they differ in their basic beliefs

Page 129: Origins of Hinduism: The Indus Valley Civilization
1. artifacts and relicts found through archeological digs
2. a. bath tank at Mohanjo-Daro: ritual bathing important to Hindus

   b. terra-cotta figurines: represent fertility, strength, rebirth, and continuity, central to the Hindu faith

   c. bulls: represent virility, sacred to the Hindus
3. agricultural people, dependent on water; water still sacred to Hindus

Page 146: The Ramayana: Comprehension
1. (map)
2. King Dasharatha, Queen Kaushlya, Lakshmana
3. by destroying demons
4. by stringing Lord Shiva's bow
5. She believed Rama would have her son sentenced to death.
6. because his father's promise must be honored
7. Bharata is very upset. Rama tells him to rule the kingdom.
8. because she could not live without him
9. Ravana, the giant, has ten heads and twenty arms.
10. because he knew Rama would die of a broken heart. He disguises himself.
11. Jatayu, the old vulture
12. (map)
13. Hanuman is a monkey, son of the wind god.

Answer Key *(Cont.)*

Page 146 *(cont.)*

14. She would be rescued only by her husband.
15. He did not want to be involved with Ravana's evil.
16. The Lord of the Ocean appeared with instructions.
17. Rama would not kill an unarmed enemy.
18. (map)
19. A husband cannot take back a wife who has lived with another man.
20. She is hurt.
21. She leaps into a funeral pyre to prove her loyalty.
22. The royal couple return to Ayodya as rulers.

Page 167: Hindu Crossword Puzzle

Across

1. Indus
2. karma
3. Vedas
4. Ganges
5. ascetic
6. Sarasvati
7. moksha
8. untouchables
9. snakes
10. Kali

Down

1. Upanishads
2. Lakshmi
3. Shiva
4. dharma
5. Aryan
6. reincarnation
7. creator
8. Brahmin
9. caste
10. Vishnu

Page 168: Quiz and Review

Part One:

1. honey; Aum
2. sacred thread
3. seven
4. cremation
5. Agni
6. Divali; Lakshmi
7. spring; Krishna
8. mandir
9. shrine
10. meditation; Divine Mother

Part Two:

1. *Indus*–ritual bathing, fertility symbols
   Arvan–fire worship, the Vedas
2. ascetic focused on individual, not on authority of Brahmin and Vedas
3. *dharma*–balance of universe
   karma–cause and effect of one's actions
   samsara–reincarnation
4. caste system based on Aryan tradition; born into a caste because of personal merit; endeavor to do better for next lifetime.
5. fire means renewal, cleansing. Husband and wife circle it, used for cremation.
6. in temple would see offerings to shrine, circling shrine, taking of prasad, prostration, meditation, chanting, prayer to dieties
7. (1) worship God (2) recite scripture (3) honor parents and elders (4) help poor (5) feed animals

Page 174: Buddha's Enlightenment: Comprehension

1. 563 BCE; "the one who brings all good"
2. A. white elephant pierced her wom
   B. She would give birth to a great leader
3. because he will not live to hear Siddhartha's teachings
4. He will be either a great ruler or a great teacher.
5. She dies shortly after giving birth.
6. He showers him with pleasure and protects him from ugliness.
7. communing with nature
8. He rescues it.
9. King Suprabuddha needed proof of Sidhartha's bravery.
10. archery, wordsmanship, horsemanship
11. two palaces to protect them from the outside world
12. a sick man, an old man, a dead man
13. shaves his head; 29 years old
14. to transcend the body
15. Bodh-gaya; under the Bodhi tree

Page 216: Vocabulary

1. G	6. O	11. E	16. D
2. H	7. P	12. N	17. M
3. J	8. T	13. B	18. F
4. L	9. R	14. I	19. S
5. C	10. Q	15. K	20. A

Pages 217-218: Quiz and Review

Part One:

1. 563 BCE, Lumbini
2. desire
3. Answers will vary.
4. Answers will vary.
5. Answers will vary.
6. Tipitaka
7. meditation
8. koans
9. stupa
10. right

Part Two:

1. because the King was afraid Siddartha would become a saint after seeing the realities of the world.
2. suffering, cause of suffering, end of suffering, truth of the Middle Way.
3. to cleanse the mind, sitting quiet, eyes closed, focus on breathing, focus on mandala, chanting sounds, koans
4. spiritual and political leader of Tibet; baby is sought with information given by Dalai Lama, then baby is tested for special knowledge.
5. Zen emphasizes focus on individual insight, not dependent upon boddhisattvas or scriptures, quietude, meditation.
6. see page 197, 198 for diagram of stupa, pagoda, monastery
7. Deer Park, Lumbini Grove, Adam's Peak, Palace of Dalai
8. compassion, inner peace, right action

Answer Key *(Cont.)*

Page 223: Origins of Sikhism: Comprehension

1. approximately 1500 CE; April 15, 1469
2. The Punjab, northern India
3. He refused to participate in the Ceremony of the Sacred Thread.
4. A cobra shaded his face.
5. "There is neither Hindu nor Muslim."
6. Mardara, a Muslim servant who played music
7. Nanak squeezed the bread of each. The rich man's gave blood and the poor man's gave milk.
8. (map)
9. Lehna, Guru Angad, which means "part of me"
10. It turned into flowers. The Hindus and Muslims divided the flowers and the sheet covering them.

Page 250: Vocabulary Wordsearch

1. turban
2. kangha
3. service
4. golden temple
5. khalsa
6. Punjab
7. angad
8. kesh
9. langar
10. guru
11. kara
12. gurdwara
13. *Guru Granth*
14. Singh
15. Nanak
16. kaccha
17. Kaur
18. amrit
19. rivers
20. kirpan

Pages 251-252: Quiz and Review

Part One:

1. 1500 CE
2. Muslims
3. (any two) Indus, Chenab, Ravi, Jhelum, and Sutlej
4. Ram Das
5. Arjan
6. Tegh Bahadur
7. Gobind Singh
8. gurmurki
9. Hymns
10. Iran; Afghanistan
11. 5 K's
12. gurdwara
13. destroyed
14. gupurbs
15. Mata Sahib Kaur

Part Two:
Answers will vary.

Page 268: Quiz and Review

Part One:

1. 6th
2. Analects
3. Tao Te Ching
4. popular
5. Heavenly
6. immortality
7. Immortals
8. Yellow Springs
9. yin; yang
10. charm

Part Two:
Answers will vary.

Pages 278-282: World Religions Final Exam

Part One:

1. C	6. D	11. A	16. A
2. A	7. B	12. D	17. C
3. B	8. C	13. C	18. D
4. A	9. B	14. B	19. B
5. D	10. A	15. C	20. C

Part Two:

21. T	26. F
22. F	27. T
23. F	28. F
24. T	29. F
25. T	30. T

Part Three:

31. Mary and Joseph
32. The Torah or the Ten Commandments
33. Dalai Lama
34. Hajj
35. Ganesh
36. Khalsa
37. Tao Te Ching
38. meditate
39. turbans
40. Last Supper
41. rabbi
42. Vedas, Upanishads
43. Ka'bah
44. desire
45. Golden Temple
46. Western Wall
47. Roman Catholic, Eastern Orthodox
48. relationship
49. Rama, Sita
50. Judaism, Hinduism

Part Four:
51–64. Answers will vary.

Part Five:

65. Islam, Koran, Muhammad
66. Sikhism, Guru Granth, Guru Nanak
67. Christianity, Greek Scripture (or New Testament), Jesus
68. Hinduism, Rig Veda
69. Buddhism, The Sermon at Deer Park, Buddha
70. Judaism (Since it comes from the Hebrew Bible, Christianity is also an acceptable answer); Tanakh (or Hebrew Bible); Moses (the speaker), God, or unknown
71. Taoism, Tao Te Ching, Lao Tzu

#624 Interdisciplinary Unit—World Religions   288   © *Teacher Created Resources, Inc.*